HALF A HUNDRED THRALLS TO FAUST

Half a Hundred Thralls to Faust

A Study Based on the British and the American Translators of Goethe's Faust
1823-1949

BY

ADOLF INGRAM FRANTZ

WITH A FOREWORD BY
CARL F. SCHREIBER

CHAPEL HILL

The University of North Carolina Press

1949

Copyright, 1949, by
The University of North Carolina Press

TO HELEN

*Loyal Companion
for Three Decades*

Foreword

Mr. Frantz states in his Preface that "in its thesis form, the manuscript of *Half a Hundred Thralls to Faust* was placed at the disposal of an eminent Goethe scholar. His gratuitous remark, after reading it, was to the effect that these pages contained more useful material than most of the theses written for the Ph.D. degree." I was greatly pleased because the dissertation had been done under my direction. Since then I have learned to my discomfort that the word "useful" is only praise of a sort, and a subordinate sort at that. It would seem that scholars who produce "useful" works "do not belong" in the council of the Amphictyons; they are to all intents and purposes considered as "hewers of wood and carriers of water." It seems a pity that in the realm of scholarship the Upper and the Lower Houses should be drifting ever further apart. It is conceivable that these helpers could get on without the scholars, but the scholars will always be dependent on the products of the "honest, industrious workers" of a different but loyal class. As it is, our scholarship is tending more and more to hover about in the

"Misty mid region of Weir,"

where assurance is lacking and presumption has its unstable abode. Of this condition von Hofmannsthal speaks eloquently at the end of *Der Tor und der Tod:*

> Wie wundervoll sind diese Wesen,
> Die, was nicht deutbar, dennoch deuten,
> Was nie geschrieben wurde, lesen,
> Verworrenes beherrschend binden
> Und Wege noch im Ewig-Dunkeln finden.*

---

* Herbert Edward Mierow's translation of these lines reads:
    How wonderful these human beings are,
    Who find a meaning in the meaningless

Undoubtedly the finest "tool" in the Goethe field is Hans Gerhard Gräf's *Goethe über seine Dichtungen.* These nine stout volumes containing from 443 to 711 pages apiece have done more to advance Goethe scholarship than any other single work. In his Foreword to the volume "Lyrik I" Gräf illumines the "tool" aspect of research so admirably that it ought here to be quoted at some length:

First and foremost these volumes will prove to be an aid and a convenience which has long been lacking. But, strange to say, just in this particular sense has the publication of this work evoked a strong regret in certain quarters! Indeed, Herman Grimm, when I sent him a section of my unpublished manuscript for his comment, indicated a like regret in his letter to me. He advised me on this score in emphatic terms, that I should carefully consider a rearrangement of the material; I should abandon the strict chronological order; I should add some suggestions of my own to give my volumes somewhat more character than that of a bare *Stoffsammlung*; I should stamp it in some way as my own work. Unless I could manage this somehow, he greatly feared that scholars would shamelessly appropriate to themselves what I had so skillfully arranged, as though the labor of gathering this material had been theirs and not mine. I am frank to confess that I have never been able to share these fears; indeed, to this day it remains a complete enigma to me how a regret can be uttered about the aid to scholarship which this work truly represents. I am of an entirely opposite opinion: would to heaven we had or could count on having, many such time-and-labor saving devices! Isn't scholarship, as well as the state and society, dependent on one great cooperative venture? And whom do we scholars really serve? Certainly not the sluggards and the parasites (and what harm will it do in the last analysis if a few lazy-bones do undeservedly devise something with ease with the aid of our books?) but surely the honest industrious workers, and above all the truly great spirits whose original work is advanced and hastened perceptibly by such time saving means. To my way of thinking, then, it is of the greatest consequence that we be provided with more and ever

---

Who read the words which never have been written
Who bind like masters tangled skeins of things,
And still trace paths in the eternal dusk.

more of such reference works, for the bounds of the knowable expand unabated from year to year, daily, and by the hour.

Gräf, I dare say, would have bade Mr. Frantz enter the inner circle of "honest, industrious workers" who serve the "truly great spirits."

It is my expectation that this book will occupy a worthy place among the publications scheduled to appear in 1949, the two-hundredth anniversary of Goethe's birth. It merits the earnest attention of an understanding public. Between its two covers there is contained virtually all that can be said on this subject. Little of importance will be added for the dates between 1823 and the present. Perchance the individual concealed behind "Beta," the next to the last in the anonymous column, will step forward into the light; it may be that a few dates can be added, but by and large this topic has been exhausted. Of course, new translations will appear; they usually come in waves. It was Mr. Frantz's good fortune to write his book at a time when eight of the translators were still living and willingly gave him firsthand information on their ventures. But, however *Faust* may fare in the English world of the future, whatever translations appear, they will be in the nature of addenda to what has been gathered together here.

Over a period of nineteen years Mr. Frantz has not tired in gathering facts and information; he has rewritten the whole body of material a number of times; he has moved it to a new vantage ground where it now stands bare of the immaturities of incipient authorship. The short *aperçus* heading each chapter have a definite charm. The quotations are skillfully woven into the body of the text; the charts are illuminating, and the bibliography carefully compiled. Two cases of great delicacy have been handled with admirable discretion.

Mr. Frantz, in his capacity of biographer and historian, has obliged us with an entertaining chapter on the Shadowy Figures. It is a surprisingly large group. Of these literary titmice we know neither the date of birth nor the year of their death. It matters little to the world at large, but it does rise up to vex the library cataloguers. What a veritable swarm of these animalculi settled on the *Faust!* Their names will live on despite their utter lack of personality. One is reminded of that great line in Act III, Part II:

> Nicht nur Verdienst, auch Treue wahrt uns die Person.

Their accomplishment (Verdienst) was virtually nil, but their fidelity (Treue) to a great cause will keep their names on the roster of those who attempted to translate a world masterpiece. And how should you rate those who body forth as persons, running the gamut from a great lord to a small clerk in the Pension Office, Washington, D. C.? What were their literary attainments? I dare say that Anna Swanwick and Bayard Taylor are the fairest names. Mr. Frantz does not rank the translators as authors. But how would you rate Taylor? The question is posed for your own answer. Such, alas, is the way of this world, that Shelley and George Borrow made only partial translations of the *Faust*.

By bringing the whole group of translators conveniently together, Mr. Frantz has given us the opportunity of making discoveries on our own. From the chart on the number of editions issued, for instance, it becomes fairly clear that something like a quarter of a million English *Fausts* have gone forth into the world in a century and a quarter. Furthermore, it is no bare assumption that the translators of the *Faust* were a fairly vigorous sort. Apparently they enjoyed good health and lived carefully. Of the twenty-eight for whom we have both dates, Bayard Taylor died at fifty-three and Sir Theodore Martin lived on to ninety-three. The average age of the entire group exceeds three score and ten. The Parts translated do not seem to have affected the span of life. Taylor, who translated both Parts, was the youngest to die and Martin, who performed a like task, became the Nestor of them all. I am uncertain whether this proves or disproves Lord Kelvin's dictum: "When you cannot measure, your knowledge is meagre and unsatisfactory."

I doubt whether the facts and the arrangement in this book

Foreword   xi

will be challenged; there will, however, be disagreement about what Mr. Frantz considers well done and what is remiss. It was ever thus; from *de gustibus*-times to the present. No one who knows two languages well can ever be quite satisfied with a translation of one language to another. Germanisms or anglicisms weave their way back and forth. We hear the tones issuing from the original and are annoyed that they do not harmonize with those of the new rendition. Translations were never designed for language experts, but they are usually judged by them. It is the expert's sole mission to point out gross errors, extremely loose renditions, and banalities. Offhand illustrations of these three categories will make this point clear.

> Keines der Viere
> Steckt in dem Tiere

is scarcely

> None of the four
> Stands in the door.

He who has the Faust at his tongue's end would have to wrack his brains long and hard to place the two lines from Lord Gower's translation:

> He called for his confessor,
> Left all to his successor.

And, finally, what could be in worse taste than Galvan's horrific:

> Whom are you coaxing here! Hell-fire!
> You curs'd, infernal, old rat-catcher!
> To the devil I first pitch the Lyre!
> Then to the devil the vile gut-scratcher.

There will also be lack of agreement on rhyme and meter—and interpolated lines. On the latter point it should be said that as unreasonable an expansion as Anster allowed himself cannot be condoned. Taylor, who chose to adopt a mosaic-method of lifting a German line from its place to substitute for it an English line of equal length and fashion, goes to the other extreme—and not always happily so. Anna Swanwick, whose translation was very well received, stands somewhere in the middle; her version has seventy-six lines more than the original.

The German word order with its separable prefixes and its legitimate transpositions and its abundance of feminine endings is much more adaptable for certain rhymes and meters. Why blink the matter further; the English language is lacking in certain poetically acceptable rhymes. The great poetry in English has deliberately dodged these meters. If then they have been consciously avoided by the great English poets, why should the puerile insistence on them in translation bar the translator from the German who would fashion a graceful and pleasing rendition of a foreign masterpiece! The English language is so powerful in most respects that it seems a pity to expose one of its real weaknesses in so ruthless a manner. "As poetry ought always to be beautiful," says Anna Swanwick, "the charm of the original must never be sacrificed to the endeavor to be literal."

In a trenchant article entitled "Faust-Translations and Faust-Mosaics" (*Monatshefte*, Vol. XXX, No. 2), Heinrich Henel states the whole problem boldly:

A quality which it is difficult to define, but which every discerning reader recognizes at once, constitutes the true essence of a poem; its poetry. From this there follows that nothing less than English poetry can be accepted as a valid translation of celebrated poetry in a foreign language. Unfortunately, it also follows that it takes a poet to translate poetry, and that his product cannot be more than an approximation to the original. It is conceded by almost everyone that a translation, at least in some respects, offers less than the original. The only way to compensate for the loss is to have a translator who, in other respects, is able to offer more. It is time that someone had the courage to say this. The hypocritical excuse that the original must not be distorted, perverted or wronged opens the door to the mediocre and shuts it to the inspired.

Foreword xiii

Mr. Frantz's *Half a Hundred Thralls to Faust* should lead to a thorough re-evaluation of the aims and purposes of translation.

Carl F. Schreiber
Yale University

New Haven, Connecticut
May, 1948

Preface

THE WRITER HAS set forth in bold relief on the pages which follow the pertinent and ascertainable facts concerning the lives of the English and the American translators of Goethe's *Faust*. He offers to a selected reading public, especially to that segment of it which is interested in international literary relationships, much new, highly significant, and engaging biographical material concerning the goodly company of high-spirited men and women, who, from Lord Leveson-Gower (1823) on down to Professor John F. L. Raschen (1949) have, in many instances, spent the best years of their lives in the difficult endeavor to English the greatest German classic of all time.

The author attempts, moreover, to evaluate the various translations, to bring them into relationship with each other and with past and contemporary critical opinion. In order to give the reader an intelligent understanding of the breadth and significance of the subject matter here treated, he draws, in the Epilogue, a composite picture of the translators and their works and considers the tantalizing question as to why such a host of men and women on two continents should engage in the almost impossible task of making an acceptable English translation of *Faust*, and why nearly half a hundred of them should intellectually fall under its spell and become *thralls* to *Faust*.

The reader will find also that in this volume bibliographical errors of long standing are corrected. For instance, Bayard Taylor's translation of Part I was first published in 1870 and not 1871.* Similarly, Anna Swanwick's version of Part I was

---

* This fact was first pointed out by the author in the original Thesis version of this book which was deposited with the Graduate School of Yale University in 1931. Carl Van Doren's article on Bayard Taylor in the *Dictionary of American Biography* (Vol. XIX, published 1936) also refers to it.

first published in 1850 and not in 1849. The author has uncovered in the William A. Speck Collection of Goetheana at Yale University an 1851 *Titelauflage* of the *Dramatic Works of Goethe* containing *Faust, Iphigenia in Tauris, Torquato Tasso,* and *Egmont* translated by Anna Swanwick, and *Götz von Berlichingen* translated by Sir Walter Scott. This work is mentioned in no other bibliographical volumes published to date. The translation of *Faust* commonly attributed to Professor Hjalmar Boyesen is found to be merely a reprint of Anna Swanwick's translations of both parts.* Moreover, the authorships of two English translations of *Faust*, one of Part I, published in 1834, and the other of both parts, in 1838, have been established for the first time beyond a reasonable doubt as being those of Warburton Davies and Arthur Taylor respectively.

Something should be said about the scope and the plan of this volume. It confines itself to the English and to the American translators of Goethe's *Faust*. No attempt is made to deal with partial translations, such as the anonymous publication by Boozey and Sons, 1821, or with those by Percy Bysshe Shelley, George Borrow, Alexander H. Everett, and others. The most significant life interest of the individual translators has usually determined the chapter in which they appear in this volume. Since, however, some of them followed more than one profession, either simultaneously or chronologically, it was not always possible to be exact in this respect. One chapter, unfortunately, must deal with a group of translators about whom personally or about whose life work little or nothing is known up to the present time. To give them more prominence, the two women translators have been treated in a group by themselves.

For the sake of convenience, the dates of each translator, and the year in which the first edition of his translation of *Faust* appeared, are placed, together with the translator's name, at the top of the section devoted to him. The position of the

* For bibliographical notes on the translations of *Faust* attributed to L. E. Peithmann, G. G. Zerffi, J. Cartwright, and H. Boyesen, see pp. 302, 304, 304, 305 respectively.

Preface xvii

chapters themselves, headed by appropriate selections from the *Faust*, the order of each section in these chapters, and of the separate items comprising the Notes, the Bibliography (Editions and Reprints), and the Bibliographical Notes, are based mainly on chronological considerations. Moreover, the references pertaining to the translators and their respective translations are numbered consecutively in each chapter as well as in the body of Notes corresponding to it.

A chronological list of the translators, grouped according to nationality, will be found following the Bibliography, and, similarily placed, a table of the number of editions which each translation has enjoyed gives a vivid picture of the dispersion of the *Faust* in English. The starred editions and reprints are available in the William A. Speck Collection of Goetheana, housed in the Sterling Memorial Library of Yale University.

It was Professor Carl F. Schreiber, Curator of the William A. Speck Collection of Goetheana, who first suggested the subject of this study to me and called my attention to the fact that, in possessing a virtually complete series of the English and the American translations of Goethe's *Faust*, this collection offered many unusual opportunities for research. I gratefully acknowledge my debt of gratitude to him for important bits of information, numerous helpful suggestions, and the wholehearted and deep interest in this work so signally expressed in his Foreword to this volume.

I desire to express my appreciation to the members of the staff of the Sterling Library and the Speck Collection at Yale University for their valuable assistance and the permission to use some of the manuscript material in connection with the preparation of this volume.

I have been given much help also by the eight translators: Albert G. Latham, Geoffrey Montagu Cookson, C. Fillingham Coxwell, Alice Raphael, F. G. G. Schmidt, George M. Priest, Carlyle F. MacIntyre, and John F. L. Raschen, several of whom are still living. Courtesies of great assistance have been received from Professor Karl E. Weston of Williams College,

Professor A. E. Lang of the University of Toronto, Professor William Rose of the University of London, Professor J. T. Krumpelmann of St. Stephen's College, Professor Victoria E. Mueller of Vassar College, Professor B. Q. Morgan of Stanford University, Professor R. Priebsch, London, Mr. A. G. Berry, Foreign and English Bookseller, London, and from Mr. E. J. Dingwall, Hon. Asst. Keeper, Printed Books of the British Museum.

It is only fair to say that I have made free use of all available bibliographical books on the subject, and to the best of my knowledge due credit in the proper places has been given to these sources of information.

In its thesis form, the manuscript of *Half a Hundred Thralls to Faust* was placed, a few years ago, at the disposal of an eminent Goethe scholar. His gratuitous remark, after reading it, was to the effect that these pages contained more useful material than most of the theses written for the Ph.D. degree. Encouraged by these and similar observations made by others, and by the continuing world-wide interest in the *Faust* "überhaupt," the writer now offers the original work in a revised and considerably expanded form to the public. As a ready reference book, presenting between its two covers a closely drawn account of the English and the American *Faust* translators in relationship to their endeavors, this volume should be welcomed by all who lay some emphasis on a broader study of Goethe and his works and on international literary relationships as a whole.

Adolf Ingram Frantz
Bucknell University

College Park
Lewisburg, Pennsylvania
February, 1949

Contents

FOREWORD by Carl F. Schreiber	vii
PREFACE	xv
I. STATESMEN AND *FAUST*	3
Lord Francis Leveson-Gower	4
Sir George Buchanan	11
II. JURISTS AND *FAUST*	16
Abraham Hayward	17
John Anster	24
The Honorable Robert Talbot	30
Sir Theodore Martin	36
Thomas J. Arnold	45
Thomas E. Webb	50
III. MEPHISTOPHELES DONS CAP AND GOWN	54
John Stuart Blackie	55
Albert George Latham	61
William H. Van der Smissen	69
George Madison Priest	76
John Shawcross	80
F. G. G. Schmidt	83
Carlyle Ferren MacIntyre	86
John Frederick Louis Raschen	94
IV. SHADOWY FIGURES AMONG THE TRANSLATORS OF *FAUST*	100
David Syme	101
v. Beresford	103
John Wynniat Grant	105
Charles Hartpole Bowen	108
W. H. Colquhoun	110
Beta	111
R. McLintock	113
V. THE DISCIPLES OF AESCULAPIUS AND *FAUST*	118
Sir George William Lefevre	119
John Todhunter	123
C. Fillingham Coxwell	126

Contents

VI. MEN OF LETTERS AND *FAUST* 131
Arthur Taylor 132
William Bell Macdonald 135
Jonathan Birch 140
John Hills 147
Lewis Filmore 151
Bayard Taylor 155
Frank Claudy 166
Alfred Henry Huth 176
William Page Andrews 180

VII. THE MANSE AND *FAUST* 188
Warburton Davies 189
Leopold J. Bernays 195
Archer Thompson Gurney 200
Charles Timothy Brooks 204
Charles Kegan Paul 210
William Dalton Scoones 214

VIII. SOLDIERS AND *FAUST* 217
Captain Charles Henry Knox 218
Geoffrey Montagu Cookson 222

IX. SCIENTISTS AND *FAUST* 226
John Galvan 227
William Barnard Clarke 230
James Adey Birds 233

X. WOMEN AS TRANSLATORS OF *FAUST* 236
Anna Swanwick 237
Alice Raphael 244

EPILOGUE 255
NOTES 261
BIBLIOGRAPHY 275
BIBLIOGRAPHICAL NOTES 301
A LIST OF THE TRANSLATORS 306
A NUMERICAL TABLE OF THE EDITIONS AND
  REPRINTS OF EACH TRANSLATION 308
INDEX 311

Illustrations

	PAGE
1. A passage from Theodore Martin's translation of *Faust*....	39
2. A page of manuscript from Carlyle Ferren MacIntyre's translation of *Faust*...............................	89
3. Page 106 of Jonathan Birch's manuscript copy of his translation of *Faust*...............................	141
4. A page from Bayard Taylor's manuscript of his translation of *Faust*	165
5. A page from Frank Claudy's manuscript of his translation of *Faust*	173
6. The title-page to a copy of the translation of *Faust* by Warburton Davies.............................	191
7. A page from Alice Raphael's translation of *Faust*........	249

HALF A HUNDRED THRALLS TO FAUST

So ist's mit Aller Bildung auch beschaffen
Vergebens werden ungebundene Geister
Nach der Vollendung reiner Höhe streben.
Wer Grosses will, muss sich zusammenraffen.
In der Beschränkung zeigt sich erst der Meister,
Und das Gesetz nur kann uns Freiheit geben.

> Goethe: *Natur und Kunst*

I

Statesmen and Faust

Mephistopheles:
Such a condition no man dared abuse.
Each would be something, each set forth his dues;
The smallest even as full-measured passed:
Yet for the best it grew too bad at last.
The Capable, they then arose with energy,
And said: "Who gives us Peace, shall ruler be.
The Emperor can and will not!—Be elected
An Emperor new, anew the realm directed,
Each one secure and sheltered stand,
And in a fresh-constructed land
Justice and Peace be mated and perfected!"[1]

NAPOLEON IS REPORTED to have read Goethe's sentimental classic the *Sorrows of Werther* no fewer than seven times and to have carried it with him even on his military campaigns, so that, during the lulls in hostilities, he might divert himself by perusing its pages. What about Napoleon and *Faust?* He probably did not read it, for no French translation of Goethe's *Faust* appeared before his death in 1821. However, others in high places, leaders of men, found *Faust* fascinating, even enthralling. In the character of Faust we have one of the classic examples of a person striving successfully for self-expansion, for power, and for place. In time, Faust, albeit in a very fantastic way, assumes the duties and the honors of a statesman and an imperial adviser, and in old age he becomes a ruler over extensive domains.

Lord Leveson-Gower and Sir George Buchanan, like Faust, came to explore "die grosse Welt" and its ways. In spite of their busy routine, these statesmen found the time and believed it worth while to make Goethe's *Faust* understandable to their countrymen by translating it into their native tongue.

4 Half a Hundred Thralls to Faust
LORD FRANCIS LEVESON-GOWER
(1800-1857)
Translation of *Faust I* First Printed in 1823

Among those who have translated Goethe's *Faust*, Leveson-Gower is of emphatic interest. His personal acquaintance with Goethe and his pioneer position as the first European to attempt a virtually complete translation of this great drama give him a place of unique distinction in the long line of those who have Englished the *Faust*.

Goethe himself in 1826 draws this significant portrait of the English peer: "Lord Gower, who translated parts of my *Faust*, in his hasty journey from Petersburg, whence he has accompanied the Duke of Devonshire, spent only a quarter of an hour in Weimar; a pause whose precious fifteen minutes he graciously accorded me. By a longer stay here he could have caused great mischief. He is a very handsome man, and, as ladies would say, interesting. His restless attitude indicates that he feels the lack of something or other, and I think some haste were necessary to supply this deficiency in order to fill the gap in his existence."*[1a]

It must be said to Goethe's credit, that at the ripe age of seventy-seven his understanding of human nature had by no means flagged. After an interview of fifteen minutes, so graciously accorded him by the migrant lord, Goethe does not shoot wide of the mark. We are indebted to Dr. Maginn, a close associate of Christopher North, for a complete verification of Goethe's statement concerning Leveson-Gower's interesting personality. Dr. Maginn has this to say: "He is a general favorite with all classes whose favor is most to be coveted, with Theodore Hook and the wits . . . with A. B., X. Y. Z., and the beauties . . . and with Howley, Philpots, Carr, and all the other ornaments of the episcopal bench. And being himself witty, good-humored, a tall man of his inches—and as handsome a fellow as you can pick out in the round town, in the very

---

* The longer quotations from Goethe's writings are given in my own translation.

flower and vigor of his days, too, and a most staunch and pious disciple of Mother Church, to say nothing of having the best cook after Ude, there can be but little doubt that he might enjoy all the aforesaid honors and luxuries, even if he had never incurred the smallest risk of inking his fingers by anything more serious than a sonnet in an album, or an autograph, upon Duchess Coutts."[2]

Lord Leveson-Gower was born in London in 1800. He received his early education at Eton and took the B.A. degree at Christ Church, Oxford, in 1821. At the age of twenty-two he was elected a Member of Parliament. In later life he became a Lord of the Treasury, Secretary of War, Privy Councilor, Chief Secretary for Ireland under the Duke of Wellington, and held still other important offices. On the death of his father, about 1837, he inherited several huge estates and changed his name to Lord Francis Egerton, Earl of Ellesmere and Viscount Brackley, by which title he was known until his decease in 1857. He was a liberal patron of the arts as well as of literature.[3]

The translator appears to have visited Germany only once, in 1826. But his admiration for the German poet continued active; for in 1831, together with fourteen other Englishmen, he sent the author of *Faust* a birthday gift in the form of a handsome gold seal ring.* This bore the slightly altered Goethean legend: "Ohne Hast, aber ohne Rast."

Just when Gower's interest first turned toward German literature in general and Goethe in particular is a matter of speculation. We know that at the age of twenty-two he be-

* Each of the fifteen friends contributed two guineas toward the gift. Carlyle wrote the greeting. The group consisted of Thomas Carlyle; his brother Dr. Carlyle; W. Fraser, editor of the *Foreign Review;* Dr. Maginn; J. Heraud, editor of *Fraser's Magazine;* G. Moir, translator of Schiller's *Wallenstein;* Churchill Jerdan, editor of the *Literary Gazette;* Professor Wilson, editor of *Blackwood's Magazine;* Sir Walter Scott; his son-in-law Lockhart; Lord Francis Leveson-Gower; Southey, Wordsworth, and Procter (Barry Cornwall).—George Henry Lewes, *The Life of Goethe* (3rd ed.; London: Smith, Elder and Co., 1875), p. 560. The original poem, "Den fünfzehn Englischen Freunden," sent by Goethe as a message of thanks, bearing one of the first imprints of the seal, is one of the most treasured items of the William A. Speck Collection of Goetheana in the Yale University Library.

came a Member of Parliament. In reporting this event the London *Times* states that "he had, however, at an earlier date displayed a taste for literature and the fine arts; and long before he has risked the broad glare of publication, he had printed for private circulation some poems which were at least respectable. He then published a translation of *Faust*, accompanied by free and spirited versions of popular lyrics selected from the works of Goethe, Schiller, Bürger, Salis, and Körner, which passed through several editions before he resolved to withdraw it from further circulation."[4] Abraham Hayward, who translated *Faust* in 1833, states that Gower was "a man of rank, of acknowledged taste and talent, and a profound student of German literature for years."[5]

That distinguished purveyor of literary gossip, Henry Crabb Robinson, has a further bit of testimony to offer concerning Lord Leveson-Gower. Recalling the conversation he had enjoyed with Goethe during a visit to Weimar in 1829, Robinson says: "He [Goethe] was alive to his reputation in England, and apparently mortified at the poor account I gave of Lord Leveson-Gower's translation of *Faust;* though I did not choose to tell him that his noble translator, as an apology, said he did it as an exercise while learning the language."[6] Robinson's telltale reference to the translator's own words probably brings us nearest to the sad truth, that Gower still was submerged in the grammar and the tantalizing sentence pattern of the German language at the time he began translating *Faust*. His translation is proof indeed that he did not bring "to his task a thorough knowledge of German." When Gower attempted to render *Faust* into English, he had just recently received his B.A. degree from Oxford, and he was then only in his early twenties.

It is likely that Gower was induced to translate *Faust* by the prevalent interest in German literature. The *Westminster Review* (1824) observes that "within a short period German literature has become a study among our younger poets, and a copious anthology might already be collected from the versions which have recently appeared in our popular magazines."[7]

Moreover, it is likely that Gower had seen William Taylor's translation of the Domszene from *Faust*,[8] made as early as 1810, and Shelley's prose translation of individual passages[9] dating back to 1815 as well as the Walpurgisnacht in verse, 1822.[10]

It was, of course, in the nature of a courtesy that Gower should send his translation of *Faust* to the author himself, and we have evidence showing that Goethe received several copies in various states. In his diary for May 11, 1825, we find this entry: "A parcel from London sent by Gower containing a translation of *Faust*. Read in the same."[11] This copy was probably one of Gower's second edition published in 1825. There is also a record of the impression the translation made on Goethe. In a letter written to Ottilie von Goethe, June 1, 1825, not quite three weeks after he had received Gower's version, Goethe says: "But now [I pass on] to the very highly esteemed English literature. Lord Gower's translation is in reality a complete recasting, for since he had to omit so much which he did not understand, hardly anything has remained of the original."[12] However, Goethe must have preferred to keep this opinion to himself when Gower visited him in 1826; for, as we shall see, the translator continued very anxious that Goethe should tell him what he thought of the *Faust* in its English dress.

That Goethe's opinion of this first English translation of his *Faust* became, if anything, more unfavorable as time went on, is clear from A. B. Granville's report of his conversation with the poet on January 2, 1828. "He [Goethe] observed to me, that most assuredly it was not a translation, but an imitation of what he had written. Whole sentences of the original, added he [Goethe], have been omitted and chasms left in the translation where the most affecting passages should have been inserted to complete the picture. ... No doubt, the choice of expression in the English translation, the versification, and talent displayed in what is original composition of his lordship's own well-gifted mind, may be deserving of his countrymen's applause; but it as the author of *Faustus travesti* not as the translator of Goethe's *Faustus*, that the popular applause has been obtained."[13]

But Lord Gower's efforts to elicit from Goethe a direct expression of opinion relative to his translation of *Faust* were not yet at an end. He went to the length of plying the author with inducements. This interesting approach Goethe relates in a conversation with Förster on October 16, 1829: "About six or eight weeks ago an Englishman, who occupies himself with our literature, sent me a translation of *Faust* in a neat handwriting, with the request that I pass my judgment on it. However, with the very civil apology that an affection of the eyes would not permit me to read the manuscript copy, I asked him to excuse me, should I not be able to fulfill his wish within a reasonable time. Thereupon, I received yesterday from the noble Lord a unique copy printed for myself with splendid large letters on vellum, accompanied with an expression of the hope that it might be possible for me to read this type without injuring my eyes."[14] Since only two editions of Gower's work appeared, the first in 1823, and the second in 1825, we must conclude that the translator, besides sending Goethe a copy of the 1825 edition, had two additional copies prepared, the one in "zierlicher Reinschrift" and the "auf Velin gedrucktes Exemplar," and forwarded them to the author.

Whether or not Goethe ever sent Gower a criticism of the translation we do not know, but the work continued to be a frequent topic for discussion between Goethe and his friends at Weimar. The next day, October 17, 1829, after Goethe had received the last of the above-named copies, he spent some time again reading and discussing the translation with Förster. Goethe seemed well pleased with Gower's rendering of the Dedication, but he deplored the omission of the larger part of the Prologue in Heaven. In this connection the poet said to Förster: "Not the difficulty of the translation troubled the noble Lord; there were religious or more probably high-churchly scruples; possibly not his own but those of the distinguished society in which he moves. Nowhere are there as many hypocrites and dissemblers as in England; it probably was different in Shakespeare's time."[15]

Then Förster criticized Gower's rendering of the ballad Es war ein König in Thule and pointed out especially the amusing translation of the two lines:

> Gönnt alles seinem Erben,
> Den Becher nicht zugleich.*

as:

> He called for his confessor
> Left all to his successor.

Therepon Goethe laughed heartily and remarked: "Had his father confessor called! We are going to make it plain to the noble Lord, that the King of Thule reigned before the Flood; at that time there was no father confessor!"

When Goethe says of Gower's translation that it is "a complete recasting" of the original, that there were parts left out "which he could not master," that certain other portions, like the Prologue in Heaven, were omitted on account of "high-churchly scruples," he has put his finger on the principal defects of this version. Gower has used too much freedom in the handling of the subject matter, making of the translation practically a new work. He has omitted portions which he either did not understand in the original or could not translate on account of a lack of facility in handling both languages, or because he was prejudiced against them. These portions include the Prologue in Heaven, with the exception of the Angels' Chant, the Rustics' Song under the Lime Tree, and the song of the Invisible Spirits which follows the Curse; large parts of Auerbach's Cellar; the Flower scene between Faust and Margaret; the Summer House scene; and the whole of the Interlude played upon the Blocksberg.

A single example, to which many others could be added, will suffice to show the general lack of fidelity to the thought

---

* The quotations from *Faust* appearing in this book are taken from the Weimar edition of Goethe's Works.

of the original. The first ten lines of Faust's monologue in the scene Night I read in the original:

> Habe nun, ach! Philosophie,
> Juristerei und Medizin,
> Und leider auch Theologie!
> Durchaus, studiert mit heissem Bemühn.
> Da steh' ich nun, ich armer Tor!
> Und bin so klug als wie zuvor;
> Heisse Magister, heisse Doktor gar,
> Und ziehe schon an die zehen Jahr,
> Herauf, herab und quer und krumm,
> Meine Schüler an der Nase herum.

This passage Gower translates:

> With medicine and philosophy
> I have no more to do;
> And all thy maze, theology
> At length have waded through:
> And stand a scientific fool,
> As wise as when I went to school.
> 'Tis true, with years of science ten,
> A teacher of my fellow men,
> Above, below, and round about,
> I draw my scholars by the snout.

In a large part of the translation Gower follows Goethe's metre with a fair degree of accuracy, even attempting the feminine rimes with some success; but in other passages which he found difficult, he departs from Goethe's metrical scheme altogether. Where the original of Gretchen's Prayer in the Zwinger scene reads:

> Ach neige
> Du Schmerzenreiche,
> Dein Antlitz gnädig meiner Not!
>
> Das Schwert im Herzen,
> Mit tausend Schmerzen
> Blickst auf zu deines Sohnes Tod.

Gower translates:

> Thou, who hast woe
> Greater than mortals know,
> Thy brow incline!
> Thou, with unceasing love,
> To him who sits above
> Pray'st for thy Son divine.

Gower was badly prepared for his task, and the translation, therefore, at least if judged by present-day standards, must be regarded as a failure. Carlyle felt this to be the case when he wrote apologetically to Goethe: "Lord L. Gower's translation is now universally admitted to be one of the worst, perhaps the very worst, of such a work, ever accomplished in Britain; our Island, I think, owes you some amends; would that I were the man to pay it."[16]

SIR GEORGE BUCHANAN
(1854-1924)
Translation of *Faust I* First Printed in 1908

One of the most prominent of all the English *Faust* translators was the Right Honorable Sir George William Buchanan, the son of Sir William Buchanan, a former British ambassador. Born in Copenhagen, 1854, he received his scholastic training at Wellington College and then entered immediately the diplomatic service as Attaché in 1875. For nearly half a century he represented his country with effective dignity.[17] He was in turn Attaché at Vienna, Rome, and Tokio; Second Secretary at Tokio in 1879; and Chargé D'Affaires at Darmstadt from 1893 to 1900. While at the latter place, Buchanan was called upon to represent England and the United States to settle the Venezuela boundary dispute.[18]

In later years he came to hold even more responsible positions, such as Secretary of the Embassy at Rome, 1900, and at Berlin, 1901-1903; Minister Plenipotentiary at Sofia, 1903-1908; Minister at The Hague, 1908-1910; Ambassador to Petrograd, 1910-1918; Ambassador to Rome, 1919-1921. Russia honored Buchanan by bestowing upon him the freedom of the city of Moscow, 1916, and by making him an honorary member of the University of Moscow and Petrograd, 1917. He retired from the diplomatic service in 1921 and died in 1924.[19] He became a member of the Privy Council and was made the recipient of high honors: G.C.B., G.C.M.G., and G.C.V.C.[20]

The London *Times*, December 22, 1924, paid the following tribute to the deceased veteran British statesman: "With Sir George Buchanan . . . has passed away the British ambassador who had to bear the heaviest burden of any during the war, for he represented his country at Petrograd up to the time when the Russian Revolution entered into its second phase, and relations were broken off between Great Britain and the Bolshevist masters of Russia. . . . Sir George Buchanan called himself a diplomatist of the old school. One can only hope that the new diplomacy, if there is such a thing, will produce men of the same admirable type. Upright, urbane, tactful, and patient, imbued with the highest sense of duty, and perhaps for this very reason hypersensitive to ignorant or passionate criticism when it imputed to him any neglect of duty, he could make no enemies among all those that knew him well."

Thoroughly engrossed in his work as a diplomatist, Sir George Buchanan had little time left for literary activity. It is significant, however, that, of the two important products from his pen, one should be a translation of Goethe's *Faust*. The volume, *My Mission to Russia*, published just before his death in 1924, discusses the most important and difficult period of his life as a wartime ambassador, while his *Faust* translation, finished and published as early as 1908, represents the efforts of less arduous days as British Minister at Sofia and The Hague.

Buchanan himself relates in the Introduction to his work how he came to make the translation: "One day last summer [1907] as I was reading *L'espoir en Dieu* of Alfred de Musset, I turned to the passage in *Faust*, in which Margaret taxes her lover with his unbelief. In order the better to compare Faust's confession of faith with the appeal addressed to the Deity by the French poet in the Lines commencing—

> 'O toi que nul n'a pu connaître,
> Et n'a renié sans mentir,'

I translated it into blank verse. This led me to translate other passages and, finally, the whole of the first part."[21] He is also indebted, he continues, to Countess Otto Czernin, "who has kindly gone through with me the text of my translation and rendered the greatest assistance by her criticisms and suggestions."

While he endeavors in his rendering of the First Part to adhere as closely as possible to the original, the translator says his aim has been to reproduce the spirit of the play rather than to translate the work word for word. For this purpose, he deemed blank verse the best vehicle, and proceeded on this principle with the exception of Dismal Day and a few lyric parts.

The quality of the translation as a whole is mediocre. By adopting blank verse as the medium for his translation, although the task was thus made easier for the translator, he has failed to reproduce the tonal beauty and variety of the original. The lyric passages, especially the shorter ones in which the verses have a varying number of metrical feet, have become little better than rhythmic prose in the translation and are by no means a faithful reproduction of the metre of the original. As an example let us take a passage from Night beginning with line 501:

> In Lebensfluten, im Thatensturm
> Wall ich auf und ab,
> Webe hin und her!
> Geburt und Grab,
> Ein ewiges Meer,
> Ein glühend Leben.
> So schaff' ich am sausenden Webstuhl der Zeit
> Und wirke der Gottheit lebendiges Kleid.

Buchanan translates:

> In the tides of life, in the storm of deeds,
> I rise and I fall,

> I move here and there!
> The cradle and the grave,
> An eternal sea
> A changeful weaving,
> A life filled with fire,
> Thus work I at the whirling loom of time,
> Weaving life's forces for the Godhead's needs.

Buchanan's blank verse becomes somewhat smoother in the longer, more sustained passages. An example of his best work is the Forest and Cavern scene, where he follows the original in the use of the iambic pentameter:

> Erhabner Geist, du gabst mir, gabst mir alles,
> Worum ich bat. Du hast mir nicht umsonst
> Dein Angesicht im Feuer zugewendet;
> Gabst mir die herrliche Natur zum Königreich,
> Kraft, sie zu fühlen, zu geniessen. Nicht
> Kalt staunenden Besuch erlaubst du nur,
> Vergönnst mir in ihre tiefe Brust,
> Wie in den Busen eines Freunds, zu schauen.

In the translation this passage reads:

> Spirit sublime, thou gav'st me, gav'st me all
> That I did ask. Thou hast not then in vain
> Revealed thy presence to me in the fire.
> Thou gav'st me glorious nature for my realm,
> With power to feel and to delight in her,
> Not as a stranger with cold wondering glance,
> But as a friend, who reads a brother's heart,
> Deep down into her breast thou bid'st me gaze.

In Margaret's Song at the Spinning Wheel and the Zwinger scene, the translator reproduces the metre but not all the feminine rimes of the original, while his version of the ballad König in Thule is more inexact and only masculine rimes are used. In each stanza every first and third line is rimeless. Other scenes partly in rime are the Peasant's Song in Before the Gate, Mephistopheles' Song of the Flea in the Auerbach's Cellar scene, and parts of the Witches' Kitchen.

One gains the impression that the whole translation was done somewhat in the nature of a set task. Buchanan began the translation by accident, and finished it as a matter of duty toward himself. There is hardly a single passage which one could call good poetry. The best that can be said of it is that it reproduces the thought of the original with a fair degree of accuracy. The *Athenaeum* in reviewing this translation remarks: "It is not easy to say much in commendation of Sir George Buchanan's translation of *Faust,* which is not in any respect an improvement upon the best of its predecessors. Its form may perhaps lay claim to a certain novelty, for with the exception of some of the songs and one or two lyric passages, it is written in unrimed verse, the metre being for the most part an approximation to that of the original. . . . The verse is often wooden and the diction prosaic, and the meaning is not always so accurately given as it should be."[22] The reviewer closes by saying that since it is of such a poor quality, it is a superfluous translation. We may add, however, that it constitutes an interesting experiment, and shows at least how *Faust* should not be translated.

II

Jurists and Faust

The Student:
For Jurisprudence I feel no call.

Mephistopheles:
I do not blame you there at all;
I know this calling through and through.
Law and Justice eternally descend,
Direful as a disease which has no end.
They drag themselves from race to race,
Cautiously moving from place to place.
Reason becomes nonsense, benevolence a pest;
And woe to you, heir to this bequest!
Yet of the law which is our inborn right
That question, alas! never comes to light![1]

THE MULTIPLICITY OF Goethe's personal interests is reflected on almost every page of *Faust*. The Sage of Weimar was, for instance, no stranger in the field of jurisprudence. As a university student, although only to indulge his insistent father, he finished the work for a degree in law and later even engaged for a short time in active practice. Goethe's allusions in *Faust* to the law and to the legal profession are grounded in his own life and, therefore, possess the realistic appeal which only experience itself can engender. That *Faust* captivated some of the ablest English legal minds of the nineteenth century, including Abraham Hayward, John Anster, the Honorable Robert Talbot, Sir Theodore Martin, Thomas J. Arnold, and Thomas Webb, is no small compliment to this classic and its author.

Jurists and Faust

ABRAHAM HAYWARD
(1801-1884)

TRANSLATION OF *Faust I* FIRST PRINTED IN 1833

Abraham Hayward, the first of the three translators to make a version of *Faust* in English prose, was a prominent character in the public life of his day. In enumerating the traits of another person in one of his writings, Mr. Hayward has given us an apt characterization of himself: "He is not a specimen of a period, an illustration of a calling, or an example of a class. He is in no sense a representative man. He stands alone in his peculiar and personal description of celebrity—He starts with no advantage of birth or fortune, and he never acquires wealth: he produces no work of creative genius: he does not intrigue, cringe, or flatter: he does not get on by patronage: he is profuse without being venal: he is always on the side he thinks right: yet we find him, almost from the commencement to the very close of his career, the companion and counsellor of the greatest and the most distinguished of his contemporaries, the petted member of the most brilliant and exclusive European circles."[1] Here we may also add Bernal Osborne's characterization of Hayward as the "connecting link between the political and literary magnates"[2] of his time.

Hayward was born at Wilton, England, 1801. After attending several private schools, where he picked up some Greek but more Latin, he was tutored at home for several years, and it was during this period that he studied German and French. In 1818 he was articled to George Tuson, a solicitor in whose library he read widely in English literature. However, since he detested the office work which he was forced to do here, he went to London in 1823 to enter himself as a student of the Inner Temple to study law. After finishing his course, Hayward practiced as a special pleader until he was admitted to the bar in 1832.

In the meantime, however, in the autumn of 1831, he made his first visit to Göttingen, Germany, which at that time was a great center for legal studies. Here, already known as the editor of the *Quarterly Review of Jurisprudence*, he was received with so much kindness and was so well impressed by the German legal minds that upon his return to England he translated Frederick Charles von Savigny's tract *Of the Vocation of our Age for Legislation and Jurisprudence*. Since this immediately attracted the attention of the English lawyers and scholars, Hayward, who was in many ways a shrewd and aspiring person, set out once more for Göttingen. Again he came back with a new inspiration, namely, to translate Goethe's *Faust*. This he did with dispatch.

The translation of *Faust*, together with his legal knowledge, proved to be the sesame that opened the doors for him into polite society, distinguished literary circles, and the world of politics. Hereafter Hayward was feted and dined; his counsel was sought out by the most distinguished men of the age; he became a connecting link between British statesmen and foremost statesmen abroad, as well as between the leading literary men of England and those on the continent.* He continued to act in this manifold role† and to travel much abroad until death closed his eventful career in 1884.[3] One of the last to visit him on his death bed was the great Gladstone.

As we already know, Hayward's first acquaintance with German dates back to the two years he spent at home, 1817-1819, under the guidance of a private tutor. At this time he

---

* In politics Hayward's name is associated with those of Disraeli, Lord Derby, Lord Palmerston, Gladstone, and Lord Aberdeen; in literature with Macaulay, Lockhart, Thackeray, Mrs. Shelley, Froude, Mignet, Merimée, Ottilie von Goethe, Tieck, and the Brothers Grimm. The dinners he gave in his chambers in the Inner Temple were brilliant affairs and were attended by the celebrities of the day. It is said that Lord Macaulay and Hayward were the two best-read men in all England. Hayward was a most gifted and witty raconteur and wrote entertainingly on the *Art of Dining*.

† Hayward was also on the staff of the *Morning Chronicle*, wrote articles for the *Quarterly Review* and the *Edinburgh Review*, and was a member of the Athenaeum Club. He published *Lord Chesterfield, his Character, Life and Opinions; George Selwyn, his Life and Times*, 1842; *Specimens of an Authorized Translation from the French*, 1856; *Goethe*, 1878; and *Sketches of Eminent Statesmen and Writers*, 1880. The British Museum Catalogue, 1888, credits him with twenty-six separate articles and works. His biographical volume on Goethe is a general discussion of the poet's life and works and contains nothing new on *Faust*.

must have mastered the rudiments of the language; for, although he seems to have engaged in no further study of German meanwhile, immediately after his first short visit to Göttingen in 1831 he translated Savigny's legal tract with a satisfactory degree of accuracy. In his Journal, kept during his second visit at Göttingen, in the latter part of the same year, we find the following entry for August 19: "Went to call on Miller, found him at home and talked to him mostly in German about England." This implies that he had a fair command of the German language at the time.

Hayward's interest in German literature and Goethe's *Faust* was, no doubt, also stimulated by these visits to Göttingen and other German cities and by his intercourse with German scholars and friends of Goethe. While the author of *Faust* was still living at this time, there is no evidence that Hayward ever met him. But we know that Hayward had become so interested in *Faust* that soon after his return to England he made a prose translation of it for his own use and for private circulation.

This initial attempt of 1833 was followed in the same year by the first published edition. In the advertisement prefixed to this volume he dwells on the circumstances that led him to bring the second printing before the public: "I commenced this translation without the slightest idea of publishing it, and even when, by aid of preface and notes, I thought I had produced a book which might contribute something towards the promotion of German literature in this country, I still felt unwilling to cast it from me beyond the power of alteration or recall. I therefore circulated the whole of the first impression amongst my acquaintance and made up my mind to be guided by the general tenor of the opinions I might receive from them. I also wished the accuracy of my version to be verified by as many examinations as possible. . . . The result of the experiment has been so far satisfactory, that I am now emboldened to lay the work before the public, with some not unimportant alterations and additions, suggested by subsequent inquiry or by friends."

In the Preface to the revised edition of 1834, Hayward further expatiates on the motives that led him to make an English version of *Faust*. He says that he was urged on by an encouraging remark made by Charles Lamb to an honored friend of his. Moreover, Hayward also felt that it was necessary to make a new version of *Faust* because a previous attempt had been unsatisfactory: "I venture to think that it may possess some interest and utility now; when at the distance of nearly half a century from the first appearance of the work (1790), nothing at all approximating to an accurate version of it exists. With one or two exceptions, all attempts by foreigners (foreigners as regards Germany, I mean) to translate even solitary scenes or detached passages from *Faust* are crowded with the most extraordinary mistakes, not of words merely, but of spirit and tone; and the author's fame has suffered accordingly."[4]

To make sure that he himself did not misconstrue *Faust* in the original and translate it inaccurately, Hayward, on his visit to Germany in 1833, consulted many prominent German scholars, friends, and contemporaries of Goethe, such as Jacob Grimm, A. W. Schlegel, Tieck, Chamisso, Franz Horn, the Baron de la Motte Fouque, Dr. Hitzig, Retzsch, Varnhagen von Ense, Eckermann, and Madame de Goethe. Several letters that passed between German scholars and Hayward are still extant. Jacob Grimm wrote to him from Göttingen, November 4, 1832, and again on November 23, 1833. Then there are two letters from August Wilhelm Schlegel, the famous German translator of Shakespeare. The one written April, 1832, contains a negative reply to Hayward's request for a necrolog of Goethe by Schlegel. As an excuse for not complying with the request, he writes: "Besides, in my position I cannot write in a superficial manner about Goethe, but you or Mr. Carlyle would do that capitally. Farewell, sir, etc."[5]

The second letter from Schlegel, relative to the translation of *Faust*, was written from Bonn, December 31, 1832. On account of its length, only short excerpts can be given here. It reads: "Sir . . . I had resolved to answer immediately, but I have been overwhelmed with work; there is left for me but little time for interesting correspondence, and it is only today, the last day of the year that I find an hour of leisure to discharge my obligation.*

"Here is the explanation of the passages from *Faust* that you ask.

" 'Haupt- und Staats-Action.' This is the title which we apply to marionette dramas when they treat heroic and historical subjects.

" 'Sie ist gerichtet', refers to the sentence of death pronounced by the judges; the following words: 'Sie ist gerettet', to the salvation of her soul."

Then follows Schlegel's unfavorable opinion of a prose translation of *Faust:* "I doubt whether a prose translation of *Faust* is able to give a just idea of *Faust*. The poet has indulged himself in a very great variety of metres and always in a characteristic manner. There is an astonishing flexibility and a perfect naturalness in the dialogue."[6]

But we know that in spite of Schlegel's strong doubts as to the success of the venture, Hayward chose prose as the medium for his translation, even for some of the especially poetic portions as the Zueignung and the König in Thule. As authority for this innovation, he cites the words of Goethe himself concerning the introduction and the spread of Shakespeare in Germany: "Shakespeare, translated into prose first by Wieland, then by Eschenburg, being reading [*sic*] generally intelligible and adapted to every reader, was enabled to spread rapidly and produce a great effect. I honor both rhythm and rime, by which poetry first becomes poetry; but the properly deep and radically operative— the truly developing and quickening is that which remains of the poet when he is translated into prose."[7] Of course, it is extremely doubtful whether the great poet would have sanctioned a prose translation of a work so varied in form, and so dependent on metre, rime, and all other poetic devices for its highest effectiveness.† But Hayward's

---

* Schlegel's letter, written in French, is here translated into English.

† Hayward, no doubt, laid too much stress on the particular passage quoted above. It would have been very beneficial for him to have read and to have taken to heart also the passage in the *West-Easterly Divan:* "Translation is

opinion was that a translator must inevitably sacrifice either metre or meaning, and he chose to reproduce the meaning at the expense of the metre.[8]

Hayward's translation was highly acclaimed. Southey, Wordsworth, Rogers, Hallam, Coleridge, and many others wrote letters in which they congratulated him upon his splendid achievement, and some years after its publication Carlyle stated that of the nineteen translations then existing "Hayward's was the best."[9] In Germany it was regarded as "word true and spirit true."[9a] Herman Kindt in *Die Gegenwart* remarks: "Die bedeutendste der ersten Jahre ist die schon eben erwähnte von A. Hayward."[10]

But not all the critics joined in this chorus of praise. We do well to quote the following from the *Westminster Review*. "He [Hayward] had, therefore, not the least vocation for the work he has undertaken; but his industry, unhappily obscured by too much pretension, has notwithstanding enabled him to produce a translation which is remarkable under such circumstances . . . but at the same time we must warn every learner of German, who seeks for assistance in the understanding of the original, from paying any attention to the translation of Mr. H. which must lead him into continual errors, as it always obscures or annihilates the sense of the original under a translation of mere words and phrases."[11]

At the present time, when we possess the verse translations of Bayard Taylor, Anna Swanwick, Theodore Martin, Alice Raphael, and John F. L. Raschen, it is more difficult for us to appreciate a prose translation to the same extent that Hayward's contemporaries did, even if it were faultless. Exactly thirty years after he published his second edition, Hayward reissued his *Faust* translation for the eighth time with many improvements and additions of new notes. The eleventh edition appeared in 1890, and in 1908 a new edition with thirty illustrations. This is sufficient proof of its popularity.

---

of three kinds: First, the prosaic prose translator with new ideas, but gives up all poetic art, and reduces even the poetic enthusiasm to one level watery plain."—William Page Andrews, "On the Translation of Goethe's Faust," *Atlantic Monthly*, December, 1890, p. 733.

Considered from the standpoint of a prose translation, this popularity was not unmerited. While the language of the translation is still too latinized and lacking in the simplicity of the German original, it is difficult to find any considerable number of such glaring mistranslations as are only too common in most of the early poetic versions. Hayward is by far at his best in the narrative and reflective passages, with only occasional errors marring his work. The last line of the first stanza of the Dedication, "Der euren Zug unwittert," he translates too boldly and inaccurately as, "Which atmospheres your breath." Here and there he fails to catch the exact shade of meaning conveyed by the original, as in lines 1583 and 1584. The original has:

> Wenn aus dem schrecklichen Gewühle
> Ein süss bekannter Ton mich zog;

but Hayward translates: "Since a sweet familiar tone drew me from those thronging horrors."

The poetic parts were more difficult for him to render, and occasionally, casting these passages into a dubious sort of rhythmic, rimeless form, he contents himself with a paraphrase. In the closing lines of the Chorus of Angels in Night I, where the original has:

> Thätig ihn preisenden,
> Liebe beweisenden,
> Brüderlich speisenden
> Predigend reisenden
> Wonne verheissenden
> Euch ist der Meister nah,
> Euch ist er da!

Hayward translates:

> Ye in deeds giving praise to him,
> Love manifesting,
> Living brethren-like,
> Travelling and preaching him,
> Bliss promising—
> You is the master nigh,
> For you is he here.

In conclusion, it may be said that Hayward's translation was very useful in popularizing Goethe's *Faust* in England. Many people, no doubt, read the prose version who probably never would have become interested in a poetic translation. It is also to his credit that after great labors, and, to be sure with the liberal aid of others, Hayward made a version, which, if still far from reproducing the style and the varying moods of the original, yet is virtually more correct in rendering its thought than most of the verse translations up to the present time. His version also served as a model for Leopold Bernays in his attempt to render *Faust*, Part II, into prose in 1839 and for F. G. G. Schmidt's translation of Part I in 1935. But Hayward offered little or nothing to that class of readers who insisted on fidelity to form and spirit as well as verbal correctness in a translation. It took many more years of constant effort and dozens of trials by as many translators before an acceptable version appeared.

JOHN ANSTER
(1793-1867)

TRANSLATION OF *Faust I* FIRST PRINTED IN 1835;
Faust II, 1864

John Anster, the first Irishman to make a translation of Goethe's *Faust*, was born in 1793 at Charlville in the county of Cork. At the age of seventeen he entered Trinity College, Dublin, and was called to the Irish bar in 1824. His Alma Mater granted him the LL.D. degree one year later. In 1837 he was appointed Registrar to the High Court of Admiralty in Ireland, but during the latter part of his life he served his Alma Mater as Regius Professor of Civil Law. He died in 1867.[12]

By nature Anster was somewhat timid and reserved. He was "called to the Irish bar in 1824, but from causes originating in all probability in his own retired habits and his distaste for the turbulent element in which the Bar appears to live, move, and have its being, his labors have for the most part been confined to chamber practice."[13] However, "his social charm, kindly wit, and wide literary culture rendered Anster a delightful companion."[14]

The one outstanding friendship of this Irishman's life was with Samuel Taylor Coleridge, and Anster's name occurs from time to time in the latter's correspondence.[15] They seem first to have met as a result of Anster's publication of certain of his translated portions of *Faust* in *Blackwood's Magazine*, "where they had attracted the attention of the late Samuel Coleridge, who was led to express, upon more than one occasion, a high opinion of their merits: this sentiment ripened into a warmer feeling when the 'old man eloquent' became acquainted with the personal qualities of the writer, and the enthusiastic reverence cherished for his works by his young disciple."[16]

In a letter to T. Allsop, Esquire, dated November 17, 1821, occurs this cryptic but relevant sentence by Coleridge: "My anxiety to consult you on the subject of a proposal made to me by *Anster* before I return an answer, which I must do speedily."[17] In another letter soon after, he (Coleridge) refers to "The Dublin scheme" promoted by Anster, namely, that Coleridge should deliver a course of lectures in that city.[18] Once more, in the postscript to a letter written to Allsop, April 27, 1824, Coleridge says, "To my great surprise and delight, Mr. Anster came in on us this afternoon, and in perfect health and spirits."[19] Finally, we find Dr. Anster's name linked with that of Coleridge in the former's review of Coleridge's *Aids to Reflection* published in 1825.[20]

The friendship between the two grew out of their mutual compatibility and their similar literary interests. Coleridge was so deeply interested in the Faust lore that he at one time determined to write a Faust play himself. He says: "Before I had ever seen any part of Goethe's *Faust*, though, of course, when I was familiar enough with Marlowe's, I conceived and drew up the plan of a work, a drama, which was to be, to my mind, what the *Faust* was to Goethe's."[21] This plan, which was never carried out, has been preserved with the rest of his works.

We find that Anster's literary interests date back to his

university years at Dublin. While in residence there as an undergraduate, he wrote a prize poem in English on the death of Princess Charlotte, in which "he gave evidence of those poetic powers which in after years, when matured by study and thought, placed him amongst the best writers of his day."[22] His interest in German literature was also aroused at this time, for we find that in 1819 Anster published his *Poems: With Translations from the German* and, during the following year, some translated fragments of *Faust* in *Blackwood's Magazine* which included parts of the Dedication, The Prelude at the Theatre, the whole of Night I, part of the Witches' Kitchen scene, Gretchen's Song at the Spinning Wheel, and almost the entire Prison scene.*

Although Anster's interest in *Faust* is thus evident at an early age, and in spite of the fact that he translated these fragments even before Gower's version was published, he did not complete Part I until 1835. For this long delay he blames his temporary lack of interest in the subject. In his Preface he says: "I was in this state of mind when Mr. Hayward's mention of the extracts in *Blackwood* in the Preface to his translation recalled my attention to the subject. The result has been completion of the task."[23]

On the other hand, Hayward was not slow to state in self-laudatory terms that he had encouraged Anster to complete the project: "The author of the most admired [translation], Dr. Anster, has generously given me the credit of encouraging him to the completion of his task, and this alone must be deemed no unimportant service to literature."[24] However, we should bear in mind also Coleridge's favorable remarks about the fragments in *Blackwood's Magazine* and his friendship with Anster, which stimulated the latter to literary activity.

The translation of Part I† was received by the critics with

---

* In the biographical volume *Men of the Time* we read that "These [scenes] were at once received into favor. Their truth and vigor were at once acknowledged, and it is said that the great German poet himself recognized their excellence."—*Men of the Time* (London, 1856), p. 25. See note 13.

† To spare tender consciences Anster relegates the first Walpurgis Night to the Appendix. Here is also included a translation of Goethe's poem "The Bride of Corinth."

a considerable difference of opinion. Favorable comment, however, is not lacking. The *Edinburgh Review* finds that "it is the genius, the fire, the characteristic mind and tone of Goethe which we find here, and here alone, transfused into our native tongue; and it is easy to trace how the possession of this fellow-feeling with his author has smoothed away for him many of the difficulties with which other translators have contended unsuccessfully; so that he is carried, with grace and dexterity, through portions of the work where the others labor in much perplexity, and do not think themselves safe unless they have fast hold of the words and idiom of Goethe, in default of his spirit."[25]

But from the start there were dissenting voices. In the Preface to his second edition (1839), Talbot, whose first version appeared in the same year (1835), criticizes Anster's translation with a large measure of justice when he remarks: "He has, however, far exceeded his prototype [Shelley, whom Talbot thinks Anster is taking for his model] in redundancy, and at least doubled the original matter, by interpolations purely arbitrary, notwithstanding a declaration in his preface, that he had in no instance, ventured to substitute anything of his own for Goethe's. . . . The greater part of Goethe's rhymed dialogue is by him turned into blank verse, an innovation upon the very frame work of the original by no means commendable."[26]

Not quite so unfavorable is an article by "Z" in the *Westminster Review* for 1836: "The *Faust* of Dr. Anster has obtained considerable reputation. Like the *Faust* of Lord F. L. Gower, it is no translation, but an imitation; we might almost say an original English work built upon the ideas of Goethe. It is unjust to try such works by the standard of translation—by a standard taken from the original. Such works must stand or fall by their own intrinsic value and we cannot hesitate to say that the perusal of Dr. Anster's *Faust* must give pleasure to any unprejudiced reader."[27]

This serious lack of fidelity to the original must be traced back largely to the fact that Anster only tries to communicate the effect produced on his mind and ear by the poem which he has translated, that he lays no claim to verbal fidelity, and that his knowledge of German was deficient. He confesses that he has in some instances not been familiar with the spoken language and fallen into erroneous interpretations of the German text.[28]

In the following passages Anster is both at his best as far as his individual poetic powers, his ability to recapture the spirit of Goethe, as he would call it, are concerned, but also at his worst as a translator in that he more than doubles the number of lines in the translation.

Lines 447-53, Part I:

> Wie alles sich zum Ganzen webt,
> Eins in dem andern wirkt und lebt!
> Wie Himmelskräfte auf und nieder steigen
> Und sich die goldenen Eimer reichen!
> Mit segenduftenden Schwingen
> Vom Himmel durch die Erde dringen,
> Harmonisch all' das All durchklingen!

Anster translates:

> Oh! how the spell before my sight
> Brings nature's hidden ways to light
> See! all things with each other blending—
> Each to all its being lending—
> All on each in turn depending—
> Heavenly ministers descending—
> And again to heaven uptending—
> Floating, mingling, interweaving—
> Rising, sinking, and receiving.
> Each from each, while each is giving
> On to each, and each relieving
> Each, the pails of gold, the living
> Current through the air is heaving;
> Breathing blessings, see them bending,
> Balanced worlds where diffused is harmony unending!

In addition to the enormous expansion of the thought, scarcely a single line is true to the rhythmic movement of the original. Interesting is Anster's superabundant use of the feminine rime, but all are in words used as present participles and by no means argue for any great amount of skill in the translator's handling of this type of rime. The blank verse, which Anster uses to replace the original metre in a number of passages, is rather pale and feeble.

In regard to the motives for translating Part II, which was completed and published in 1864, Anster says at the end of the lengthy Preface to this volume: "It has grown up under my hands from day to day and from year to year silently with no thought of publication. If asked, Why then translate it? I can only reply that this intellectual exertion, such as it is, is, in the enjoyment it affords, its own great reward. A member of my family became interested in the subject, and felt it desirable to arrange such passages as could be found among papers, disregarded and almost forgotten by me. This accident led me to complete the poem."

It seems, then, that for the translating and publishing of both parts of *Faust* by Anster, we have to thank his friends as much as the author himself. He was dominated by no overwhelming desire, nor was he urged forward by any sense of duty as were Blackie, Taylor, Claudy, and other later translators.

Anster's translation of Part II shows little improvement over his rendering of Part I. He still is more or less independent in his handling of the original, in regard both to the thought and to the rhythmic variations of the different parts. Where, as in portions of Act III, he substitutes iambic pentameter for Goethe's hexameter, the metre is harsh and halting. Lines 8568-78 read:

> So spake my Lord—this further mandate followed:
> When thou hast seen through all things in their order,
> Then take as many tripods as thou deemest
> Needful—as many vessels as the priest
> Requires when perfecting the holy rite—
> Caldrons and bowls and flat round altar-plates—
> The purest water, from the holy fount,
> Be in high pitchers a short space apart,

Have dry wood ready, quick to catch the flame;—
And let not a well-sharpened knife be wanting!

In spite of the fact that Dr. Anster's translation of both parts was accepted in Germany for a time as the standard English translation of *Faust*,[29] we must insist that it gives a distorted idea of the original. After reading Anster's version, one fully understands why the writer in the *Athenaeum* was led to sum up his view of this work in these tart words: "Now, whoever is for poetry, in lieu of translation, may find his object here; but if anyone, as whimsical as ourselves, desires to meet in a version an impress of the original, he must look elsewhere."[30] Nevertheless, the "poetry" in this translation caused it to go through a remarkable number of editions. It was reprinted as late as 1909.

THE HONORABLE ROBERT TALBOT
(1776-1843)

TRANSLATION OF *Faust I* FIRST PRINTED IN 1835

The two translators who published their English versions of *Faust* in 1835 were John Anster and the Honorable Robert Talbot, both of them Irishmen, at least by birth, and both barristers. The former was a well-known figure in his day and considerable information about him is at hand. Concerning the latter, however, although he is distinguished by the title "Honorable," our knowledge is still very limited.

However, by using this "Honorable," which is a courtesy title bestowed upon children of certain ranks of the nobility, as a clew, we are able to identify the translator with a well-known family of the Irish nobility, the Talbots of Malahide, who resided in Dublin County, Ireland. *The Genealogical and Heraldic History of the Peerage and Baronetage*[31] lists among the children of Lord Richard Talbot of Malahide one "Robert who was a barrister-at-law, b. 1776; m. 7 Oct., 1828, Arabella, dau. of Admiral Sir Chaloner Oglo, 1st bart., widow of the Hon. Edw. Bouverio, M. P.; and d. 17 March, 1843." In this brief article are two convincing arguments for assuming that this Robert Talbot is the translator. The first is that his dates, 1776-1843, satisfy the time requirement for the translation, which was published in 1835; the second is that his family connections explain the appellation of dignity which goes with his name.

When Talbot made his translation of Goethe's *Faust*—the only work of which he is known to be the author—he lived at Hampton Court, London. Previous to this, however, he also resided in Germany for some time. The *Gentleman's Magazine*, 1835, refers to him as one who "has resided much in Germany."[32] In the Preface to the second edition of his *Faust*, published in 1839, Talbot remarks, "Such incongruities [as copying German idioms in the English] remind me of having seen in Germany, many years ago, a dandy of that nation exhibit himself at a dress ball, a l'anglaise in yellow buckskins, and topboots; so that the dress, being quite out of place, his appearance was neither German nor English."[33]

From the Advertisement to the 1835 edition, written in June, 1834, it is clear that Talbot finished his translation the year previous to its publication, "before the writer was aware, that he had been anticipated, either by Mr. Blackie, or Mr. Symes [*sic*]."[34] The Postscript, written March 21, 1835, informs us that "a few sheets of this work were struck off, as early as last July; but the writer was advised to suspend the printing of it, till November; that being considered a more favorable season for publication. When he was, accordingly, about to proceed with it, in November, a translation of *Faust*, from the pen of Mr. Anster, was announced, as already in the Press. This occasioned the further delay, which has since taken place; the Translator having been desirous to give precedence to Mr. Anster; but that Gentleman's announcement not having been reported during the last three months, he now ventures to come forward with his own version."[35]

Talbot was acquainted with Abraham Hayward and had read his prose translation of *Faust*. He remarks in his Advertisement to the first edition that "Mr. Hayward has most obligingly allowed the translator to make what use he pleased of the information contained in his Notes; of which permission he would avail himself to a greater extent, than he has done, did he not consider that Gentleman's Work to be an indispensable companion to all, who would obtain a proper knowledge of *Faust*."

Talbot holds that since the German language "admits of certain modes of expression, so peculiar, and sometimes apparently so capricious, as to defy all attempt, on the part of a translator, to produce an exact imitation,"[36] and since the German writers are so arbitrary in their formation and use of compounds, it is useless to attempt an exact verbal translation. Therefore, he has "endeavored to collect the spirit of his Author's meaning without confining himself to a mere verbal interpretation, or attempting to furnish an exact echo to the almost endless variety of measures employed in the original— Still less has he thought of finding equivalents in kind for the female rhymes which so abound in the German language and are comparatively so rare in our own."[37]

Despite the fact that Talbot translates the whole of *Faust* including the Prologue in Heaven, his version of 1835 has but slight literary merit. Mistakes of every conceivable kind abound, and it is little better than Gower's. The translator recognized its deficiencies before the whole version was published, and, therefore, remarks in his Postscript that "he has to regret that he did not allow himself the advantage of a general revise; as he now perceives several necessary corrections."*

Still, Talbot's version of 1835 is interesting because of Ottilie von Goethe's connection with it. The *Gentleman's Magazine*, 1835, remarks that "Mr. Talbot . . . has resided much in Germany, and his translation was for sometime in the hands of the widow of Goethe, the poet's son August, who understands

---

* Talbot refers to this again in the Advertisement to his second edition, published in 1839: "The greatest part of the first edition of this work was unluckily put to press, without the writer's knowledge, while he was on a sick bed; and he thus lost the benefit of a general revise. He trusts, however, that most of the errors, whether of the press or of any other description, which disfigured the former, will be found corrected in the present edition."

English perfectly."³⁸ However, one cannot subscribe to her reactions to the translation. This same periodical reports her as pronouncing "it to be not only the most literal translation of *Faust* which has yet appeared, but to have entered completely into the spirit of the work."

Not satisfied with this initial attempt, Talbot made a further revision of the first edition in preparation for its republication at a later time. Among the "literary remains" of August Wilhelm Schlegel is a letter from Talbot dated July 18, 1836, in which the latter asks the noted German scholar for advice concerning the translation of certain passages in *Faust*. It reads in part: "Having an opportunity of sending . . . to Bonn, I take the liberty of presenting to you, who have so eminently succeeded in naturalising our Shakespeare in the language of Germany, with a copy of an attempt to render *Faust* in English rhymes. I am not a little ashamed of the many awkwardnesses which will be found in it, owing to its having been printed off without my knowledge, while I was upon sick bed, and before I had given it the least corrections. Should it ever be reprinted, I hope, it will appear in a less slovenly condition. In the meantime, however, I have altered with a pen a few of its many glossing errors.* Being very anxious that a Second Edition (if I might look forward to such a thing) should be as little exceptionable as possible, I venture to propose to you, Sir, a few queries, with regard to certain passages of the exact meaning of which I am in doubt, and even to hope, that you would certainly favor me, by mentioning any other mistakes; many of which doubtless you would discover, should you do me the honor of casting your eye upon my performance." Then follow questions about these passages: "Die Gegenwart von einem braven Knaben," "Nur was der Augenblick erschafft, dass kann er nützen," "Harmonisch all' das All," "Mit ahnungs-voller Gegenwart," and "Werdelust." Several of Talbot's suggestions with respect to the meaning of these expressions show how

---

* The copy of this first edition in the Speck Collection has the abovementioned alterations in pen and ink. Since not only the errata have been corrected, but other additional alterations have been made, it would appear that this is the very copy which Talbot corrected for Schlegel.

helpless he was in making the translation. In regard to the first one, for instance, he says: "[It] leaves me in doubt whether the word 'Gegenwart' . . . means *presence* or the *present time*." He closes his letter with a show of great servility. "What adequate apology," he says, "can I make to you, Sir, for this letter? but I trust you will be inclined to excuse an ardent admirer of the *Faust*, and one who is anxious to have the opinion of the most distinguished Critic in Europe on all literary subjects."[39]

When the second edition appeared in 1839 with the English and the German text on opposite pages,* it was dedicated to "Thomas Carlyle, Esquire . . . as the individual best qualified, in the writer's opinion, to estimate the degree of consideration to which it may appear entitled, this volume is, without his permission, respectfully inscribed." In the Preface Talbot points out that Hayward's prose translation gives no "notion of the graceful movement which distinguishes the original,"[40] and he criticizes Anster severely for his looseness as well as diffuseness. He then adds at the close: "I confidently hope that my version will be found, by German scholars, to the full as true to the original even in the minutest particulars, as any that has yet appeared, either in verse or prose."[41]

The revision of the first edition, which Talbot effected from 1835 to 1839, was not as thorough as one might wish that it had been. Essentially the same faults which marred the former are still evident in the latter. The poetic value of the translation is small. The lyrics, including those at the end of Scene 1, are a total failure in the English dress which Talbot has given them. By the altering of the number of lines or the metrical feet, by rendering the thought in a loose, inexact way, and by his conventional language, Talbot has robbed these parts of all resemblance to the original. The following four verses from the Chorus of the Disciples:

> Hat der Begrabene
> Schon sich nach oben
> Lebend Erhabene,
> Herrlich erhoben!

* The attractive and costly paper and type used for this edition indicate that Talbot must have been a man of means and taste.

Talbot translates:

> The buried One is raised on high!
> Living He treads His native sky.

The Soldier's Song in Outside the Town Gate is another example. The first stanza:

> Burgen mit hohen
> Mauern und Zinnen,
> Mädchen mit Stolzen
> Höhnenden Sinnen
> Möcht' ich gewinnen!

Talbot translates:

> Castles, with lowering
> Battlements—
> Maidens, with towering
> Sentiments,
> Allure our eyes!

Nearly every page of Talbot's translation, even in the more sustained and conversational portions, is marred by some inaccuracies. One more passage taken from The Cathedral will suffice to give us a general notion of the nature of this translation. The Evil Spirit speaks the opening lines of this scene:

> Wie anders, Gretchen, war dir's,
> Als du noch voll Unschuld
> Hier zum Altar trat'st,
> Aus dem vergriffnen Büchelchen
> Gebete lalltest,
> Halb Kinderspiele,
> Halb Gott im Herzen!

In Talbot's version this passage reads:

> How different, Margaret, was't with thee,
> When thou, still full of innocence,
> Camest before the altar here,
> Out of thy well-thumbed little book
> Lisping thy prayers,
> Half childish play
> Half God within thy heart.

The thought is well reproduced here but not the metre. In the first two lines the translator has added one foot to each verse; the feminine endings are lacking altogether; and in several verses the metre is rough. Talbot has no musical ear; hence we listen in vain for rhythm and the melody of the original. But if he does not have the poetic gifts of Anster, he has at least avoided Anster's diffuseness.

SIR THEODORE MARTIN
(1816-1909)
Translation of *Faust I* First Printed in 1865; *Faust II*, 1886

> You, too, can measure well how great
> His perils are, who would translate
> The thoughts on aptest language strung,
> And wed them to another tongue.*

Sir Theodore Martin will be remembered not so much for the brilliance he displayed in his vocation as a lawyer as for the success he achieved as a man of letters. Born in Edinburgh in 1816, he was educated to follow his father's profession, the law.[42] He practiced as an attorney in his native city until 1846, when he became a member of a London firm of parliamentary solicitors. In 1881 Martin was elected Lord Rector of St. Andrew's University, and in 1896 he was made Knight Commander of the Royal Victorian Order.[43] For a number of years he was an intimate friend and adviser of Queen Victoria.[44] He remained a barrister nearly all his life, and died at Bryntysiliv, Wales, in 1909.[45] A biographer in *Blackwood's Magazine* aptly compares Martin's nature and life to that of Goethe: "While he was fortunate in the length of years allotted to him, he was still more fortunate because in the bad sense he never grew old. He preached incessantly the gospel of work, which he rightly welcomed as the true preserver of youth. 'Frivolous pursuits', said he on his ninetieth birthday, 'base passions un-

---

* These are Martin's lines in a dedicatory espistle to Froude.—*Blackwood's Magazine*, September, 1909, p. 454.

subdued, narrow selfishness, vacuity of mind, life with sordid aims or no aims at all—these are the things that bring age upon the soul. Healthful tastes . . . a happy remembrance of youthful pleasures, a mind never without some active interest or pursuit—these are the things that carry on the feelings of youth into old age!' "[46]

If, as Martin says in the Preface written in 1903 for the *Bon Gaultier Ballads*, literature had occupied the smallest part of his long and crowded life, it was certainly the intensest and the happiest. In turn he was magazine writer, translator, stage critic, and biographer. His first literary attempt, a paper, "Flowers of Hemp," written in 1841 for *Fraser's Magazine*, won for him the good will of Professor Aytoun, and as a result a close literary friendship sprang up between the two, which Martin himself calls "a kind of Beaumont and Fletcher partnership." This bore fruit in a series of humorous papers called *Bon Gaultier Ballads*, published in *Tait's* and *Fraser's* magazines from 1842 to 1844, which brought the authors immense popularity.*

These early literary efforts were followed by various translations from German, Latin, Italian, and Danish authors. *Faust*, Part I, appeared in 1865; translations from Heine in 1878; *Faust*, Part II, and Schiller's *Song of the Bell* in 1886. The *Life of his Royal Highness the Prince Consort*, which Queen Victoria asked him to write and which many regard as Martin's best work, was finished in 1880.† Later appeared translations from the *Aeneid*, *Essays on the Drama* in two volumes, and various biographical works, such as the lives of

* "Bon Gaultier" was a pseudonym Martin used when he wrote for current periodicals. The *Bon Gaultier Ballads* were verses that parodied the leading poetry of the day, especially the "new" poetry of Tennyson.

† At the time Martin wrote this biography he was a very close friend and adviser to the Queen. His helpful relationship to her is revealed in a letter of appreciation written to him by the Queen in 1869. She says: "The Queen really is at a loss to say how much she feels his constant and unvariable kindness to her and how deeply grateful she is for it. The Queen likewise feels that in him she has found an impartial friend who can tell her many important things which her own unbiased servants cannot hear or tell her."—*Blackwood's Magazine*, September, 1909, p. 457. Martin was chosen to write this biography largely on account of the fluency of his pen and his superior knowledge of German.

Garrick, Macready, Rachel, and Stockmar, and finally *Queen Victoria as I Knew Her* in 1908.

We find that Martin's interest in German goes back to his student days at the University of Edinburgh in 1830-1833. Here he developed a love for literature, interested himself in music and the stage, and studied German. The first fruit of these early studies is the volume called *Poems and Ballads of Goethe*, translated together with Aytoun during 1843 and 1844. So close was the collaboration that Aytoun wrote later in a letter to Martin: "I was very much struck by the occasional resemblance of our styles. There is one of yours, *To my Mistress*, which I could almost have sworn to be mine from the peculiarity of the cadences, if I did not know it to be yours."[47]

Martin's next translation was that of Goethe's *Prometheus, a Dramatic Fragment*, which appeared in the *Dublin University Magazine*, in 1850. He was charmed by "the simplicity and concise energy of the original, which has all the effect of exquisitely chiselled sculpture standing against a crisp, clear sky."[48] Then he proceeded to the translation of "Helena," the third act of the Second Part of *Faust*, which was published in *Fraser's Magazine* in 1858. Next there appeared in 1863, in the volume *Poems: Original and Translated*, printed for private circulation, large portions of both parts of *Faust*: the Dedication and the first two scenes of Part I, the first four scenes of Act I, the first six scenes of Act II, and the whole of Act III, from Part II. Part I was completed and published in 1865. On March 28, 1865, Martin wrote to Hermann Kindt, a German literary critic and friend, as follows: "It has been a dream of mine since boyhood to translate *Faust*, of which we have truly no version in English worthy of the name. At last I have been able to realize my dream; but I need not say how far short I feel my work must be of the matchless original."* Still, the translation was in demand, for on November 3, 1865, Martin wrote to his printers, Messrs. Whittingham and Wilkins: "I enclose my check for £67 in payment of your account

---

* All the letters here quoted from are in the Speck Collection.

for printing *Faust*. The publishers tell me I must go to press at once with a second edition."

Although Martin published his translation of "Helena" as early as 1858, and additional portions from Part II in 1863, he

> Fill thy heart thence even unto overflowing,
> And when with thrill ecstatic thou art glowing,
> Then call it whatsoe'er thou wilt,
> Life! Heart! Love! God!
> Name for it have I none!
> Feeling is all in all;
> Name is but sound & smoke,
> Shrouding heaven's golden glow!

To Hermann Kindt
From
Theodore Martin

Reproduction of a passage from Theodore Martin's translation of *Faust*, Part I, lines 3451-3458, enclosed in a letter to Hermann Kindt

was very slow in completing the Second Part. He did not do so until 1886, after having published his translation of *Poems and Ballads of Heinrich Heine* in 1878. Why did he hesitate? On November 28, 1866, he wrote to Professor Edward Dowden: "I send you by book post the volume (printed for private circulation) which contains my translation of a portion of the Second Part of *Faust*. Whether I shall ever complete my version is doubtful. I fear it would not repay the labor."* Did Martin feel that he lacked the necessary ability to make an acceptable translation, or did he believe that the Second Part of *Faust* was not worth the effort? It becomes clear from certain statements in the Preface to the Second Part that to some extent both were the case. In the following words he emphasizes the difficulty of the task before him: "In none of Goethe's works are the marvellous beauty and finish of his style carried to a higher point. In many parts the charm lies almost exclusively in the execution; and a translator may well despair of making his readers tolerant of the matter by rivalling the exquisite manner of the original, with all the odds so heavily against him in the much less plastic character of our language as compared with the German. And when Goethe is at his best, he is simply untranslatable. Such as it is, the present version is offered, in the hope that it may assist English readers in the study of what Goethe regarded as the masterwork of his life."[49] That Martin reacted rather unfavorably to certain portions of Part II is evident when he says: "Such parts of it as demand the exposition of elaborate commentary, most lovers of poetry will agree, can scarcely deserve one. The moment poetry begins to deal in mysticism or philosophical problems, and to demand elaborate exposition, it ceases to be poetry."[50]

The criticisms of Martin's version by two fellow translators are of interest. William Barnard Clarke, who published his translation of *Faust* the same year in which Part I by Martin appeared, remarks in his Preface: "I have taken a glance through

---

* The British Museum Catalogue lists the translation of both parts as having been published in 1870. No complete translation of Part II by Martin existed prior to 1886.

the numerous translations already offered to the public, from the earliest fragments down to the last offered to the world by Mr. Theodore Martin, and as I have heard that he has a high reputation as a German scholar, I have expected to see something, when not preeminent, yet superior to all the metrical and rhythmical productions of his predecessors. I regret to say that I was disappointed." Like all the other translators before him, Martin has, Clarke states, "taken an unwonted freedom with sense, metre and rhyme."

William Page Andrews in his excellent article, "On the Translation of Faust," likewise finds little to praise in Martin's version. After stating that the translator according to Goethe must aim to reproduce the simplicity of the style of the original, to avoid latinized words and purely literary expressions, he continues: "Sir Theodore Martin seems to be the only translator who has kept this aim of Goethe's always in view; but he undertakes to make a new poem, and follows Shelley in altering at will the melody of the versification, and loses at once the spiritual aura and all the impressions which the poet strives to or does convey by the music which is the accompaniment and illumination of the words."[51]

With these trenchant criticisms in mind, it will be worth while to compare Martin's version with several other contemporaneous translations, such as those of Miss Swanwick and Bayard Taylor. Let us consider the following lines from Study I, Part I:

> Geschrieben steht: "Im Anfang war das Wort!"
> Hier stock ich schon! Wer hilft mir weiter fort?
> Ich kann das Wort so hoch unmöglich schätzen;
> Ich muss es anders übersetzen,
> Wenn ich vom Geiste recht erleuchtet bin.
> Geschrieben steht: "Im anfang war der Sinn."
> Bedenke wohl die erste Zeile,
> Dass deine Feder sich nicht übereile!
> Ist es der Sinn der alles wirkt und schafft?
> Es sollte stehn: "Im Anfang war die Kraft!"
> Doch, auch indem ich dieses niederschreibe,

> Schon warnt mich was, dass ich dabei nicht bleibe.
> Mir hilft der Geist! Auf einmal seh ich Rat!
> Und schreib getrost: "Im Anfang war die That!"

Bayard Taylor translates:

> 'Tis written: "In the beginning was the Word."
> Here am I balked: Who now, can help afford?
> The Word?—impossible so high to rate it;
> And otherwise must I translate it,
> If by the Spirit I am truly taught.
> Then thus: "In the beginning was the thought."
> The first line let me weigh completely,
> Lest my impatient pen proceed too fleetly.
> It is the thought which works, creates, indeed?
> "In the beginning was the Power," I read.
> Yet, as I write, a warning is suggested,
> That I the sense may not have fairly tested.
> The Spirit aids me: now I see the light!
> "In the beginning was the Act," I write.

In Taylor's version, the metre of the first and the last lines varies slightly from that of the original. "Word" and "afford" in the first and second lines are impure rimes. "Indeed" in the ninth line is padding, and the twelfth line is rendered somewhat too freely. But Taylor is the only translator here considered who attempts the feminine rimes. Miss Swanwick's version reads:

> 'Tis writ, "In the beginning was the Word!"
> I pause, perplext! Who now will help afford?
> I cannot the mere word so highly prize;
> If by the spirit guided as I read,
> I must translate the passage otherwise.
> "In the beginning was the Sense!" Take heed,
> The import of this primal sentence weigh,
> Lest your too hasty pen be led astray!
> Doth sense work all things, and control the hour?
> 'Tis writ, "In the beginning was the Power!"
> Thus should it stand: Yet while the words I trace,
> I'm warned again the passage to efface.

The spirit aids: from anxious scruples freed,
I write, "In the beginning was the deed!"

Miss Swanwick's lines possess all the faults of Bayard Taylor's version in a more exaggerated form. While Goethe's metre is very regular here, Miss Swanwick's is rough and irregular in a number of lines and half of them have been translated too freely. Martin translates:

"In the Beginning was the Word!" 'Tis writ.
Here on the threshold I must pause, perforce:
And who will help me onwards on my course?
No, by no possibility is't fit,
I should the naked Word so highly rate.
Some other way must I the words translate,
If by the spirit rightly I be taught.
"In the Beginning was the Sense!" 'Tis writ.
The first line ponder well. Is it
The sense, which is of each created thing,
The primal cause, and regulating spring?
It should stand thus: "In the Beginning was
The Power!" Yet even as I write, I pause.
A something warns me, this will not content me.
Lo! help is from the Spirit sent me!
I see my way; with lightning speed
The meaning flashes on my sight,
And with assured conviction thus I write:
"In the Beginning was the Deed!"

Martin's translation of this passage does not measure up to those of Taylor and Anna Swanwick. They both exceed him in verbal and metrical accuracy. His rendering is diffuse; while the original, and also Taylor and Miss Swanwick, have only fourteen lines, Martin has nineteen. Instances of outright padding are "I pause" in line thirteen and "with lightning speed the meaning flashes on my sight" in lines sixteen and seventeen. However, Martin is not always as diffuse as in this passage. Here he also leaves out a part of the original, namely, the line "Dass deine Feder sich nicht übereile!"

In the case of a purely lyric part such as the König in Thule,

Taylor again has made the best version as far as meter, rime, and accuracy of translation are concerned. Miss Swanwick falsely renders, "Er leert ihn jeden Schmauss" as, "And drained its purple draught." Martin uses a sprinkling of objectionably archaic words like "leal" for "treu" and "leman" for "Buhle"; he attempts no feminine rimes but reproduces the simple language and the atmosphere of the original far better than Taylor or Miss Swanwick. The lines:

> Er sah ihn stürzen, trinken
> Und sinken, tief ins Meer,
> Die Augen thäten ihm sinken,
> Trank nie einen Tropfen mehr,

Martin translates very inaccurately:

> He saw it flash then settle down,
> Down, down into the sea,
> And, as he gazed, his eyes grew dim,
> Nor ever again drank he.

Martin's translation of Part II is more satisfactory as a whole than Part I. Some lyric passages, however, are very loosely and incorrectly rendered. A good example is the one from the Gardener's Song in Act I, scene 4. The lines:

> Bieten bräunliche Gesichter
> Kirschen, Pfirschen, Königspflaumen,
> Kauft! denn gegen Zung' und Gaumen
> Hält sich Auge schlecht als Richter,
>
> Magnum bonums, cherries, peaches
> Dusky are of hue; but buy!
> Worst of judges is the eye;
> Trust what tongue or palate teaches.

However, the reflective and the straight narrative passages in Martin's translation of Part II are much superior to those of Part I.

The footnotes at the end of Act V reveal that Martin has made a close study of Bayard Taylor's version, without, however, being dependent on him to any extent in his translation.

But Martin does accept Taylor's rendering of the last two lines of Part II:

> The woman-soul draweth us
> Upward and on,

as the best translation of these lines that can be made in English.

It may be said, then, that while Theodore Martin's translation of *Faust*, Part I, is hardly on a level with those of Anna Swanwick or Bayard Taylor, his version of Part II shows with some exceptions great improvement over his version of Part I and compares favorably with those of his fellow translators. Moreover, Martin has reproduced the style as well as the spirit of the original in many instances better than either Swanwick or Taylor, and Andrews' severe criticism, quoted above, that Martin "undertakes to make a new English poem—altering at will the melody of the versification" is certainly much more applicable to the translation of Part I than to Part II.

THOMAS J. ARNOLD
(1803-1877)

Translation of *Faust I* First Printed in 1877

Another barrister to translate *Faust* was Thomas James Arnold, who was born on Downing Street, Westminster, London, 1803. After he had finished the course of studies at St. Paul's School, Arnold, like Hayward, resided for some time at Göttingen, to which place a distinguished faculty in jurisprudence attracted students from foreign countries.

Upon his return to England, he was called to the bar at Lincoln's Inn, 1829, and received an appointment as Commissioner of Bankruptcy at Liverpool some time afterward. In 1847 he was made Stipendiary Magistrate at the Worship Street, London, police court, but he removed from there to the Westminster court in 1851. This position, together with the appointment to Senior London Police Magistrate late in life, he held until his death in May, 1877.[52] He was made an F.S.A. in 1869. Arnold "was a man of great culture and accomplishments, an intimate friend of Shelley's friend, Thomas Love Peacock, and the son-in-law of Shelley's biographer, Thomas Jefferson Hogg."[53]

As an author Arnold is known for his writings in two fields, jurisprudence and literature. His *Treatise on the Law Relating to Municipal Corporations, the Office of the Justice of the Peace, the Labor Laws and other Subjects* was published in 1852. His literary works, most of which appeared later, are all translations: Schiller's *Song of the Bell*, 1842; Goethe's *Reineke Fuchs*, 1860; *Anacreon*, 1869; and Goethe's *Faust*, 1877.[54]

It is likely that Arnold received most of his knowledge of the German language as a student at Göttingen some time before 1829; here also was awakened in him an admiration for Schiller and Goethe. Probably because Schiller was still more popular in England in the first half of the nineteenth century than Goethe, Arnold first made a translation of the *Song of the Bell* and then later, when Goethe had become better known to the English public through numerous translations of his poems, dramas, and other works, he attempted an English version of *Reineke Fuchs*. These two works were, as it turned out later, preliminary efforts to the rendering of *Faust* itself.

Since Arnold died in 1877, the same year in which his translation appeared, it is a moot question whether he saw his version through the press or whether it was made public after his death by the joint publishers, Theodore Stroefer of Munich, and George Kirchner of New York. Inasmuch as the only edition of this translation which has ever been published was printed, not in England, the home of the translator, but in Germany by the Gebrüder Kröner, Stuttgart, and since it was copyrighted in the United States by George Kirchner, it is probable that the publication of this version was entirely a German-American venture.

Although the translation of *Reineke Fuchs* is referred to as being a very creditable work, "that of *Faust* is respectable, but inferior to some other recent versions, and having been published in folio form as an accompaniment to a volume of illus-

Jurists and Faust

trations,* is but little known."[55] As far as the faithful reproduction of the thought of the original is concerned, this version is only fairly reliable. It does not, therefore, compare favorably with such translations as Bayard Taylor's, but it is fair to say that it stands on a level with Kegan Paul's. Let us examine lines 711-722 from the scene Before the Town Gate:

> O glücklich, wer noch hoffen kann
> Aus diesem Meer des Irrtums aufzutauchen!
> Was man nicht weiss das eben brauchte man,
> Und was man weiss kann man nicht brauchen.
> Doch lass uns dieser Stunde schönes Gut
> Durch solchen Trübsinn nicht verkümmern!
> Betrachte, wie in Abendsonne-Gluth
> Die grünumgebnen Hütten schimmern,
> Sie rückt und weicht, der Tag ist überlebt.
> Dort eilt sie hin und fördert neues Leben.
> O, dass kein Flügel mich vom Boden hebt,
> Ihr nach und immer nach zu streben!

Taylor translates:

> O happy he, who still renews
> The hope, from Error's deeps to rise for ever!
> That which one does not know, one needs to use;
> And what one knows, one uses never.
> But let us not, by such despondence, so
> The fortune of this hour embitter!
> Mark how, beneath the evening sunlight's glow,
> The green-embosomed houses glitter!
> The glow retreats, done is the day of toil;
> It yonder hastes, new fields of life exploring;
> Ah, that no wing can lift me from the soil,
> Upon its track to follow, follow soaring!

Arnold's version reads:

> How blest is he who still hopes on
> To raise himself aloft from error's ooze;

---

* This large folio volume in beautiful de luxe binding contains, besides fifty illustrations by Liezen Mayer which are richly ornamented by Rudolf Seitz, thirteen steel and copper engravings by J. Bankel, J. F. Deininger, G. Golberg, E. Forberg, Fr. Ludy, and eighty-five woodcuts from Wilhelm Hecht's Xylographisches Institut.

> Man wants to turn to use what is unknown
> And what is known he cannot use;
> But let us not this blissful moment's flow
> Disturb with gloomy thoughts like those!
> Behold how yon in the sun's evening glow
> Shimmer the green-girt cottages.
> He yields, gives way; the day is over-lived;
> He hastes to make a new creation live.
> Oh, why of wings to soar am I deprived,
> Ever and ever after him to strive!

Paul translates:

> Oh happy he who still may trust
> That he from these bewildering floods may swim!
> Need of the unknown is on each man thrust,
> The known is ne'er of use to him.
> But let us not disturb these fair sweet hours
> With any idle thoughts of sorrow!
> Look how the cottages in leafy bowers
> The sun's low rays of evening borrow.
> He hastens hence a newer life awaking.
> Oh that a wing might sweep me through the sky
> On after him, the earth forsaking!

Taylor's translation of "Meer des Irrtums" as "Error's deeps" is decidedly better than Arnold's "error's ooze." Paul's rendering "bewildering floods" is no closer than Arnold's. "Blissful moments flow" in Arnold's version does not translate "stunde schönes Gut" as well as Taylor's "fortune of this hour." Paul again reproduces this loosely as "fair sweet hours." Although Taylor translates line 9 of this passage too freely, Arnold's version is a bit too literal. "Overlived" does not usually connote the same idea as the German "überlebt."

But Arnold's version must be still more severely criticized for its ragged metre, and its harsh-sounding lines. The original in the Witches' Kitchen scene, beginning with line 196, reads:

> Gut! ein Mittel, ohne Geld
> Und Arzt und Zauberei zu haben:
> Begieb dich gleich hinaus auf's Feld,

Jurists and Faust

> Fang' an zu hacken und zu graben,
> Erhalte dich und deinen Sinn
> In einem ganz beschränkten Kreise,
> Ernähre dich mit ungemischter Speise,
> Leb' mit dem Vieh als Vieh, und acht' es nicht für Raub,
> Den Acker, den du erntest, selbst zu düngen!
> Das ist das beste Mittel, glaub'
> Auf achtzig Jahr' dich zu verjüngen!

Arnold translates:

> Good! The means thou'dst wish to have revealed
> Without gold or physician
> Betake thyself straight to the field,
> Hoe and dig there sans intermission;
> Restrict thyself and senses too
> Within a very narrow sphere,
> Be unmixed food thy best cheer
> With thy beasts live as beast, nor count it robbery
> That thou thyself manur'st the land thou reapest;
> This is the best of means, trust me,
> That young at eighty thou keepest.

The first and second lines of this passage are as rough as can be found in any translation, while a number of other lines read very haltingly. In most parts of the translation the "original metres" have not been followed very closely.

Finally, the rime at times seems to be a hit-and-miss affair in this version. "Word" and "Lord," "curl" and "devil," "fry" and "ancestry," "center" and "venture" are a few of the imperfect rimes of which any number may be found without trouble all through the work.

This version too, then, is far from satisfactory. Arnold was poorly prepared for his task, and though his translation is clothed in a splendid outward garb, it does not reproduce the thought, the style, the metre, and the melody of the original with any degree of felicity and truthfulness. It cannot, therefore, be called an acceptable version of Goethe's *Faust*. This is, perhaps, the reason why it was never printed in a smaller, handier edition.

THOMAS E. WEBB
(1827-1903)
TRANSLATION OF *Faust I* FIRST PRINTED IN 1880

It is rather striking that so many English translators of Goethe's *Faust* should have been men who made law their profession, or who at one time, at least, pursued legal studies. Among this group Hayward was the first, and perhaps the most widely known in his day. He was followed by Blackie, Syme, Anster, Martin, Arnold, Webb, and Beta (?).

Of Thomas E. Webb it is said that "like many other famous Irishmen, he was not an Irishman at all."[56] Born the son of a Methodist minister in Cornwall in 1827, he was educated in Kingswood School and Trinity College, Dublin.[57] The first notice we have of his being in Ireland is as a scholar in the latter institution in 1845. We are told that "like all other invaders of Ireland, he soon made himself at home, and his very Celtic temperament made this easy for him, though his tongue never compassed the Irish Brogue."[58] His connection with the university turned out to be a long and honorable one. As a student of the House in Trinity College and "grinder" in philosophy, he obtained all the prizes to be had for English essays and occasional poems.[59] He received the B.A. degree in 1850; M.A., 1857; and LL.D., in 1859. He was elected Professor of Moral Philosophy in 1857 and made a Fellow in 1863.[60] However, since he did not like the tutorial work required of him, Webb soon resigned his fellowship, read for and was elected to the bar, and received the appointment of Regius Professor of Law in Trinity College.[61] In 1888 he accepted a country judgeship at Donegal which afforded him great leisure and a comfortable emolument until his death in 1903.[62]

Webb was a man of broad culture. "It was in society that he attained his real success. He had his wide and varied reading so perfectly in hand that epigram and illustration made his talk sparkle, and gave grace and lightness to the deep and subtle arguments supplied by his philosophy."[63] He was a keen student of philosophical systems, and his essays, *The Intellec-*

tualism of Locke and *The Veil of Iris,* are called "not only brilliant but profound."⁶⁴

Judged also from the purely literary side, Webb's career was one of no mean importance. In his time he was considered to be an authority on Scott's novels, the letters of Junius, the Elizabethan poets, and the life of Napoleon, and like his fellow translator, Sir Theodore Martin, he also took a keen interest in Shakespeare. *"An Article on the Soundness of the Expurgation of many Passages in Shakespeare's Quartos from the Text of the Folio* was written but yesterday when he was over eighty years old and already touched by his fatal disease. He was indeed somewhat of a Baconian heretic, as his clever book *The Mysteries of William Shakespeare* showed. But he was mainly busied with the difficulties of Shakespeare's life, and repudiated most of the rubbish written by his silly supporters."⁶⁵

If, on the one hand, Webb interested himself greatly in the literary genius of his own country, he was broad enough in his sympathies to include among his studies the works of the German literary master-mind, Goethe, who himself throughout his life was an apt student of Shakespeare. Webb's enthusiasm for the German poet was by no means a short and passing one, for in 1880 he published his translation of *Faust,* and as a charter member and vice-president of the English Goethe Society, founded in 1886, he manifested a lively interest in Goethe research until his own death in 1903.⁶⁶

In the Preface to the first edition, the translator remarks that "the desire of the English people to naturalize the great German poet is unabated after forty efforts . . . and it will never be satisfied till under some happy conjunction of the planets, an English translator appears who has converted the German masterpiece into an English poem." The desire to be this final translator, we take it, induced Webb to attempt his English version of *Faust.*

That he did not regard his task lightly may also be gathered from his Preface to his version of *Faust.* This and the Notes to the volume disclose the fact that Webb made himself thoroughly familiar with the Faust tradition, Faust criticism, and the earlier translations before beginning his version. According to traditional dramatic technique, he divides the drama into five acts. "The division into acts," he says, "though not authorised by Goethe, is made in order to mark the movement of the action and display the unity of the plot which underlies the drama."[67] Act I (The Sage) comprises three scenes, Night, Before the Gate, and Study I. The time of the action is supposed to occupy twenty-four hours. Act II (The Transformation) includes the scenes Study II, Auerbach's Cellar, and the Witches' Kitchen. The time of the action is two days. Act III (The Temptation) includes the scenes The Street, Evening, The Promenade, Martha's House, The Street, and The Garden. The time of the action comprises four or five days. Act IV (The Fall) includes the scenes Martha's Garden, At the Fountain, The Esplanade, Night, and Cathedral. The time of the action is one day. Act V (The Catastrophe) includes the rest of the drama. Webb remarks in his explanatory Notes to this act: "An interval of some twelve months must be imagined between the Walpurgis-night and The Gloomy Day, which closes with The Night Upon the Wold and The Scene in the Dungeon."

A study of Webb's translation shows that although he made a valiant effort to convert "the German masterpiece into an English poem," as he says in his Preface to the first edition, like so many others before him, he failed to achieve his goal. The *Athenaeum* finds his translation "devoid of any poetic charm, of any grace or attraction," and his verse is "sad doggerel." It calls attention to Webb's curious translation of the line in Faust's Monologue, "Oh sähst du, voller Mondenschein," as, "Oh, would that thou, full moon, didst shine."[68] It must be added to this criticism that Webb throughout translates too freely. While not possessing the Ansterian gift for versification, he follows his predecessor to a large extent in the loose way in which the former reproduces the original. A good example of Webb's harsh, unmusical lines, together with his latinized, stilted phraseology, is found in the Soldier's Song. Where the original reads:

> Burgen mit hohen
> Mauern und Zinnen,
> Mädchen mit stolzen
> Höhnenden Sinnen
> Möcht ich gewinnen!
> Kühn ist das Mühen,
> Herrlich der Lohn!

Webb translates:

> Town with its rampire
> For the campaigner!
> Charmer still prouder,
> Scorner still vainer,
> Fain would I gain her!
> Bold is the venture,
> Fair is the prey!

Webb's second revised edition of 1889 is interesting because, in addition to Part I, it contains the Death of Faust translated from Part II, beginning with the line, "Come on, ye shambling rogues, come on," and ending with the rueful words of Mephistopheles, "'Twere better there were one Eternal Void." The translator expresses the opinion in the Preface to this edition that by thus combining the two parts he has removed "all the objections that have been advanced against Goethe by his critics."* But it must be added that, while Webb thus shortens the play and endeavors to provide it with a satisfactory ending, he is not giving the English reader the work of Goethe, but his own. He deserts his role as a translator and offers to the public a new adaptation of Goethe's *Faust*. Thus this edition, besides possessing all the defects of the earlier version, has the additional fault of introducing the Second Part of Faust to the English reader as a torso.

* Webb has omitted the Prologue in Heaven as unnecessary for the drama in the form he has given it and holds the novel but erroneous view that the words "Sie ist gerettet!" refer not to the redemption of Gretchen's soul but to her present rescue from public execution.

III

Mephistopheles Dons Cap and Gown

Mephistopheles:
Use well your time, for all too soon it flies;
But system will teach you to save time, My friend,
Here is the first step I advise—
Follow a course of logic to the end.
There your spirit will be drilled to think,
Cramped tight as if in Spanish boots; so taught,
Then it will circumspectly slink
Along the path of stodgy thought,
And cannot zigzag to and fro
As a will-o'-the-wisp is wont to go.
Days will be spent in teaching you
To eat, to drink, to sleep anew;
And all you once did easily
Is done by rule of one, two, three![1]

SOME OF THE very earliest scenes of *Faust* composed by Goethe include Night I and Study II. No one, especially no teacher or university professor, can read these portions of the drama and forget Faust, the disillusioned, the disgruntled, the despairing schoolmaster at his study table in the high-vaulted, narrow, Gothic chamber, brooding over his desultory past. No matter whether one's educational philosophy and "Lebensanschauung" are destructive or constructive in nature, one is forced to admit that this pedagogue raises many fundamental questions about the art of teaching and the nature of life as a whole.

In the second scene referred to above, Faust, the scholar, the translator, has forgotten for the time being the irksome routine of the classroom; for once he is free to revel in the pure joy of intellectual activity. And who can help chuckling over the clever, the misanthropic Mephistopheles as, toward the end of the scene, he dons Faust's cap and gown to play the role of his professorial friend. John Stuart Blackie, Albert G. Latham, William H. Van der Smissen, George Madison Priest, John Shawcross, F. G. G. Schmidt, Carlyle Ferren MacIntyre, and John F. L. Raschen joined in the long procession of those who worthily wore the cap and gown, the symbol of all that is best in academic tradition. They have honored themselves by honoring Goethe with a translation of his *Faust*.

JOHN STUART BLACKIE
(1809-1895)
TRANSLATION OF *Faust I* FIRST PRINTED IN 1834

Versuch ich's, mich so kühnlich hoch zu heben
Zu den Gefilden reiner Lebenstrahlen?
Und wag' ich's frech, mit schwacher Hand zu malen,
Was Dir nur ziemt, das buntbewegte Leben?
Wie soll der Kinderzunge lallend Streben
Aussprechen, was des Mannes Kraft gesungen?
Wie soll des Menschen Stimme wiedergeben,
Was aus der tiefen Götterbrust entsprungen?
O! wenn der Liebe ungestümer Drang
Mich trieb, das ich das Heiligste entweihe,
Und zu berauschter, frecher Sünde zwang:
So schaue Du, aus der Verklärten Reihe,
Aus Himmelsharfen, liebevollem Klang,
Und wenn du mich nicht loben kannst, verzeihe.[1a]

Like Bayard Taylor, John Stuart Blackie said of Germany that it was his second fatherland, and like the American poet, he dedicated his translation to the memory of Goethe with a well-phrased poem in German. Blackie, who commends himself to our attention by his above-quoted dedicatory poem, was born in Glasgow in 1809, of Border extraction. After finishing the elementary schools, he entered Marischal College, Aberdeen, at the age of twelve and three years afterward enrolled at the University of Edinburgh. Then for two years, 1829-1831, he attended the universities of Göttingen and Berlin, where he continued his preparation in theology and law, and at the same time made an intensive study of the German language and literature. Later he extended his continental tour to Italy and Greece, acquiring there the rudiments of the languages of both countries.

By 1834 Blackie had returned to Scotland where he was made Regius Professor of Humanity (Latin) at Marischal College in 1841. Ten years later he was appointed to the Chair of Greek in Edinburgh University. From this position he resigned in 1882, but his scholastic and literary interests continued until his death in 1895. All together he visited Germany four times.[2]

Professor Blackie was not a figure "of the first importance either in social or in literary life, but he was the one recognisable figure about which not even the merest tourist perambulating Princes Street [Edinburgh] could be mistaken."[3] His clearcut features, his shrewd eyes, and his long white hair, together with his clever wit, his gay repartee, his unconventionality, and his eccentricities singled him out from among his countrymen. "A swarm of laughing stories, not one with any sting in it, like harmless butterflies floating about him, arise over his grave. Some of them were true, many only invented, not one unkind."[4] Although not a very thoroughgoing scholar, he was nevertheless extremely industrious. The British Museum Catalogue in 1885 lists forty-one different titles under his name, and his interests manifested themselves in such varied fields as theology, law, educational reform, literature, and linguistics. He was known as one of the foremost Greek scholars of his day.

Professor Blackie's interest in German literature dates back to his two years' residence at the universities of Göttingen and Berlin. From the first day he devoted himself very faithfully to the study of the German language. Writing from Göttingen, June 9, 1829, he says: "You must know that we* are all fired with a flaming zeal for mastering the German, our temptation is very small to speak English, so soon as we have acquired sufficient knowledge of German to speak it—Not a day passes without German conversation; the consequence is that whereas formerly we could scarcely put three or four words together,

---

* Other young Scotsmen were studying at Göttingen at the same time.

we now have no difficulty in expressing our meaning in long sentences. So determined were we to speak German that a fine has been imposed on those who, at certain hours, utter a single word of any other language. During breakfast or dinner, or other meals, he who is so bold as to puff out his English, must forthwith forfeit two Pfennings, and this law is most strictly enforced. We study the language six or eight hours every day, and seize every other opportunity of acquiring words, phrases, and pronunciations. I conjecture that in two months not a single English word shall come across our lips."[5]

A few weeks later he wrote his aunt that "from three to five days weekly we hear a German lecture on Modern History; once a week, from 6 to 7, a lecture on Fine Arts. Our German Reading was at first confined to translations of Walter Scott's romances. Afterwards, however, having acquired considerable facility, we thought it high time to betake ourselves to the German classics, and Schiller has been chosen as our first study. Goethe is too difficult for a beginner."[6] But after a half year's residence in Germany, he has advanced still more in his studies and writes from Berlin: "My father will be glad to hear that I am continuing to receive from all hands great commendation on my fluency and accuracy in German.* I have really Germanized myself at such a rate that I know the German for many things the English of which I cannot so easily tell, and I speak German so naturally and instinctively that if I begin to speak English with anybody, I unconsciously recur to my familiar German expressions."[7] About *Faust* he adds: "I am at present reading Goethe's *Faust* with a German friend whom I am teaching English as a recreation from my German."[8]

By the time Blackie left Germany he was so well Germanized that few recognized him to be a Scotsman, and his newly acquired culture was to remain a deciding influence for the rest of his life.†[9] But he did not attempt to translate *Faust* until

---

* At Göttingen Blackie studied under Heeren, Ottfried Müller, and Saalfeld; at the University of Berlin he attended the lectures given by Schleiermacher, Neander, Bockh, and Raumer.

† In his fragmentary autobiography *Notes of a Life*, he says: "I left

1834, when he had been appointed Professor of Latin at Marischal College, Aberdeen.

Many years afterward Blackie attempted to make clear to himself just why he had been so forcibly drawn to Goethe and *Faust*. This is his explanation: "What it was that drew me so powerfully towards Goethe at this period, I do not find it quite easy to explain. Certainly the mere juvenile sympathy with the serious problems of life, touched with such grace in the greatest of German dramas, may have had something to do with the matter; unquestionably also the thorough Germanism of the work must have laid powerful hold of me, steeped as I then was both in the popular and the academic life of Germany. But there was something deeper and of more moral nature that bound me to Goethe. The mere genial misanthropy of Faust I could have found in Manfred—What I sought from poetry was not merely amusement or a pleasant exercise of the imagination but wisdom, culture, harmony, 'Bildung,' as the Germans call it. Byron, therefore, whether in his Manfredian or Don Juanic presentation, was utterly useless to me. I flung him away once and forever."[10]

Turning to the positive aspects of Goethe's influence on himself, Blackie continues: "In Goethe I found the reverse of Byron, and this, I presume, was what attracted me.—The phrase 'Das Gleichgewicht der Seele', the equilibrium of the soul, which I had picked up somewhere in the great German's work, seemed to be the great secret of his quiet, weighty, manly, and yet womanly inspiration; and this equipoise of the soul was what I had long been struggling after in my own dim way, and which I seemed to catch a glimpse of among all my German guides, who were then supreme with me, chiefly in Goethe."*[11]

Germany with a warm side towards the German people, which I have retained through life. There were not a few things about the external habits and general tone and style of the Germans towards which the regular thoroughbred Englishman feels a repulsion. But I was no Englishman, and had not the most remote notion of looking down on any class of my fellow-beings, and in respect of sympathies and antipathies, had been left to wander at my own sweet will without any binding at all."—See note 9.

* Blackie's copy of Goethe's works *Ausgabe letzter Hand* with numerous marginal notes is in the William A. Speck Collection of Goetheana, Yale University Library.

Thus we see that a high motive actuated Blackie when he translated *Faust*. He felt that he had received definite spiritual aid from the German master, and that he now wished to make the source of his inspiration known to his countrymen. In the dedication to the volume *The Wisdom of Goethe*, "a manual of wise words, for guidance in fruitful action and sound thinking,"[12] Blackie refers especially to his recent translation of the *Faust*. He says: "I am perfectly aware of how far anything, that I can produce, must always fall beneath what a translation of *Faust* ought, according to my ideas, to be. But we might wait long enough before an English Goethe should arise, who would be fitted to do perfect justice to such a work; and in the meantime, if the present attempt shall but serve to draw public attention, in some degree, to what still remains to be done in the wide domain of German literature, I shall have my reward."

It would appear that John Stuart Blackie was much better equipped for his task as translator of the First Part of *Faust* than Gower had been a few years before. His practical knowledge of German, as we have seen, surpassed by far that of his predecessor, and, on account of his own sympathetic attitude, he no doubt understood Goethe better than Gower did. In consequence of his growing appreciation of Goethe and *Faust*, Blackie's opinions changed considerably from the time when his translation was first made in 1834 to 1880 when it was "carefully revised and largely rewritten" for the second edition.[13] This is shown by his more favorable attitude toward the Prologue in Heaven, which he like Gower had omitted in 1834, but which the broad-minded Scotsman included in the later edition. His reactions toward Part II also became quite favorable.[14] But it must be admitted that Blackie's genius was remarkable rather for its breadth than for its brilliance and profundity.* His translation of Faust, although still too free, is as a whole somewhat superior to that of Gower in fidelity both

---

* Other works by Blackie, relating to Germany and German literature, besides the translations of *Faust* and *The Wisdom of Goethe*, are *Musa Burschicosa*, 1869; and *War Songs of the Germans, with Historical Illustrations of the Liberation War and the Rhine Boundary Question*, 1870.—*Dictionary of National Biography*, Supplement, I, 204.

to the thought and to the metrical peculiarities of the original. In the following passages (lines 1064 ff. from the scene Vor dem Tor), both Gower and Blackie have given us little more than a paraphrase of the original. Where the German reads:

> O Glücklich, wer noch hoffen kann
> Aus diesem Meer des Irrthums aufzutauchen!
> Was man nicht weiss, das eben brauchte man,
> Und was man weiss kann man nicht brauchen,

Gower translates:

> Happy in error's sea who find the land,
> Or o'er delusion's waves his limbs can buoy;
> We use the arts we cannot understand—
> And what we know, we know not to employ.

In Blackie's version of 1834 we find the following translation:

> O happy he who yet hath hope to merge
> Forth from the night of error's troubled surge!
> What most we need to know can ne'er be known,
> And what we know were better still unknown.

He has changed the wording of every line in his "carefully revised and largely rewritten" edition of 1880:

> O happy he who yet hath hope to float
> Above this sea of crude distempered thought!
> What we know not is what we need to know,
> And what we know, we might as well let go;

The first two lines of the earlier version render Goethe's thought more accurately than those of the latter, but the situation is reversed in the case of the following two. Gower in this passage follows Goethe more closely in his rimes than Blackie; but neither uses feminine rimes where the original has them. Still, Blackie's lines read more smoothly than Gower's.

A comparison of passages from such scenes as Dedication, Night I, Gretchen's Song at the Spinning Wheel, Wood and Cavern, and others has convinced me that Blackie's final version is little, if any, better than the first. Inaccuracies to a larger degree in thought rather than in metre are abundant in both. Perhaps in judging Blackie's version one should remember the principles that guided him in his work. He says in his Preface: "The great principle on which the excellence of a poetical translation depends, seems to be that it should not be a mere transposing, but a recasting, of the original. On this principle, it has been my first and chief endeavor to make my translation spirited to seize, if possible, the very soul and living power of the German, rather than to give a careful and anxious transcription of every individual line, or every minute expression."[15] Naturally such a theory of translation has led Blackie to be satisfied with inaccuracies which a more modern translator would not tolerate.

ALBERT GEORGE LATHAM
(1864-1940)

TRANSLATION OF *Faust I* FIRST PRINTED IN 1902;
Faust II, 1905

> As unto some cathedral's echoing aisles,
> Vast and mysterious in the failing light,
> Where soaring arches melt into the night,
> And massy pillars stretch out shadowy miles,
> We enter here, O Master of many styles!
> Without, grim gargoyles wing their frozen flight;
> Martyrs and saints the storied windows dight,
> Triumphant victors o'er the Tempter's wiles,
> A crucifix o'er the high altar towers,
> Great symbol of unconquerable Love;
> Baffled the evil spirit limps away;
> The air is heavy with Mother Mary's flowers;
> Whiter than 'gainst an angry sky the dove,
> With streaming eyes, a white soul kneels to pray.[16]

With these inspired lines, which so aptly compare Goethe's *Faust* to a great Gothic cathedral, begins another English version of *Faust*. Albert George Latham, the translator, a versatile scholar, linguist, and educator, for some time Emeritus Professor of Modern Languages, Armstrong College, University of Durham, Newcastle-upon-Tyne, was born in 1864, the son of Edward and Mary Wakefield Latham. His mother appears to have been the more gifted of the two parents, for from her pen came numerous volumes: *Christobel, Christobel in France, The Young Crafters, Little French Plays,* and other works.

The translator studied at the Borough Road Training College for Teachers, and at the universities of Bonn, Cäen, Paris, Florence, and London. From the last-named school he received the B.S. degree with first class honors in French, and the M.A. with high honors in French and German. As a teacher Latham served as Assistant Tutor at Borough Road College, 1888-1889, and as Lecturer in charge of French and Italian at Armstrong College, Newcastle, in 1893. He was External Examiner in Modern Languages at the University of Aberdeen, 1909-1913, and in French, 1919-1923. Among the books and articles Latham published are: translations of Goethe's *Faust,* Parts I and II, and Schiller's *Wilhelm Tell; Old Tynside; Oxford Treasury of French Literature, Volume I;* verses serious and otherwise in *Longman's Magazine, Punch Almanac, Westminster Gazette;* articles in the *Cornhill Magazine* and in the daily press. He was literary editor (with Dr. W. G. Whittaker as musical editor) of *Selected Arias from Handel's Operas* and *Adaptations from Gluck; Rounds of Schubert, Mozart, Beethoven and Haydn.* He also published *Oxford Choral Songs from the Old Masters;* some lyrics, original and translated, in the *Clarendon Song Books;* and other musical and literary compositions.[17] Latham died in 1940.[17a]

From this factual record of Latham's life, we pass on to the translator's story of his version of *Faust.* It seems that Latham's interest in German literature and *Faust* began in his twentieth year. On April 12, 1883, he witnessed the presentation of Gounod's opera *Faust.* Of this, his first experience at the theatre, he writes: "The tragic story gripped my imagination as in a spell, and I still remember coming out into the work-a-day world and moving through it as through a dream, my mind still held captive by the world of fancy in which it had dwelt for the last three hours. I made haste to lay my hands on an English translation of *Faust* which I devoured in two days. It was Filmore's translation."[18] Latham's interest in German literature thus aroused, he read *Wilhelm Meister's Apprenticeship*, in translation, and much of Carlyle, including *Sartor Resartus*, which also helped to maintain his interest in German writers. Again, in 1886, in London, as a student at the Borough Road Training College for Teachers, Latham's interest in *Faust* "was rekindled to a flame" when he saw the play produced at the Lyceum Theatre, with Henry Irving as Mephistopheles and Ellen Terry as Gretchen. Since the translator still knew no German, he again had to satisfy himself by reading various English translations of *Faust*, and as yet no thought of making an English version of *Faust* had occurred to him.

After Latham completed his term of study at the Borough Training College for Teachers and had taught there several years as Assistant Tutor, he spent some time in study on the continent. For nearly two years he was a student at the University of Bonn, where he steeped himself in German. Moreover, he visited the haunts of Goethe's childhood at Frankfurt-am-Main and, of course, the Goethe House with all its interesting memories and relics. Here, Latham says, he was permitted by the guardian as a special privilege to strum on "Lotte's Spinet" a few tunes, "Studentenlieder," which he had so often sung in chorus "auf der Kneipe" with his old fellow students at Bonn. This was in 1896. The idea of translating the *Faust* had not yet occurred to him, but this visit to Frankfurt was another step on the road to it.

Two years later Latham actually began the translation of Part I. He was then lecturer in French, German, and Italian and had already published in college magazines translations of several of Heine's poems. With this valuable preparation, he was able to complete the English version of Part I for publication in 1902. The translation of the Second Part, which was begun in 1903, but interrupted by a version of Schiller's *Wilhelm Tell*, was finished in 1905. Of the time and the place of the *Faust* translation, Latham writes: "The translation occupied the greater part of my leisure from University duties and of my vacations during the period from 1900-1905 excepting approximately the period 1902-1903, when I was busy with the *Tell*. It was made either in my homes at Whitley Bay and Monkseaton on the North East Coast of England, or in the places where I spent my summer vacations. Amongst these, I remember in particular working at it in the old fashioned village of Egton Bridge in Yorkshire, at Braithwaite between Lakes Derwentwater and Bassenthwaite in the English Lake Country, and in a garden standing high above the North Shore of Loch Tay in Scotland, with the beautiful lake gleaming in the sunshine below me."

Although the most powerful of the motives that led Latham to begin the translation of *Faust* was his deep personal interest in the drama, he felt also that his training and his talents fully entitled him to attempt this difficult task. "The present translation, however," he says, "was at first undertaken in no spirit of rivalry with any of its predecessors. The translator would indeed have shrunk from entering the lists with champions of such approved worth. It began with the translation of some favorite passages as a pastime for leisure hours. A not unnatural curiosity prompted the comparison of these when done with other versions, and their author persuaded himself, he trusts not too easily, that they did not suffer in comparison. And so he found himself launched upon the perilous slope."[19] Thus, Latham says in his correspondence, he "shouldered the burden and went through to the end with it. It was no light task, but it was a labor of love."[20]

The manner in which the translation was made is interesting also. Here, as with Bayard Taylor and Frank Claudy, it was more or less a family affair. Although the translation was all his own work, Latham says he profited greatly by the encouragement given him by his wife, to whom he read his version passage by passage as it was finished. Another part of the translator's letter gives an interesting sidelight on the actual mental process involved in the work. "I recall one experience that interested me very much at the time. When I was at a loss for the particular word for the turn which I felt that the occasion demanded, after turning it over in my mind for a time, I would dismiss it from my thoughts and let the ground lie fallow, and quite frequently it was my experience to find that my obliging self-conscious self had in the meantime been busy rummaging about as it were on the shelves of my mind, and like a helpful librarian would hand me out—often at a most unexpected moment—what seemed to me a charmingly appropriate word or expression."

As far as any theory of translation is concerned, Latham is content to say in his Preface that he agrees with Bayard Taylor, and that he "does not propose to 'thresh old, old straw.'" But he states further that he believes his version possesses a "general nearness to the rhythm of the original," and "fidelity—frequently an all but literal fidelity to the thoughts of the original." He hopes finally that "his version may be indeed found to give on the whole a truer and livelier picture of Goethe's great poem in all its aspects than any of those that have gone before it."[21]

Upon the publication of his translation, Latham received a number of complimentary letters. One from the Very Reverent George William Kitchin, Dean of Durham and Warden of the University of Durham, says in part: "... I have been through the main part of your fascinating *Faust*—and thank you heartily for the pleasure of it. No one but one who has struggled with the concentrated difficulties of old Goethe can appreciate the vastness of your task, of the extraordinary skill and poetical taste with which you have achieved the work. One thing strikes me especially—your words are so well chosen that they don't set one's teeth on edge! And even the roughness of metre and rhyme please." Dr. F. B. Jevons, Professor of Philosophy in the University of Durham, and Master of Hatfield College, writes: "I have only had time of course to look at bits of it; and naturally I have turned to what appeals to me most, viz. the lyrics. Personally I think that they are the severest test which can be applied to a translator; and I do feel that your versions are English poetry, having merit as such and quite independent of their value as translations. I say 'a merit' but really mean a good deal more: if I had to praise them as poetry I should rank them high. It is marvellous to me that you should combine the fidelity of strict translation with the freedom of verse which is not merely verse but poetry; and I cannot say how proud I am to be a colleague of one before whom there is the prospect of wide and lasting poetic fame."[22]

However, after extensive reading in both parts of this translation, I am not inclined to be so eulogistic about the version as Latham's friends. Its strength lies more in its metrical than in its verbal fidelity. One is able to read the translation side by side with the German text for many lines without being struck by any disturbing metrical divergences from the original, but much less can be said for Latham's reproduction of the original spirit, language, and thought. The liberties the translator takes in his work are evident in the very first lines of his version:

> Ihr naht euch wieder, schwankende Gestalten,
> Die früh sich einst dem trüben Blick gezeigt.
> Versuch ich wohl euch diesmal festzuhalten?
> Fühl ich mein Herz noch jenem Wahn geneigt?

which Latham translates:

> Ye wavering phantoms, yet again my leisure
> Ye haunt, as erst ye my troubled gaze.
> Still doth mine heart the old illusion treasure?
> Now shall I fix the dream that round me plays?

In the first line "yet again my leisure" is padding used by the translator to meet the exigencies of rime. The fourth line is a very free rendering of Goethe's third line. Much more direct and truer is the rendering of these lines in Alice Raphael's version:

> Once more ye come, ye wavering forms that passed
> In earlier days before my troubled sight,
> Shall I endeavor now to hold ye fast?
> In that illusion do I still delight?

Or let us take a passage from the Witches' Kitchen scene. Beginning with line 2086, Mephistopheles says to Faust:

> Natürlich wenn ein Gott sich erst sechs Tage plagt
> Und selbst am Ende Bravo sagt,
> Da muss es was gescheites werden.
> Für diesmal sieh dich immer satt!
> Ich weiss dir so ein Schätzchen auszuspüren,
> Und selig, wer das gute Schicksal hat,
> Als Bräutigam sie heimzuführen.

This passage Latham renders:

> Aye, marry! if a God six days doth toil and moil,
> And cries: Well done! i' the end o' the coil,
> It must be something well worth seeing.
> Gaze now thy fill, and presently
> I'll look thee out just such a pretty sweeting;
> And happy man be his dole, say I,
> Who on her lips shall press the bridegroom's greeting.

Most of these lines represent a fair translation, but some, especially the first two, are spoiled by such stilted expressions as "toil and moil," and "i' the end o' the coil." The worst passage is perhaps in Part II, Act II, lines 7644-7647. Here Latham translates the Generalissimo's words:

> Mit Pfeil und Bogen
> Frisch ausgezogen
> An jenem Weiher
> Schiesst mir die Reiher.

as:

> With bow and arrow
> Search every narrow
> Every mere on
> Shoot me the heron.

Here the second line is largely the product of Latham's fancy instead of what he found in the original. The third line not only contains a mistranslation of "jenem," but it constitutes also a very clumsy inversion for the sake of rime. This verse is similar to the second line in Ariel's Song in the beginning of Part II which reads: "flutter down all men upon."

The word "mere," in the verse quoted above, also gives the occasion to speak of Latham's tendency in so many places to use the older, the archaic, the unusual, rather than familiar terms. Hence, we find an abundance of such words as wassail, quaffed, woebegone, wot, nonce, lorn, beshrew. What is still more objectionable to the modern reader is the use of Latin in rendering the German text. A case in point is lines 2346-2347 of Part II, Act II. Here Latham translates:

> Mich langweilt's; denn kaum ist's abgethan,
> So fangen sie von vorne wieder an.

as:

> It irks me. Scarce 'tis ended when de novo
> With the whole force they start again ab ovo.

The two Latin expression are quite superfluous, but the translator used them because they supplied what he was much in need of—a rime.

Some of the lyrical parts Latham has rendered more acceptably than the more sustained, reflective, or narrative portions of the drama. Such are lines 1093-1151 of Part I, Act I; the Song of the Spirit; the rousing drinking songs in Auerbach's Cellar; Gretchen's Song at the Spinning Wheel; and a number of shorter songs at the end of Part II. But many of the lyrics are spoiled by imperfect rimes, incorrect metre, and awkward inversions, as well as stilted diction. This version as a whole does not measure up to the high standard set by some of the other English *Faust* translations. It is too uneven in quality. Like so many others it fails to reproduce in any marked degree the language, the varying moods, and at times also the rhythm of the original.

WILLIAM H. VAN DER SMISSEN
(1844-1929)

TRANSLATION OF *Faust I and II* FIRST PRINTED IN 1927

"And now, having finished my task at almost exactly the same age at which my poet sealed up his manuscript, I may say, like him, that henceforth it does not matter what I do, or whether I do anything at all."[23] These words of restrained exultation were uttered by William H. Van der Smissen in 1926 at the conclusion of the greatest endeavor of his life, the translation of both parts of Goethe's *Faust*. They rounded out the career of one who for nearly half a century was an enthusiastic teacher of German literature and a diligent scholar and interpreter of Goethe and his works.

Professor Van der Smissen was born in Toronto, Canada, August 18, 1844. He attended the Upper Canada College and then the University of Toronto, from which he received the B.A. degree with classical honors in 1864. Two years later he was awarded the M.A. degree by the same school and was appointed Lecturer in German in University College. Although also acting in the capacity of University Librarian from 1873 to 1890, and as President of the Canadian Institute from 1886 to 1888, Van der Smissen remained on the college staff as a teacher until 1913. He was made Associate Professor of German in 1890, Professor in 1901, and received the Ph.D. degree from the University of Toronto in 1912. His interest in public affairs is further attested by the fact that he took part in and was wounded at the Ridgeway fight in 1866, and later became Captain of the University Company of the Queen's Own Rifles. His "fine sense of humor and unusual skill in kindly mimicry made Professor Van der Smissen one of the best of story tellers."[24] He died January 3, 1929, at the age of eighty-five.

Robert A. Falconer, President of the University of Toronto, says of the career of Professor Van der Smissen in his Introduction to the translation: "He has made for himself a right to be heard, because of his scholarship and the position he occupied for half a century. In 1866, at a period when no University on this continent had a separate and independent department of German, Professor Van der Smissen was given full charge of this subject in University College. . . . He was not long in taking rank in Canada, his native country, in his own subject, and no one challenged his supremacy."

Professor G. H. Needler, for many years the translator's colleague in the department of German, in his necrolog of Van der Smissen also stresses the fact that the latter played a prominent part "in raising German and the other modern languages from lowly beginnings to an equality with the Classics on the University curriculum."[25] Professor Van der Smissen wrote or edited numerous college textbooks in his chosen field. "*The High School German Grammar*, made by him and Professor Fraser, first laid a solid foundation for the study of the subject in Ontario schools. His excellent edition of the *Shorter Poems of Goethe and Schiller*, in which the poems are arranged chronologically and annotated with reference to their natural setting in the lives of the authors, was among the early books of its kind."[26] To these volumes must be added Van der Smissen's editions of Grimm's *Kinder- und Hausmärchen*, Hauff's *Das Kalte Herz*, and Leander's *Träumereien*.

The outstanding literary work of his life, is of course, the translation of *Faust*. That Professor Van der Smissen should have had the physical stamina, the mental freshness, the courage to attempt such a difficult task at the age of seventy-seven and bring it to a successful conclusion five years later, as well as to add a translation of the *Urfaust* for good measure, is amazing. It took Bayard Taylor, when in the full flower of manhood, fifteen years to make his version. Of course, Van der Smissen's accomplishment is explained to some extent by the fact that he had been a student of the German language for over sixty years, and that "he has not published hastily, but has pondered upon *Faust* and its problems for an average lifetime."[27]

In the Preface to his translation, Van der Smissen states that he first planned to edit an existing translation, making certain necessary emendations and adding commentary and notes of his own. But this he soon found impracticable and attempted an original translation. He explains further that his "chief object in undertaking this work has been to offer English readers who have not such a knowledge of the German language as to enable them to benefit directly by the labors of recent German editors and critics, a new guide for the better understanding of Goethe's *Faust* . . . a sort of compendium of German criticism up to date."[28] Moreover, since "readers of the poem are wont to stop short at the end of the First Part and give up the Second as hopelessly obscure," he is particularly anxious to bring out the "real beauty and significance" of this part of the drama.

The translator treats the German text with a considerable degree of freedom. For instance, he omits the Intermezzo "because it interrupts the continuity of the dramatic action and is," he feels, "utterly devoid of interest to English, and indeed, to most readers."[29] Again, he divides Part I into five acts corresponding quite closely to Goethe's own plan as he outlined it for the first stage production at Weimar. Finally, he transposes the last thirty-one lines of the Forest and Cavern scene to what he considers to be their original place, namely, Act V, Scene 4, since they seem to him most effective there.

Van der Smissen enumerates the principles which have guided him in his work. The first of these is "to use pure, idiomatic, readable English verse, in which no alien tone shall offend the English ear."[30] But an ill-chosen expression, an outright Germanism, occurs in Margaret's Song at the Spinning Wheel. Here the translator renders the lines:

> Nach ihm nur schau ich
> Zum Fenster hinaus.

as:

> For him at window
> I look about.

Although Van der Smissen's thorough knowledge of both English and German grammar should have enabled him to use "pure, idiomatic, readable English verse," it has not saved him from employing a language in his translation which is neither simple nor natural, and in both of these respects he fails to do justice to the original. The language in many passages is far too stiff and formal. Van der Smissen translates the two lines in Part I, Act II, Scene 1:

> Soll ich mit dir das Zimmer teilen,
> Pudel, so lass das Heulen.

as:

> If thou with me the room would'st share
> Poodle, leave howling sir.

The reader gets the feeling here that the rules of linguistic propriety have been violated. It would have been better to carry over into the translation the informal and natural tone of the original as is the case in Alice Raphael's translation. Her version reads:

> If we are to share this cell,
> Dog, stop growling.

Most translators, including Van der Smissen, have failed to make Mephistopheles' utterances consistent with his character. He is no less a wisecracker and a gossipy old wag when he appears before God than when he impersonates Doctor Faust. In excusing his speech before the Lord, Van der Smissen has him say:

> Pardon! This troop, I cannot follow after
> With stilted speech, though I incur their scorn;
> Pathos from me would but excite thy laughter.[31]

Cookson, although his rendering is often too free and at times slangy, has succeeded best in this respect. As an example let us take the passage from the Prologue in Heaven where Mephistopheles gives the Lord his opinion of man. Here are the original lines:

> Er scheint mir, mit Verlaub von Euer Gnaden,
> Wie eine der langbeinigen Zikaden,
> Die immer fliegt und fliegend springt
> Und gleich im Gras ihr altes Liedchen singt.
> Und läg er nur noch immer in dem Grase!
> In jeden Quark begräbt er seine Nase.

Van der Smissen translates:

> And, by your Grace's leave, he seems to me
> Like some long-legged grasshopper to be,
> Which ever flies and flying springs
> And in the grass the same old ditty sings.
> Would he but lie on the grass reposing!
> Vile froth he seeks to stick his too inquiring nose in.

Cookson, who translates too loosely but catches the flippant, derogatory note in Mephistopheles' speech to perfection, translates:

> Man, by your Highness' leave, the more's the pity,
> For all the world is like a long-legged grig,
> And flits and hops and dances the same jig
> And pipes in the green grass the same old ditty.
> I wish he'd lie there always, no such luck;
> Plump goes his nose in every bit of muck.

This point is so important that one may be pardoned for citing another example from Act V, Scene 5. Here Van der Smissen has Mephistopheles say after Valentine is fatally wounded:

> Now is the lubber tame.
> We must be off at once and disappear!
> Hark to the murderous hue and cry!
> With the police I can deal easily;
> The penal court's a different affair.

But Cookson puts these breezy words into the mouth of Mephistopheles:

> A cripple he is the lout!
> We'd best clear out: do you hear that hullabaloo?
> They're crying murder, I can square
> The watch but not the Lord High Justicer.

The criticism that has just been made of Mephistopheles' mode of speaking in Van der Smissen's translation applies more or less also to the other characters. One feels that he has not succeeded in reproducing in the English what is so splendidly done in the original, the differentiation and the portrayal of character by means of speech. Moreover, this uniformly severe and unnatural quality in the language robs the translation of much of its life and effectiveness.

Another of Van der Smissen's canons is: "When obliged to choose between an imperfect rhyme and a perversion of the sense, always to choose the former." It seems that the translator has followed the best course under the circumstances, but, naturally, it would be more desirable still to have the translator skillful enough to give both the thought of the original and the perfect rhyme. Combinations like "reposing" and "nose in," "pother" and "another" are not uncommon. By comparison it will be found that Bayard Taylor's version is marred much less by such expressions.

The translator also found it difficult in places to reproduce the feminine, dissyllabic rimes; and again, at other times, he has not infrequently rendered a masculine rime by a feminine one. In Margaret's Song of the King in Thule and in the Song of Lynceus, the warden, in Part II, he has left the odd lines rimeless, because he felt that he was thus able to obtain better results than by forcing the rime.

Van der Smissen's translation of Part II is, if anything, on a slightly higher level than that of Part I. This is the case with most of the English and the American versions where a translator has rendered both parts, and especially in Martin's translation. Van der Smissen's version of Part II compares favorably with that of Bayard Taylor. In the lyrical passages where the stanza or the poem is meant to produce an impression of supreme beauty and felicity instead of conveying any sharp and definite train of ideas, both translations render the text rather freely. In the purely narrative and the descriptive passages both seem to come almost equally close to the metre and thought of the original. For an example we may take a part of Faust's last speech in Act V:

> Ja! diesem Sinne bin ich ganz ergeben,
> Das ist der Weisheit letzter Schluss:
> Nur der verdient sich Freiheit wie das Leben,
> Der täglich sie erobern muss.

> Und so verbringt, umrungen von Gefahr,
> Hier Kindheit, Mann und Greis sein tüchtig Jahr
> Solch ein Gewimmel möcht ich sehn,
> Auf freiem Grund mit freiem Volke stehn.
> Zum Augenblicke dürft' ich sagen:
> Verweile doch! du bist so schön!
> Es kann die Spur von meinen Erdentagen
> Nicht in Äonen untergehn.
> Im Vorgefühl von solchem hohen Glück
> Geniess ich jetzt den höchsten Augenblick.

Taylor renders the passage thus:

> Yes! to this thought I hold with firm persistence!
> The last result of wisdom stamps it true:
> He only earns his freedom and existence,
> Who daily conquers them anew.
> Thus here, by dangers girt, shall glide away
> Of childhood, manhood, age, the vigorous day:
> And such a throng I fain would see,—
> Stand on free soil among a people free!
> Then dared I hail the moment fleeing:
> "Ah, still delay—thou art so fair!"
> The traces cannot, of mine earthly being,
> In aeons perish,—they are there!—
> In proud fore-feeling of such lofty bliss,
> I now enjoy the highest moment,—this!

In Van der Smissen's version we read:

> Ay! from this maxim I will never swerve,
> The last conclusion still of wisdom true:
> He only life and freedom doth deserve
> Who day by day must conquer them anew.
> And so by danger girt, shall childhood here,
> Manhood and age pass many a strenuous year.
> Such busy throngs I fain would see,
> On free soil standing with a people free.
> Then to the moment might I say:
> "Linger awhile, thou art so fair!"
> For so the traces of my earthly day,
> Though aeons roll, can perish ne'er.

In the presentiment of such high bliss
I now enjoy the highest moment—this!

Comparing the two translations in general, we discover that Taylor's language is somewhat more flexible and more suited to the individual characters. He is also the greater master of rime and metre and the greater poet, but in neither version do we find the simple style of the original. Both translators have accompanied their works with commentaries that are monuments to their scholarship and show that through long years of diligent study they had thoroughly familiarized themselves with the best that had been thought and said about Goethe and his *Faust*. In the case of Van der Smissen, the desire to publish a commentary appears to have been one of the main reasons for his translation of *Faust*.

GEORGE MADISON PRIEST
(1873-1947)
TRANSLATION OF *Faust I and II* FIRST PRINTED IN 1932

One of America's most fitting tributes to Goethe on the centennial of his death was the translation of *Faust* by Professor George Madison Priest, of Princeton University. Preceded only by Bayard Taylor in 1870 and 1871 and by the Canadian Professor William H. Van der Smissen in 1927, he became the third American to render both parts. In many ways a scholar of distinction, Professor Priest worthily takes his place among the ranks of those who have Englished the *Faust*.

George Madison Priest was born at Henderson, Kentucky, January 25, 1873. After receiving his A.B. and M.A. degrees from the College of New Jersey (now Princeton University), he prepared himself more fully in his field by further study at some of the outstanding universities of Germany. These included Berlin, 1894-1895; Freiburg, 1899; Leipzig, Marburg, and Jena, 1901-1902. The last-named school awarded him the Ph.D. degree in 1907. Priest began his teaching career at Princeton in 1895 and was Professor of Germanic Languages there until his retirement.[32] His death occurred in 1947.[32a]

Professor Priest's scholarly treatises in the field of German include a biography, *Ebernard von Erfurt*, 1907; *A Brief History of German Literature*, 1909; *Germany Since 1740*, 1915; editions of Riehl's *Spielmannskind*, 1902, and Sudermann's *Fritzchen*, 1929; a translation of Goethe's *Faust*, Parts I and II, 1932; and, finally, an *Anthology of the Classical Period of German Literature*, 1934. The revised version of *Faust* appeared in 1941.

Professor Priest's interest in *Faust* began in the early nineties when he was an undergraduate at Princeton, not anticipating that forty years later he would publish an English translation of the great dramatic poem. Begun partly as a pastime, partly at the suggestion of friends and largely, perhaps, because of his connection with the Andrews version of *Faust*, the translation took Professor Priest six years of concentrated effort to complete. While most of his predecessors found certain portions of Part I, especially the lyrics, particularly difficult to translate, Professor Priest labored longest over Act V.[33]

In the Preface to the first version, the translator tells us that "*Faust* is being presented, as nearly as possible, in the form, and only in that form, in which Goethe finally wished it to be known. . . . The numbering of the metrical and rhyming systems of the original have been preserved in the more formal, more elevated passages. In straightforward dialogue the translator has followed Goethe's example in taking liberties with the sequence of rhymes, in leaving a number of lines unrhymed, and in not straining after absolute purity of rhyme. Lines in the translation which may seem to be improperly stumbling and irregular, are in many cases reflections of the same characteristics in German . . . a device of Goethe's to vary the metre or to suggest the momentary restlessness or confusion of spirit of the speaker. In general, the translator has aimed to change nothing, and above all, to add nothing."[34]

Professor Priest also acknowledges his indebtedness to a number of earlier translations, including those of Bayard Taylor, Anna Swanwick, Albert George Latham, and, in particular, to that of William Page Andrews, from which "numerous passages—the songs of the Arch-angels and Faust's curse, for example—have been taken over . . . virtually intact. It was impossible, as it would have seemed foolish to ignore earlier translations."[35] Of course, one cannot help appreciating the candor with which the above acknowledgments are made; nevertheless, the fact that this translation admittedly approaches, in a certain measure, a composite production, detracts from its uniqueness and its interest. To confirm Professor Priest's indebtedness to the Andrews version, one has only to read and compare such parts as the Dedication, where fifteen out of thirty-two lines are identical and fourteen lines nearly so; also Night I, Outside the Town Gate, Forest and Cavern, Ramparts, and A Prison.

Since Professor Priest revised William Page Andrews' manuscript largely before its publication in 1929, one cannot know just what part of the translation was original with Andrews. Hence, one hesitates to express a definite opinion as to the peculiar merits or demerits of these two translations of Part I. In passing, however, it may be observed that where Professor Priest's version varies from Andrews', the differences do not always strike us as being definite improvements in the rendering of the thought, the reproduction of the metre, or the musical quality of the verse. In supplying the feminine endings both are remiss, and, in addition, Professor Priest occasionally adds one or more extra syllables to the original length of the lines.

Profesor Priest's version of Part II, done independently, is superior in quality to Part I, but it would be too high praise to say that it is an entirely satisfactory rendering of this difficult work. For instance, in the Song of Ariel, the original lines 4615 and 4616,

> Wenn der Felder grüner Segen
> Allen Erdgebornen blinkt,

are rendered too freely, if not inaccurately, as

> When the meadows bright with showers,
> Unto all the earth-born call.

But neither Latham, Swanwick, nor Taylor has been more accurate here. In the translation of lines 11298 and 11299 from Deep Night,

> Und wie mir's gefallen
> Gefall ich auch mir,

which Professor Priest renders as

> And as they astound me
> Myself I commend,

the same fault of inaccuracy is discernible in a still more exaggerated form. However, from a study of all the versions of Part II made by Englishmen and by Americans, the conclusion seems to be justified that the translations of Part II are usually of a higher quality than those of Part I.

Professor Priest states in the Second Preface to his new version, published in 1941, that he "has reviewed and restudied every line and every paragraph of his previous version with as keen a vision as he possesses. He has in consequence changed the translation of many lines of the play and altered numerous paragraphs in the Introduction and the Notes—to their betterment he hopes, in respect of accuracy and clarification, perhaps also in respect of poetic sensitivity and expression."[36]

A careful reading of this revised version brings to light that the translator has actually made many alterations. In a large number of lines selected from various parts of his two versions of *Faust*, only three were found to be identical. These changes involve the transposition of words from one place to another in the same line (line 568) or from one line to another; the addition or subtraction of a syllable or foot (line 6575); the substitution of a new word, phrase, or clause (lines 9632, 11810) for an old one, or of the longer form of a word for its contraction (line 1694). Sometimes both substitution and transposition occur (line 9607). Again, the translator has used passive forms for the active (line 3742), one tense for another (line 4642), and the singular for the plural or vice versa (lines 4645, 9921).

The revised version, as a whole, reflects a greater fidelity in thought and metre to the original than the older version, but the "poetic sensitivity" referred to above by Professor Priest, that peculiarly rare and crowning endowment of a translator which enables him to choose the pregnant, the melodious, the truly poetic word or phrase, is still largely lacking here. Hence, one does not yet find here the fulfillment of the century-old dream—a perfect or nearly perfect translation of Goethe's *Faust*.

JOHN SHAWCROSS
(1872-   )
Translation of *Faust I* First Printed in 1934

Although the Goethe Centennial (1932) marked the appearance of two new translations of *Faust*, it by no means signified the close of the endeavor to render this great classic into English. Only two years later, John Shawcross, Senior Lecturer in English at Liverpool University, published his version of *Faust*, Part I.

Professor Shawcross was born in England in 1872.* From 1886 to 1890 he studied at Clifton College and the following six years at University College, Oxford. The year 1897, when he registered at the universities of Berlin and Leipzig to learn the language and attend lectures, marked the beginning of his special interest in German. From 1900 to 1902 he held the post of Lecturer in English at the University of Giessen, but for the next twelve years Professor Shawcross was engaged mostly in private study. At this time he made himself especially familiar with aesthetic theory in Germany and England, and published several treatises in this field. During the war and in subsequent years Professor Shawcross was diverted to other activities, but he continued his reading in German and English literature. In 1927 he was appointed Senior Lecturer in English at Liverpool University, a position which he held for the

* Information concerning the exact birthplace of John Shawcross is not at hand.

next ten years. He now makes his home at Duddleswell, Uckfield, Sussex.[37]

The publications of Professor Shawcross include an edition of Samuel Taylor Coleridge's *Biographia Literaria* in 1908, dealing among other things with the latter's affinities with German philosophy. He also published an edition of Shelley's philosophical prose writings. From 1902 to 1912 he translated some German lyrics, including the monologues of *Faust*, which were not published. In the spring of 1932, however, partly because he was fascinated by this great work, and partly because he was dissatisfied with earlier English versions, Professor Shawcross set out to translate the entire first part of the *Faust* drama. It was published in 1934, nearly forty years after he became interested in the play during his first stay in Germany. Moreover, in a letter dated October 27, 1947, he writes: "Since then I have translated Part II. I have been trying to get the two parts published but so far without success: the war and the ensuing shortage of paper have stood in the way. I have also made some translations of short poems by Goethe and Schiller and certain of the German Romantics: but these too have not been published."

According to his own statement, Professor Shawcross particularly enjoyed the translating of the more impassioned and poetic passages, e.g., Faust's monologues. The lyrics, especially the religious ones and Gretchen's songs, as for so many other tranlators, proved the most difficult. He states also that he wished to produce a translation in good, normal English, keeping the essential sense and something of the music of the original, avoiding padding, stiff inversions for the sake of rime, and twisting of idiom—in short to make his translation as readable as possible.

According to Professor G. P. Gooch, "the perfect translation of *Faust*, like the perfect translation of Shakespeare, is beyond human attainment, for on the mountain summits of poetry, sense and sound are inextricably interfused. The more faithful the rendering of the former, the less we have a right to demand the magic of the original phrase."[38] In the case of

Professor Shawcross the least that one can say is that he has succeeded in recapturing in his translation some of the music of the original and more of its sense. The lines 184-197, taken from the Vorspiel auf dem Theater:

> So gib mir auch die Zeiten wieder,
> Da ich noch selbst im Werden war,
> Da sich ein Quell gedrängter Lieder
> Ununterbrochen neu gebar,
> Da Nebel mir die Welt verhüllten,
> Da ich die Tausend Blumen brach,
> Die alle Täler reichlich füllten.
> Ich hatte nichts und doch genug:
> Den Drang nach Wahrheit und die Lust am Trug.
> Gib ungebändigt jene Triebe,
> Das tiefe, schmerzenvolle Glück,
> Des Hasses Kraft, die Macht der Liebe,
> Gib meine Jugend mir zurück.

Shawcross translates:

> Then give me back the days when I
> Myself was ripening still and growing!
> When from my breast unceasingly,
> A fount of living song was flowing!
> When all my world was wrapped in haze,
> And every bud of magic spoke!
> When I a thousand flowers broke
> That bloomed in all the valley ways!
> Poor was I then, yet rich beyond conceit,
> In thirst for truth, in love of counterfeit:
> Those yearnings give, no force could bate,
> The happiness deep blent with pain!
> The might of love, the strength of hate,
> My youth, my youth give back again.

With the exception of line 192 where "und doch genug" is altered and expanded to "yet rich beyond conceit," and line 194 where "ungebändigt" is diluted to "no force could bate," Shawcross has made a tolerably clear, smooth, and satisfactory translation. However, he has not succeeded entirely in avoiding the padding of his lines to satisfy the requirements of metre and rime, nor has he been able to follow Goethe consistently in the use of the feminine endings. But these are faults common to most translators. Where two consecutive verses have masculine rimes, however, Shawcross has followed the original consistently.

In such a scene as Auerbach's Cellar, Professor Shawcross has succeeded particularly well in preserving the air of levity so characteristic of the German version. Nevertheless, the deeply serious scenes of the translation, whose beauty is enhanced by the splendid poetic diction and music in the original, suffer by contrast with the German. It must be said that Professor Shawcross is no inspired poet, and, therefore, the whole translation lacks the final transmuting touch of poetic genius.

F. G. G. SCHMIDT
(1868-1945)
Translation of *Faust I* First Printed in 1935

It is a far cry from Lord Leveson-Gower, the first author of an English translation of *Faust*, to F. G. G. Schmidt, the forty-sixth. Yet in this august and sizable company are to be found only two who are definitely known to have been born in Germany, namely, Frank Claudy, whose translation appeared in 1886, and Professor Schmidt, whose version was published in 1935.* The son of a Lutheran minister, the latter was born in Bavaria on November 17, 1868. There he attended the secondary schools, and then studied theology and philosophy at the University of Erlangen from 1888 to 1890. Coming to America in 1890, he pursued the study of Germanic philology and literature at Johns Hopkins University from 1893 to 1896, being University Scholar during 1894 and 1895 and University Fellow in 1895 and 1896, when he received the degree of Ph.D. After serving as Acting Professor of German at Cornell College, Iowa, for one year, he became Head of the Depart-

* The third compatriot of Goethe to publish an English translation of *Faust* was John F. L. Raschen in the bicentennial year 1949.

ment of Germanic Languages and Literatures at the University of Oregon. He died in 1945.

Thanks to Professor Schmidt's industry and learning, we possess today not only his translation of *Faust* but also various original works, textbooks, and scholarly articles. To the first group belong two works entitled *The Ries Dialect* and *Berühmte Deutsche*. His edited texts include Von Wildenbruch's *Das edle Blut* and *Der Letzte;* Sudermann's *Heimat* and *Johannes;* Münchhausen's *Reisen und Abenteuer;* Meyer's *Ludwig und Annemarie;* Scribe's *Le Verre d'Eau;* and Dahn's *Sigwalt und Sigridh*. The learned journals to which Professor Schmidt contributed articles on philology and literature include *Alemannia, Deutsche Literaturzeitung, Zeitschrift für Hochdeutsche Mundarten, Journal of English and German Philology,* and *Monatshefte für Deutschen Unterricht*.[39]

With his thorough knowledge of German and English, his many scholastic achievements, as well as his intimate acquaintance with the *Faust* drama resulting from thirty-eight years of teaching experience, it would seem that few persons could be better prepared to make an English translation of *Faust* than Professor Schmidt. He writes that he took up his task in a measure as a pastime, and partly because friends and publishers urged him, but he also felt that there was need of a simple prose translation, which would give the real meaning of the original, often conveyed so poorly by poetic translations. To attain this end more fully, Professor Schmidt employed as plain a language as possible, and avoided elevated diction.

Professor Schmidt's translation is similar in plan and purpose to Beta's, which appeared in 1895. Just as in Beta's version, the translation is printed on the page opposite the original German. The typography of the translation matches closely that of the metrical original in the length of the lines, in the strophic form of certain passages, and in its general appearance.

In most outward aspects, Professor Schmidt's prose version differs from Abraham Hayward's, but a hurried comparison with Hayward's translation is enough to convince one that the former has followed his predecessor rather closely, and, as one examines the two versions carefully, he finds a good many instances where phrases, sentences, lines, even entire paragraphs, are rendered identically. The question involuntarily arises whether we have here a new translation of *Faust* or merely a revision of Hayward's.* Many passages from various parts of *Faust* give evidence of the translator's close dependence on Hayward, but I shall cite only one taken from the beginning of Scene 3, Faust's Study. Hayward translates:

> Faust (entering with the poodle). I have left
> plain and meadow veiled in deep night, which
> wakes the better soul within us with a holy
> feeling of foreboding awe. Wild desires are
> now sunk in sleep, with every deed of violence;
> the love of man is stirring—the love of God
> is stirring now.

Professor Schmidt has:

> Faust (entering with the poodle).
> I have left plain and meadow
> veiled in deep night,
> which wakes the better soul within us
> with a holy feeling of foreboding awe.
> Wild desires are now sunk in sleep,
> with every deed of violence.
> The love of man is stirring
> the love of God is stirring now.

Other identical passages are to be found in Scene 1, the first Chorus of Angels; Scene 3, the first nine lines of the Song of the Spirits, also numerous other lines in this song; Scene 6, the Witches' Kitchen, the first ten lines of the He-Monkey's Speech beginning "That is the World"; Scene 8, King in Thule, the first four lines; Scene 14, Forest and Cavern, four lines beginning, "The silvery forms of past ages"; Scene 25, Dungeon, nearly the whole speech of Margaret beginning, "What! You can no longer kiss?" Numberless additional identical or

---

* See my article "A New Prose Translation of Goethe's Faust," *Monatshefte für Deutschen Unterricht*, April, 1936.

almost identical lines can be cited. Often, in long passages, the difference between the two renderings is only here and there a matter of a single word or a slight change in word order.

Moreover, there are also instances where the deviations from Hayward are open to exception, to say the least. Examples are found, for instance, in lines 6, 101, 104, 367, 374, 399, etc. The same applies to the substitutions of "you" for "thou" in addressing the Lord, the Earth-Spirit, nature, etc.

All of this seems to indicate that Professor Schmidt has found it rather difficult to improve upon Hayward's translation to any great extent, or he has not taken the time to do so. In his Preface he acknowledges his indebtedness to this version, though only in the same general way as to a number of more recent metrical translations, and thus he does not lay claim to strict originality. At the same time, it is to be regretted that Professor Schmidt with his excellent training for this type of work did not cast aside the versions of his predecessors and make an entirely new prose translation.

But it would seem that the venture was worth while. This small, conveniently arranged, and attractively bound work is likely to appeal strongly to the general reader who is undertaking a study of the *Faust* perhaps for the first time. Professor Schmidt has modernized Hayward's translation, or at least the larger part of it, so that we have the *Faust* in a slightly more contemporary, readable, everyday English. In some instances, Professor Schmidt has actually improved upon the clarity and exactness of his predecessor's work.

CARLYLE FERREN MacINTYRE
(1890-   )
Translation of *Faust I* First Printed in 1941

In secret work the magic and make young
old Faust for lust and life in your modern phrase.
And be the matter ever so abstruse
for brain, the tune will tingle on the tongue.[40]

The most unconventional American translator of Goethe's

Faust "was born on a limited train 'somewhere in the Middle West,' July 16, 1890," as "the only child of a Scotch furniture-maker and a part German scholarly mother."⁴¹ Seemingly impelled by the Faustian thirst for knowledge and by the urge for a broad, first-hand experience of life, in his exuberant youth, according to his own statement, he "hoboed six thousand miles in the United States" and later traveled through considerable portions of Europe and Africa.⁴²

In the romantic heyday of his late thirties and early forties, Professor MacIntyre, who began his professional career as a teacher at Occidental College and later became Professor of English at the University of California, Los Angeles, built himself a cabin "on the alluvial fan at the foot of the Sierra Madre . . . and filled it with his European loot . . . pewter, bronze, tanagras, and prints of Botticelli and Michelangelo. With a vineyard and winery back of the cabin and his neighbor a mile away, he lived the idyllic life. . . . The latchstring was always out to a few students who took him as he was and loved him for his electric individuality."⁴³

But this rather self-centered existence came to a sudden end on New Year's Eve, 1933, when a destructive flash-flood carried away Professor MacIntyre's car, his cabin, and with it his library of several thousand volumes, together with copies of a good many sentimental poems which he had written during these years. Chronologically, this event marked a turning point in his life, for from this time on he assumed a more social attitude toward the world about him, and he gave expression to this newly found social interest in his literary compositions. At the same time he developed a fondness for the classics of German literature, especially for Goethe's *Faust*.

In the following words, Lawrence Clarke Powell delineates graphically, though with perhaps some lack of restraint, the man and the translator as he appeared a few years ago: "Tall, lean, powerful, with thin, thrusting face, a hopped up, supercharged twentieth-century Byron, he excites the violent emotions of love, hate, fascination, repugnance. None are indifferent to him and to a whole cross-section of humanity he is a real friend."[44] The London *Times* succinctly sums up its impression of Professor MacIntyre as being "one of the few into whose soul the iron as well as the irony of his age has entered."[45] He has published the following works: *Cafes and Cathedrals*, Oxford (England), 1939; *Fifty Selected Poems* by Rainer Maria Rilke (translation), University of California Press, 1940; Goethe's *Faust*, Part I, New Directions, Norfolk, Connecticut, 1941; *The Black Bull*, Decker, New York, 1942; *Rilke's Life of the Virgin Mary*, University of California Press. Professor MacIntyre is also co-editor of *Elements of Discourse in English Literature*, published in 1934, and *Prose of the Romantic Period*, published in 1938. Moreover, his translation of one hundred poems by Stefan George has just come off the press, and he is now working on an English version of *Faust*, Part II.

The translator's interest in the German language and in German literature may have been strongly stimulated by his parents, for his mother was part German and we are informed that his father, although a Scotsman, liked the greatest German classic well enough to take his son to see a performance of it. This proved to be an unforgettable event in the boy's life. While attending high school he studied German for two years and continued with several other courses in the language at Drake University. Then, in the early twenties, came his first sojourn in Germany, and at this time he studied at the University of Marburg under Professors Elster, Deutschbein, and Hamann, who, recognizing his literary talents, encouraged him to make translations from the works of a number of German poets. By virtue of his meritorious work there and a thesis on *Der Gebrauch der Farbe in Rosettis Dichtung*, there was bestowed upon him the degree of Ph.D. in 1923.[46] But he says of his work there: "My German landlady and her daughter taught me more about colloquial German than I ever could learn in classes. I wanted to do a thesis on Heine, but they insisted that I take something English."[47]

Professor MacIntyre's plans to English the *Faust* became more definite during the next decade and a half, so that by

1936, as a result of the encouragement offered him by Aldous Huxley in Hollywood and by Rockwell Kent's drawings, which always kept him "steamed up," he began to work on the translation in earnest.* At the same time, he tells us, he read

> Now I must open the fundamental text, with the honest purpose, once & for all, to turn
> The holy original
> into my own beloved german.
>
> It is written: 'In the beginning was the Word!'
> I'm stopped already. Who will help me further?
> I cannot possibly rate the Word so highly.
> I must translate it otherwise,
> if I am rightly enlightened by the spirit.
> It is written: 'In the beginning was the Thought!'
> Consider the first line well,
> lest the pen write too hastily.
> Is it the Thought that works & creates all?
> Should it not be: 'In the beginning was the Power!'
> Yet, even as I write it down,
> I feel I cannot let that stand.
> The spirit helps me! Suddenly I have it,
> and confidently write:
>   'In the beginning was the Deed!'

Reproduction of a page of manuscript from Carlyle Ferren MacIntyre's translation of *Faust*, Part I, including lines 1220-1237

* A further sidelight at this point is afforded us by the following statement by Professor MacIntyre: "When my knowledge of the great scope of Goethe's mind began to force me to it, I finally read Carlyle's translation of the *Wilhelm Meister* books. Though I translated from the lesser poets ever since high school days, it was finally Rilke who made me do him more fully, and that toughened my spirit to tackle Goethe."—Letter to the writer, March 30, 1942.

the other *Faust* translations "with increasing displeasure; they simply did not function like the English idiom to which I am accustomed. . . . Hayward's seems to me the best of the lot, because his is in a prose that reads without affectations; his vocabulary is occasionally stilted. About the others, I'd say that they showed me what to avoid."[48]

In 1938, when Dr. MacIntyre received a Guggenheim Fellowship which enabled him to make a second trip to Europe, his translation of *Faust* was well advanced. He worked on the manuscript "in almost every place in Europe and even carried on in Africa. . . . Actually I did four different manuscripts . . . I worked on the 'Walpurgisnacht' on the top of the Brocken and visited Auerbach's on various occasions when I needed to absorb the real spirit of parts." He states further that he attended a number of performances of both parts of *Faust* and was able at first hand to discuss his translation with some very eminent German scholars and critics, including Hans Beutler, of the Goethehaus in Frankfurt; Anton Kippenberg, of the Insel-Verlag; and Professors Elster and Deutschbein, of the University of Marburg.[49] The finished translation of *Faust*, Part I, came off the press here in America in 1941.

What theory of translation, if any, has Professor MacIntyre followed? With the poet Dryden, he felt that every generation demands a new translation of a classic,[50] and, in spite of running the danger of shocking the literary sensibilities of conservative and classicist critics and readers, he has tried, according to his own statements, to make a version of *Faust* in the living, contemporary, English idiom, unhampered by the poetic inhibitions of the past. In fact, he boldly bases his unconventional translation approach upon the very words of the author of *Faust* himself, who, upon occasion, is reported to have said to his secretary Johann Peter Eckermann: "In these days the critics wrangle about rhymes——If I were young and reckless, I would purposely violate such caprices and use alliteration, assonance, and false rhyme, as pleased and suited me."[51]

In further elaboration of his theory of translation, Professor MacIntyre states at the close of his version that he has tried "to avoid the following major temptations: padding to eke out a line's length; inversion of the normal order; the use of 'poetic' diction, dead words, clichés, tautologies, and the like; circumlocution and paraphrase. Not forgetting the four foot doggerel line which Goethe took from Hans Sachs, I have often tried the apparently easy blank verse of the Elizabethans, a medium to which our ears are more conditioned; in order to give a different tone to other parts, I have tried meters which seemed to me to reproduce something of the feeling of the original. It is futile for anyone to work on a version employing the exact rhythms and double rhymes of the original."[52] In addition, he states that he has planned the translation for younger people, especially those who will never read German. Also he has considered its use in the theater, and this he cites as one of the reasons for not following the metres and the rimes of the original.[53]

A careful reading reveals a thoroughgoing consistency between Professor MacIntyre's theory and his practice in translating the *Faust*. The contemporary idiom employed lends the whole work freshness and interest. Here and there it even exceeds the original in the colloquial quality of its diction. In Outside the Town Gate, for instance, the first student says to the second (lines 828 and 829):

> Christ, just look how those broads walk by!
> Come on brother, let's give them a try.

The second citizen in the same scene remarks to his companion (lines 868 and 869):

> That's right, neighbor, no foreign intervention!
> Let them crack each others' heads and bust 'em.

In the hilarious Auerbach's Cellar scene, where we can rightly expect anything to happen and any sort of language to be used, Brander shouts (lines 2092 and 2093):

> That's a nasty song! To hell with politics!
> No more of that. And thank God every day
> you weren't born to rule

the Roman Empire. You can bet I'm glad
I'm not the Kaiser or his chief adviser.

Gretchen's last speech in the scene At the Well illustrates how the contemporary idiom makes itself felt in some of the more restrained and serious passages:

> Once, how boldly, I'd have run down
> any girl that got herself in trouble!
> My tongue would have found hard words
> for her sins, to smear then black and blacker
> and still not black enough. And I'd have blessed myself
> and been so good and smug—
> but now we're tarred with the same brush!
> Yet—all that led to it, O God
> it was so good! It was so sweet!

This translation is marked also by a very general departure from the rhythmic and metrical patterns of the original. Occasionally, as in the first four stanzas of Gretchen's Room, one finds a fair degree of fidelity in these respects. However, many times where the rimes are not entirely omitted their appearance seems to be dictated largely by the ease with which they could be supplied. In the scene Martha's Garden, on the other hand, there are no riming lines; neither is the rhythmic pattern of the original maintained, and the lines actually read more like prose than poetry. In some parts of the Prologue in Heaven, especially in the chants of the Archangels, and in the whole Dedication, blank verse is employed.

The possibility of a greater degree of fidelity to the original rhythmic patterns and rimes has been decreased in this translation by the tendency to reduce the number of lines and to alter their length. For instance, in Street I, seventy-six lines of the original have been reduced to sixty-five, and three hundred and fifty-one to three hundred and twenty-seven, respectively. This tendency to pack lines and thus to reduce their number is not proportionately the same, however, throughout the translation. In a further effort to hew down the size of the drama and to adapt it for stage presentation in America, Professor MacIntyre has relegated his version of the Dedication, the Prologue at the Theatre, and the Walpurgis Night's Dream to the Appendix following the translation.

Finally, we may ask, what is the intrinsic merit of this latest effort to English the *Faust?* In one respect Professor MacIntyre's version reminds us strongly of Geoffrey Montagu Cookson's translation, which appeared in 1925. Both authors have done their best work in the gay, the spirited, the unrestrained passages. Like his predecessor, Professor MacIntyre has successfully caught up in his translation the cynical spirit of Mephistopheles,* the bravado of students and soldiers, the carefree mood of the peasants under the lime tree, and the uncouth chatter of monkeys and witches on the Blocksberg. But, if Dr. MacIntyre's translation can be called slangy in places, Cookson's version is doubly so. The latter, however, has done his best or his worst, one hardly knows which, to make his lines rime in some fashion or other, in contrast to Dr. MacIntyre, who, for the most part, does not attempt to do so.

Finally, it must be said that although one misses in Professor MacIntyre's translation the poetic touch which graces the translations by Miss Swanwick, by Bayard Taylor, and occasionally the version by Latham, he has made the Faust drama live for us again by letting the characters speak naturally and in the idiom of our own day. The work is pervaded by a freshness which reawakens the interest of the reader already familiar with *Faust* and fascinates him who peruses its pages for the first time. In addition, the attractive illustrations by Rockwell Kent, so appropriately interspersed, enhance the engaging qualities of the whole volume. Hence, in spite of its obvious deviations from the original, this version will occupy

* *Werther* was the translator's favorite book when he was fifteen. In it he found much comfort for adolescent steaminess and dreaminess, but Mephisto in his red tights had long haunted him. "I enjoyed," says Professor MacIntyre, "doing the scenes in which Mephisto really put his hooks in; I feel a strong affinity with his humor and malice, and I certainly know how a frustrated professor feels! The Devil with Martha and the whole Walpurgisnacht were really fun."—Letter to the writer, March 30, 1942.

a worthy place alongside its fellows in the imposing row of the translations of Goethe's *Faust* made into English thus far.

JOHN FREDERICK LOUIS RASCHEN
(1875-   )
TRANSLATION OF *Faust I* AND PARTS OF *Faust II*
FIRST PRINTED IN 1949

Professor John Frederick Louis Raschen could hardly have chosen a more auspicious and fitting time than the bicentennial year of Goethe's birth for the publication of a translation of *Faust*. Well toward the front in the impressive list of works on Goethe scheduled to appear in the commemorative year of 1949, the most recently completed English version of this great classic bids fair to arouse considerable interest in both Europe and America among those who through the years have come to hold in high regard the genius of Johann Wolfgang von Goethe.

Professor Raschen can boast of being, at least in his very early life, one of the three among the translators of *Faust* who were compatriots of Goethe himself, for he was born in Bremen, Germany, February 19, 1875. After coming to America at the age of fourteen, he entered Baldwin-Wallace College and graduated from that school in 1895. He continued his studies at Nast Theological Seminary, at Lafayette College, at Columbia University, and at the University of Heidelberg. From Lafayette College he received the Master of Arts degree in 1905, and Dickinson College honored him with the degree of Doctor of Literature in 1912.[54]

Before entering upon his teaching career, Professor Raschen, prompted by his youthful idealism and his interest in the work of the Christian church, held Methodist pastorates at Akron and Despatch, New York. He was made Headmaster in Greek and Latin at Dickinson Seminary in 1901, Instructor in Modern Languages at Lafayette College in 1902, advanced to Assistant Professor in 1905, and to Professor in 1906. In 1914 he left Lafayette to become Professor of German Language and Literature at the University of Pittsburgh, where in 1921 he was made Professor of Modern Languages. He retired from his teaching duties at the latter school in 1945. At the present time he is Visiting Lecturer in German at the University of Michigan and lives with his younger daughter, Mrs. J. C. Tibbetts, at 1401 Iroquois Drive, Ann Arbor.[55]

During the passing years many honors both academic and otherwise have been bestowed upon Professor Raschen. At the University of Pittsburgh he was made the Executive Officer of the Graduate Council and the Secretary of the University Senate. A partial list of the academic groups of which he has been a member at one time or other includes the Modern Language Association of America, the National Institute of Social Sciences, the American Dialect Society, the Verse Writer's Guild of America, the Goethe Society of America, and the Schiller Academy of Munich.[56]

As an author the translator has contributed articles to both the German secular and the religious press. He served on the review staff of *Social Science Abstracts* and published texts in the International Modern Language Series in 1907, 1910, 1932, 1933, and 1934.[57] Professor Raschen has translated the whole of *Faust*, Part I, and a considerable number of shorter and longer scenes from Part II. These include Pleasure Garden and A Dark Gallery from Act I, Vaulted Gothic Room from Act II, Shady Grove from Act III, and Open Country, Midnight, Outer Court of Palace, and Ravines, Woodlands, Cliffs, Wilderness from Act V. Although the translation bears the imprint of the Goethe bicentennial, it actually came off the press in December, 1948. Planned for the collegian and the ordinary reader as well as the scholar, it is provided with copious notes and a bibliography.

We are informed by the translator that his interest in *Faust* has been a constant one for over four decades, in fact, ever since he sat at the feet of such famous teachers as Calvin Thomas of Columbia and Robert Petsch of Heidelberg, 1905-1907. "In favorable hours throughout the years," Professor Raschen writes, "I was 'bound to this poem,' and successive lines were typed, reshaped, and filed to retain or re-present the musical rhythm and swing."[58] In the Introduction he says further that "inasmuch as many have given time and 'sweat' to rendering *Faust* into readable form, I have no hesitancy in saying that I did not intend to displace any prior attempt. . . . I make no claims for preeminence of my endeavors. I have undertaken to be a mediator between the poet and his readers. If the work conveys the sense and meaning approximately in rhythmic lines, it has achieved its aim."

The translator claims to have followed no specific and preconceived theory in his work and to have steered clear of prior English versions. "Unconsciously," he says, "I was swept along by the rhythm of the poem, to capture both sense and the sweep thereof in phrase and form. Call it paraphrase if you will; that it also has the character of imitation may be evident in spots. At any rate, I attempted to exhibit fidelity to the poet's mind and mood. Whether I achieved this remains to be seen."[59] Professor Raschen confesses that he experienced much difficulty in reproducing the variety of metre and especially the feminine rimes.

Yet this translation definitely must be placed among the best English versions of *Faust*. Not always free from padding, due to the exigencies of rime and metrical pattern, not always equal to the perhaps impossible requirement of reproducing the feminine rime, and given here and there to a loose paraphrastic rendering of the original, still this version, as a whole, reproduces the thought and the spirit as well as the form of *Faust* to a very high degree. It can be said that it is not only a good translation but good poetry. Compared with the versions of Professor Raschen's predecessors and colleagues in the teaching profession, it fully measures up to those by Latham, Van der Smissen, and Priest, and it is definitely superior to that by MacIntyre.

To turn to some passages, first of all, where Professor Raschen's translation is vulnerable to unfavorable criticism, I quote lines 430-434 from Night. Here the original reads:

> Ha! welche Wonne fliesst in diesem Blick
> Auf einmal mir durch alle meine Sinnen!

> Ich fühle junges, heil'ges Lebensglück
> Neuglühend mir durch Nerv' und Adern rinnen.

Professor Raschen translates:

> What rapture flows and meets my sight;
> Come suddenly, in warmth my senses steeping!
> I feel life's transport, hallowed, new, with might
> Fresh-glowing through my nerves and pulses sweep.

Although the sense of the original is unquestionably present in the first three lines, the translation lacks the directness and the forcefulness of the original.

The first eleven lines of the soldiers' chorus in Outside the Gate:

> Burgen mit hohen
> Mauern und Zinnen,
> Mädchen mit stolzen
> Höhnenden Sinnen
> Möcht ich gewinnen!
> Kühn ist das Mühen,
> Herrlich der Lohn!
> Und die Trompete
> Lassen wir werben,
> Wie zu der Freude,
> So zum verderben,

read in Professor Raschen's translation:

> Castles with lofty
> Rampart and tower,
> Maids of mind haughty
> Scornful and dour,
> Fain I would capture!
> Bold is the venture,
> Glorious the pay!
> We let the trumpet
> Call us to wooing,
> Be't for pleasure
> Or our undoing.

In the first part of this passage the triple rime of the original is missing, and it would seem that the lines

> Und die Trompete
> Lassen wir werben

have been misconstrued.

Lines 4679-4685, Part II, Act I:

> Des Lebens Pulse schlagen frisch lebendig,
> Ätherische Dämmerung milde zu begrüssen;
> Du, Erde, warst auch diese Nacht beständig
> Und atmest neu erquickt zu meinen Füssen,
> Beginnest schon mit Lust mich zu umgeben,
> Du regest und rührst ein kräftiges Beschliessen,
> Zum höchsten Dasein immerfort zu streben,

which Professor Raschen translates as

> Life's pulses throb anew; revived I'm ready
> To hail ethereal dawn with tender greeting.
> Thou earth throughout the night hast proven steady;
> Before my feet refreshed, renewed art breathing
> And spreadest delights for my eyes to unravel.
> I'm stirred to firm resolve—the challenge meeting—
> Henceforth to strive t'ward mankind's highest level!

demonstrate the translator's ability to render into English the long five-stressed lines. The rhythmic pattern and the feminine rimes have been retained, but, in line 4679, "revived I'm ready" and, in line 4684, "the challenge meeting" are nothing but padding.

Definitely superior passages are to be found in many parts of Professor Raschen's *Faust*, as, for instance, his translation of the chant of the Archangels, especially lines 251-258:

> And swift beyond the mind's conceiving,
> The earth revolves, with splendor bright.
> Day's Eden-brightness wanes, receding
> Before deep, awe-inspiring night.
> The oceans foam, their waves keep hurling
> Massed weight against the rock-girt shore;
> Both rocks and waves keep onward whirling
> On spheric course forevermore.

Here we have the melodic charm, the rhythmic movement, and the thought of the original preserved in a most satisfying and masterful manner. A similar excellence is to be found in such passages as Faust's long monologue in Part I, lines 602-735, Ariel's Song at the beginning of Part II, Act I, and many others.

IV

Shadowy Figures Among the Translators of Faust

Leader of the chorus:
Who hath not won a name, and seeks not noble works,
Belongs but to the elements: away then, ye!

. . . .

All:
Given again to the daylight are we,
Persons no more, 'tis true,—
We feel it and know it,—
But to Hades return we never!
Nature, the Ever-living,
Makes to us spirits
Validest claim, and we to her also.[1]

NOT ONLY POLITICAL, social, and educational leaders, but also men of little stature and minds of mediocre intellectual acumen have succumbed to the powerful charm of Goethe's *Faust*. These figures, upon whom the glaring light of publicity never played, came to feel *Faust* to be a compelling influence which somehow reached down into their own little existences, and moved them to express his thoughts and experiences in their own native tongue. For David Syme, v. Beresford, John Wynniat Grant, Charles Hartpole Bowen, W. H. Colquhoun, Beta, and R. McLintock, the translation of Goethe's *Faust* represents the greatest achievement of their lives, a tour de force which in a sense immortalized them. It is their good fortune to live on in the reflected glory of the intellectual and spiritual Titan Goethe.

Shadowy Figures
DAVID SYME
(-)

TRANSLATION OF *Faust I* FIRST PRINTED IN 1834

The year 1834 displayed an unusual abundance of English *Faust* translations, for at this time Hayward's second revised edition and three new versions, one by Warburton Davies, another by John S. Blackie, and the third by David Syme appeared. Allibone's *Dictionary of Authors* mentions Syme as the writer of *Reports of Proceedings in the High Court of Justiciary* from November, 1826, to 1830.[2] The British Museum Catalogue credits him with a translation of *Faust* in 1834 and an additional work, *The Fortunes of Francesco Novello da Carrara . . . from the Chronicles of Catarro* in 1830.[3] Further information about him is lacking.

In the short Preface to his translation of *Faust*, Part I, which appeared simultaneously at Edinburgh and at Leipzig, Syme calls attention to the fact that he has made a careful study of the original and kept Shelley's fragment constantly before him while making the translation. Although the Prologue in Heaven seems to him strange and startling, he nevertheless included it in his version, probably because Shelley had translated it and had not taken umbrage at Mephisto's remarks to the Lord. Syme has, however, omitted as irrelevant the theatrical prologue, the Intermezzo, and a few words and lines at different places. "For a very few expressions, chiefly in the lyric passages," he believes there is "no authority in the strict letter of the text." Still he hopes that on the whole he has "taken no greater latitude in these respects than will be thought allowable in this kind of composition." Syme favors the type of translation in which "the author of a foreign nation . . . [is] brought to us in such a manner that we may regard him as our own."

This translation has all the worst faults of the early versions: omissions, an abundance of loose and inaccurately translated lines, forced and unnatural metre, little poetic inspiration, and a uniformly unnatural, uninteresting style in which all characters speak alike. The diversified moods and the spirit of the original are wholly lacking. A few examples chosen from the lyric and the conversational parts of the drama will suffice to show the nature of this version. The first two stanzas of Margaret's Prayer in the Zwinger scene read in Syme's translation:

> Ah: incline,
> Full of grief,
> Placidly thy face,
> Send: ah send relief:
>
> Deep, the sword,
> In thy heart,
> Stands as thou art gazing;
> With a voiceless smart
> On thy son's death.

How shabbily they compare with the inimitable lines of the original in every respect! It is by contrast with such a faulty translation that Goethe's lines shine forth in their true poetic beauty:

> Ach neige,
> Du Schmerzenreiche,
> Dein Antlitz gnädig meiner Not!
>
> Das Schwert im Herzen,
> Mit tausend Schmerzen,
> Blickst auf zu deines Sohnes Tod.

An extremely deficient translation also is that of Faust's words to Mephistopheles in Study II:

> Werd' ich beruhigt je mich auf ein Faulbett legen,
> So sei es gleich um mich gethan!
> Kannst du mich schmeichelnd je belügen,
> Dass ich mir selbst gefallen mag,
> Kannst du mich mit Genuss betrügen:
> Das sei für mich der letzte Tag!
> Die Wette biet' ich!

which Syme renders as:

> If ever I lie down in peace, be that
> Moment my doom,—deceive me, by your arts,
> Into a dream of happiness or comfort,
> And be that day my last. I venture!

Here he has unsuccessfully tried to compress Goethe's seven lines into four. Such attempts are frequent in every part of the translation.

All of these faults show that Syme had neither an intelligent theory of translation nor the ability to make an acceptable English version of *Faust*, and the liberties he has taken with the German text place him definitely in the same class with Gower. Syme did Goethe's reputation in England a disservice with his thoroughly inadequate translation.

v. BERESFORD
(-)
TRANSLATION OF *Faust I* FIRST PRINTED IN 1862

Another enigmatic character among the English translators of *Faust* is v. Beresford.* Frank Claudy, one of the American translators, whose version appeared in 1886, states in the Preface to his first edition: "As far as I have been able to ascertain, this is the first time that one of Goethe's own countrymen has attempted to translate *Faust* into English."[4] Was Claudy correct in his conclusion that he was the first German to translate *Faust*? The British Museum Catalogue,[5] which lists the author of the 1862 version as A. von Beresford, mentions, besides his translation of *Faust*, two other works: *Millicent; or our English Homes of the Present Day*, in two volumes, Göttingen, 1858; and a translation, *Prinz Rosa-Stramin*, 1860. The volume *Millicent; or our English Homes of the Present Day*, written in English, would indicate that he was an Englishman, for if he were a German, v. Beresford would not have been

---

* The translator's name appears as v. Beresford on the title-page and Dedication of the translation, as von Beresford in the Preface to Claudy's translation, and as A. von Beresford in the British Museum Catalogue.

so likely to write a book in English bearing such a title. This last-named volume, like the two translations, seems to have been intended for English readers.

Possibly v. Beresford's Dedication[6] also sheds some light on his nationality. Addressed to his Highness, Prince Maurice of Hanau, it reads: "In accepting of the dedication of this work, Highness adds one more to the many kindnesses already shown me, kindnesses which I shall ever think of with a grateful heart. If this little volume sometimes serves to awaken a thought of the writer, the labor bestowed upon it will be amply repaid. With every wish for Your Highness' happiness, believe me Your Highness' faithful and sincerely attached v. Beresford. Cassel, June 10, 1861." Although the *Dictionary of National Biography* contains such names as John Beresford, Lord John George Beresford, it lists no v. Beresford. Also the facts that the translator lived in Germany, that he was an intimate friend of a German prince, and that his books were published in Germany again seem to indicate that he was a German. Moreover, the faulty English of the translation, as well as its over-literalness, might also be an indication of German nationality, but since we find such shortcomings also in other translations, these facts have little value for our present purpose. Until further evidence is discovered, the supposition that v. Beresford was an Englishman by birth, who had resided in Germany for many years and obtained the title "von" by royal favor, is perhaps as satisfactory as any.

Little praise can be given this translation. As already mentioned above, it abounds in bad English constructions, mistranslations, inversions, and over-literal lines. Line 5 in Night I, which reads in the German, "Da steh' ich nun," v. Beresford translates inaccurately as: "Here stay I now." A similarly amusing rendering is that of line 207 in the same scene, where "Mir wird bei meinem kritischen Bestreben" is made to read in the translation, "Yet oft in my analysizing strife." Examples of this kind from v. Beresford's version can be multiplied ad infinitum.

The lyric portions are rendered in a still more wooden

style than the rest. The following passage from the Zwinger scene gives a sufficient idea of v. Beresford's limited abilities to reproduce these parts. The German lines:

> Wer fühlet
> Wie wühlet
> Der Schmerz mir im Gebein?
> Was mein armes Herz hier banget,
> Was es zittert, was verlanget,
> Weisst nur du, nur du allein!

he translates as:

> Who knows
> How throes
> My torment to the bone?
> How my wretched heart is breaking,
> How is trembling, how entreating,
> Know'st but thou, but thou alone!

Such futile efforts as v. Beresford's and Galvan's may be excusable when made only for private circulation, but there is no justification whatsoever for inflicting them upon the reading public at large. Like Gower's version they are but travesties of Goethe's *Faust*. The Prince von Hanau must have been as poor an English scholar as v. Beresford to have found any pleasure in this volume which was dedicated to him.

JOHN WYNNIAT GRANT
(-)

Translation of *Faust I* First Printed in 1867

Concerning John Wynniat Grant's life very little is discoverable, and that bit can be gathered only from his "Address to the Muse," which was written in Rome in 1854 and later placed at the end of his translation of *Faust*. Significant are the lines:

> The evil star that frown'd upon my birth,
> And cast me friendless on this beauteous earth . . .
>
> Or stray along the winding banks of Quair . . .
>
> When far remote from Caledonia's land.[7]

Since the translator, while in Rome, wrote in such a nostalgic vein of the banks of the Quair which flows into the Tweed, and of Caledonia, it may be fairly safe to assume that he was a Scotsman by birth. It is also within the realm of possibility that some years before he published his translation of *Faust*, his continental tour, like that of John Stuart Blackie, may have included Germany, where he became familiar with the German language and literature and especially with the writings of Goethe and Schiller. From his published works it would seem that the translator was a person of some refinement and of artistic temperament.

The literary activity of John Wynniat Grant was confined almost entirely to translation. In Allibone's *Dictionary of Authors*, the following works are listed under his name: a translation of the *Introduction to the Study of Art-Mythology* by A. E. Braun, 1856; an original work, *Historical Pictures from the Campagna of Rome: with Lyrics from Faust*, 1867; a translation of the *Lay of the Bell* by Schiller, 1867; and a translation of *Faust; a Dramatic Poem* by J. W. von Goethe, 1867.[7a]

Although, as is evident from the works mentioned above, Grant had considerable experience in translating from the German before he attempted *Faust*, his version of the drama is worthy of little praise. He is a second Anster, lacking all of his predecessor's poetic gifts; he is a mere rimester who takes unprecedented liberties, especially with the lyrics of *Faust*. In all but a very few instances the number of lines is considerably augmented, and in several of the songs, notably in the long Song of the Spirits toward the end of Study II, Grant exceeds even Anster in his diffuseness. Here Goethe has fifty-four verses, Anster fifty-nine, and Grant seventy-two. Grant cannot curb his tendency to expand on the original even in the conversational and reflective parts of the drama. A case in point is the passage from Study II in which Faust says to the poodle:

> Soll ich mit dir das Zimmer teilen,
> Pudel, so lass das Heulen,

> So lass das Bellen!
> Solch einen störenden Gesellen
> Mag ich nicht in der Nähe leiden.
> Einer von uns beiden
> Muss die Zelle meiden.

These lines Grant translates very loosely, inaccurately, and with considerable expansion:

> Now poodle leave off howling,
> And barking and growling!
> I cannot be hospitable
> If thou art not peaceable!
> Such a troublesome chum
> Must not stop in my room,
> If thy noise thou wilt not stay,
> One of us must away,
> And if no way beseems
> Me to I go to extremes,
> With the door open standing,
> No one needs commanding.

"Me to I go to extremes" is entirely unintelligible as it stands.

In every respect this is a rather meaningless and futile translation. Its language in most parts is nothing but rimed prose with many awkward inversions. Gretchen's words after singing the ballad König in Thule tumble to a low prosaic level as she soliloquizes:

> What a fine casket!—In here how did it come?
> I'm sure I lock'd the chest when I left home.
> I'm quite surpris'd! inside what can there be?

If Grant could not curb the irresistible impulse to make a translation of *Faust*, an attempt in prose might have done his reputation less harm. This version can have no more than a bibliographical interest. The copy in the William A. Speck Collection is autographed by the translator in the following amusing manner: "All genuine copies bear the signature of the translator. J. W. Grant." Surely no danger of pirating here!

CHARLES HARTPOLE BOWEN
(-)
TRANSLATION OF *Faust I* FIRST PRINTED IN 1878

On one of the preliminary leaves to Charles Hartpole Bowen's translation of *Faust*, is this short and striking legend: "Forty years have well nigh elapsed since the following translation of *Faust* was written. Put aside for so long a period, it may well seem strange that it should now appear in print. The only reason for this that the writer has to give, is a desire to save any friends who may hereafter care to read it the trouble of perusing a manuscript—Kilnacourt, Queen's County: May 24, 1877."[8]

Concerning Bowen's identity nothing more than a bit of circumstantial evidence can be mustered. The *Topographical Dictionary of Ireland* states that at the close of the reign of Queen Elizabeth, Queens County, Ireland, was settled by a number of English families, prominent among whom were the Hartpoles and the Bowens.[9] Since the translator lived in Queens County, at least at the time when the translation was about to be published, bearing a middle name Hartpole and a surname Bowen, tolerable logic would make him a descendant of these English immigrant families. After two and a half centuries of residence in Ireland, they would for all intents and purposes be regarded as Irish. Charles Hartpole Bowen, therefore, is to be assigned to the Irish group of translators composed of John Anster, John Galvan, Thomas E. Webb, and John Todhunter.

The reason why the translator finally had his version published after forty years, although his motive to accommodate his friends may be considered laudable, was no weighty one in any respect. Certainly it cannot be said that the literary merits of this version made it desirable and imperative that it should be published. It is the product of a youthful admirer of Goethe and *Faust*, who, entirely ignorant of the functions of a translator, found pleasure, nevertheless, in his dilettante efforts to reproduce the great original.

A few examples will suffice to indicate the nature of the translation. The first stanza of the Dedication:

> Ihr naht euch wieder, schwankende Gestalten,
> Die früh sich einst dem trüben Blick gezeigt.
> Versuch ich wohl euch diesmal festzuhalten?
> Fühl ich mein Herz noch jenem Wahn geneigt?
> Ihr drängt euch zu! Nun gut, so mögt ihr walten,
> Wie ihr aus Dunst und Nebel um mich steigt,
> Mein Busen fühlt sich jugendlich erschüttert
> Vom Zauberhauch der euren Zug umwittert,

Bowen translates:

> Ye wild and spectre forms, again ye rise,
> The troubled vision of my earliest youth;
> Say! Shall I grasp ye ere once more it flies,
> And do I feel that this delusion sooth
> My heart still haunts? Come then before my eyes
> Crowd forth from mist and vaporous cloud uncouth;
> My spirit feels within its inmost source
> The wizard breath that wafts your onward course.

In the opening speech in Auerbach's Cellar, Frosch says in the original:

> Will keiner trinken? keiner lachen?
> Ich will euch lehren Gesichter machen:
> Ihr seid ja heut wie nasses Stroh,
> Und brennt sonst immer lichterloh.

In Bowen's version these lines read:

> Will no one laugh, will no one booze?
> Another tune I'll make you choose.
> Wet straw were livelier stuff today,
> Yet other times you blaze away.

One detects at once that the desired qualities of a good translation are not abundant in this version. The language is prosy; the thought is rendered too freely and too loosely, and then again too literally; the metre is forced, and the lines always close with the hard, monotonous masculine rimes. The translation is a failure. The title-page, which credits *Faust* to T. W. von Goethe, shows either that Bowen was amazingly ignorant of the life of Goethe or that he was unpardonably careless as a proofreader.

W. H. COLQUHOUN
(-)

Translation of *Faust I* First Printed in 1878

Nothing can be ascertained about W. H. Colquhoun's life and calling. However, in the short Preface to his version Colquhoun remarks that he has labored for a long time on a translation of both parts of *Faust*. He now ventures to publish Part I because "there are friends who wish to see it in printed form," and because he feels encouraged by Maffei, the most famous of the Italian translators of *Faust*, who generously welcomes every laborer in such a field with the following words: "Of the great foreign authors the different interpretations and translations do not cause any harm; on the contrary, since every translator puts into it, so to say, a part of his own individuality, the translated work, being shown in different lights, acquires a unique and increased splendor."[10]

The translation of *Faust*, Part I, by W. H. Colquhoun appeared in 1878; however, nowhere can any reference be found to the publication of Part II.[11] If it never came off the press,[12] the loss has been small, for although the translator's aim was "to render the German very closely,"[13] he has succeeded in this to only a limited extent. His translation of Michael's Chant in the Prologue in Heaven:

>And storms in rival roar are striving
>From shore to sea—from sea to shore,
>And in their wrath a woof are weaving
>All, all around, of deepest power.
>Before the thunder-peal's career,
>Destruction, flashing, flames away
>But, Lord, thy messengers revere
>The placid progress of thy day,

lacks the forceful, elevated, and expressive diction of the original. Again, when Colquhoun makes the Angels sing in chorus at the end of Scene I:

> Arisen Christ hath,
> From womb of corruption forth!
> Rejoicing may ye
> From your bonds break free;
> By deed, glory giving,
> Love manifest making;
> Feeding, right brotherly,
> Voyaging in ministry,
> Blessedness promising,
> You is the Master near.
> Unto you is he there,

one feels that the language, in spite of the fact that it is in poetic form, is only clumsy, faulty, and uninspired prose. Other shortcomings of this translation are its over-literalness and frequent verbal inaccuracies. The one redeeming feature is the metre, in which Colquhoun has approximated the German more closely than in other matters.

BETA
(-)

TRANSLATION OF *Faust I* FIRST PRINTED IN 1895

Whether Beta is the real or assumed name of the translator whose prose version of the First Part of *Faust* appeared in 1895 is still a moot question. Goedeke states that it is the pseudonym of an English judge,[14] but does not give the source of this information. Since the name Beta occurs in biographical reference books, it is possible also that it is genuine. A. G. Berry, successor to David Nutt, who published Beta's translation, wrote in 1931: "The tradition is that the author Beta was purely a private student. The book has not been sold for many years."[15] Moreover, Professor Schreiber informs me that in the late summer of 1939 he called on Mr. Berry, and that together they went through the ledgers of the firm of David Nutt. Although the accounts for 1895 were inspected, no trace of Beta could be discovered. There was a slight lead that such a person lived in Greek Street, Soho, but there the trail ended. Beta issued his version with the German text and the translation on opposite pages and with notes in the back, apparently as a handy volume for students and others who had only a limited knowledge of German but were interested in *Faust*. Hence, it is not impossible that Beta may have been a somewhat obscure English pedagogue, who, uncertain of the success of the venture, preferred to leave the public in the dark about his real identity.

The translator remarks in his Preface that he has attempted "nothing more than literal fidelity" in this version. He has made another literal prose translation of *Faust*, he says, not because of the inadequacy of Hayward's version, which he himself has followed rather closely in his work, but in order that he might offer to the interested public "the light thrown on numerous passages by the advance of Faust-exegesis."[16] In his acknowledgments, Beta mentions that he has also profited from the metrical translations of Anster, Birds, Pradez, Sabatier, Swanwick, and Bayard Taylor.

The translation itself is of no great interest. Bayard Quincy Morgan has characterized it correctly when he calls it little more than a copy of Hayward's version.[17] An idea of the close correspondence between these two translations may be gained by a comparison of the following passages from the Dedication. Hayward:

> Ye bring with you the images of happy days, and many loved
> shades arise; like to an old half-expired Tradition, rises
> First-love with Friendship in their company. The pang is
> renewed; the plaint repeats the labarinthine mazy course of
> life, and names the dear ones, who, cheated of fair hours
> by fortune, have vanished away before me.

Beta:

> Ye bring with you the images of happy days, and many loved
> shades arise: like an old half-forgotten legend, comes up

first love, with friendship, in their company. The pain is renewed; the plaint recalls the mazily devious course of life, and names the good who, cheated of fair hours by fortune, have vanished away before me.

The sentence structure in the two passages is exactly the same, and, where there is a divergency in the readings, Beta uses synonyms which express the thought of the original with no more fidelity than Hayward's terms. With much the same servility, Beta follows Hayward throughout the translation. But Beta has been more consistent than his predecessor in that he has rendered in prose also the few parts which appear in poetic form in Hayward's version.

R. McLINTOCK
(-)

Translation of *Faust I* First Printed in 1897

What little we know concerning McLintock is wholly about his literary activities. He appears to have done no original work. The first record we find of McLintock is in the British Museum Catalogue, 1891, which lists a translation under his name in 1881 of *A Trip to the Brocken* by Heine.

The periodical *Academy* reports that on January 29, 1887, "after the appointment of officers and committees, a paper was read by Mr. R. McLintock of Liverpool upon 'The Five Best English Translations of Faust' before the English Goethe Society of Manchester."[18] On this occasion he discussed the versions of Miss Swanwick, Professor Blackie, Theodore Martin, Professor Anster, and Bayard Taylor.[19] McLintock condemned all of them for reproducing the original neither in form nor in meaning, and then at the close read his own version of the entire Prologue in Heaven.

The publication of the Göchhausen Manuscript of the *Urfaust* by Erich Schmidt in 1887 appears to have deepened McLintock's interest in Goethe's *Faust* and the historical problems connected with it. In the Introduction to his translation of Part I, published in 1897, he reviews the history of the development of the Faust legend. He continues with a comparison of Part I and the fragment of 1790 with the Göchhausen Manuscript and Marlowe's *Faustus*, concluding that Goethe's *Faust*, Part I, is very closely dependent upon Marlowe's work. According to his findings it is "a resetting of Marlowe's theme."[20] He further contends that the Prologue, written in 1797, is, as a prologue to *Faust*, a mere piece of self-stultification on the part of the author; that it was meant to deceive; that the Second Part also is an afterthought, and that, finally, it presents the successive periods in the later real life of its author, whereas the First Part is an intensively realistic picture of an imaginary career, ending in a catastrophe, from which no escape is thinkable.[21]

Very little can be said in favor of McLintock's theories outlined above. He has the vanity to hope that they "may help a few eyes to see the imbecility and absolute immorality of some of the current interpretations of the work."[22] But since his findings are entirely at variance with the conclusions of the large bulk of unprejudiced modern scholarship, we may do well to turn to the translation itself, a procedure which may be of greater advantage and interest at this time.

McLintock holds that a good version must possess "the clearness without which, in most cases, all else is vanity,"[23] and that it must reproduce the original in both form and spirit.[24] It is, therefore, these characteristics especially that one should expect to find in his translation. A comparison of his version with the original is somewhat disappointing, however. Throughout the conversational and reflective passages, McLintock has reproduced the metre of the original with good success, but not as much can be said of the lyric parts. In such a passage as the Angels' Chorus at the end of Scene I, in which he has attempted to reproduce Goethe's dactylic feminine rimes at all odds, the metre is forced and unnatural. The lines:

> Thätig ihn Preisenden,
> Liebe Beweisenden,
> Brüderlich Speisenden,
> Predigend Reisenden,

> Wonne Verheissenden,
> Euch ist der Meister nah,
> Euch ist er da!

read in the translation:

> Let your deeds praise his name!
> Love in you blaze and flame!
> Feed the poor! Raise his fame!
> Preach on all ways the same!
> God's promised grace proclaim!
> Then is the Master near—
> Yea, even here!

McLintock is not accurate in rendering the thought of the original, and many passages are translated too freely. The opening lines of Scene 8 serve as an example. Here Gretchen says:

> Ich gäb' was drum, wenn ich nur wüsst',
> Wer heut der Herr gewesen ist!
> Er sah gewiss recht wacker aus
> Und ist aus einem edlen Haus;
> Das könnt ich ihm an der Stirne lesen!
> Er wär' auch sonst nicht so keck gewesen.

In McLintock's version these lines read:

> I'd give a trifle just to know
> His name today who scared me so!
> And O me! but he did look brave!
> He's surely not a low-born knave—
> That much was plain in face and bearing—
> Or else he'd never have been so daring!

Otto Heller in his study entitled *Faust and Faustus*, referring to McLintock's version, writes: "His excellent *Faust* translation happens to be all but unknown in this country."[25] Again, somewhat later, he states: "This work has not received sufficient credit. It was considerably underestimated by R. Weissenfels." However, I cannot share Otto Heller's enthusiasm for this translation. Since he lists only Anster's, Bayard Taylor's, and Latham's versions in his bibliography, Heller's high opinion of McLintock's translation may be due to a lack of acquaintance with the later, more accurate versions. I have in mind such translations as William Page Andrews' and Alice Raphael's. Possibly, also, Heller's special interest in McLintock's theories may account at least in part for his lavish praise of this version. I cite a final quotation from Scene 12 lending support to the opinion already expressed above that McLintock has made only a partially successful translation. Lines 3137-3148 read in the German:

> Ich zog es auf, und herzlich liebt' es mich.
> Es war nach meines Vaters Tod geboren.
> Die Mutter gaben wir verloren,
> So elend wie sie damals lag,
> Und sie erholte sich sehr langsam, nach und nach.
> Da konnte sie nun nicht dran denken
> Das arme Würmchen selbst zu tränken,
> Und so erzog ich's ganz allein,
> Mit Milch und Wasser; so ward's mein.
> Auf meinem Arm, in meinem Schoos
> War's freundlich, zappelte, ward gross.

McLintock translates rather loosely as follows:

> I reared her, and quite fond of me she grew.
> 'Twas after Father's death—and Mother lying
> So ill we thought her surely dying,
> And every hour about to flit.
> And then she mended, O! so slowly, bit by bit!
> She lying prostrate and dejected,
> No nursing was to be expected,
> And so I reared it—I alone—
> On milk and water—'twas my own!
> And on my arm and lap it grew
> And got to know me throve and crew.

Lines four and six in the translation are pure padding. The use of the word "crew" in the last line seems odd, but it served as a rime for "grew." Andrews translates as follows:

> I brought it up and it was fond of me.
> Father had died when it was born;

> We gave our mother up for lost, so worn
> And wretched, lying there, was she.
> And she grew well but slowly, bit by bit,
> She could not think of suckling it
> Herself, the poor babe pitifully wee,
> And so I brought it up, and quite alone,
> With milk and water; so't became my own.
> Upon my arm and in my lap it threw
> Itself about, was friendly too, and grew.

With the exception of the feminine rimes, which Andrews has omitted, Andrews' translation is much more accurate than that of McLintock. And Martin and Taylor, whom McLintock criticized severely in his address before the Manchester English Goethe Society,[26] have reproduced the language and the spirit of the original more adequately than McLintock.

A point that adds interest to this volume, however, is the rendering in the footnotes of the Göchhausen Transcript where the reading of the *Urfaust* differed from that of Part I of *Faust*. The Appendix contains a translation of the scene Two Imps and Amor, the Variants of the Göchhausen Transcript, and the complete Paralipomena of the Weimar edition of 1887.

V

The Disciples of Aesculapius and Faust

> *An old Peasant:*
> To tell the truth, that you appear
> Upon a holiday seems only right—
> You, who in evil days gone by,
> Proved a friend to all the people here.
> How many a person is alive,
> Because your father in the past
> Snatched him out of raging fever,
> When he checked the plague at last.
> You entered every stricken house,
> Though at that time a young man still;
> Many a corpse was carried forth,
> Yet you came through and were not ill,
> Surviving trial and hardship to the end;
> The friend was aided by the Heavenly Friend.[1]

GOETHE'S INTEREST in the medieval pseudo-science of alchemy and its modern successors, medicine and chemistry, has left its mark on the *Faust* drama. We will remember that the hero of this work is represented in the scene Before the Gate as being the son of a well-known and beloved physician. The youthful Faust—himself an apt disciple of Aesculapius, the ancient, fabled Greek physician and demigod of the healing art—together with his father is portrayed as going from house to house to help those smitten by the plague. Although their alchemically concocted medicines were in many cases more deadly than the plague itself, the public continued to regard Faust with utmost esteem, even veneration bordering on worship, as their great helper in the time of need.

When Goethe makes the Director in the Prologue for the Theatre say:

> These masses you alone through masses can subdue,
> Each then selects in time what suits his bent.

Disciples of Aesculapius

Bring much, you somewhat bring to not a few,
And from the house goes everyone content,[2]

he expresses an idea which he himself has carried out in *Faust*. The disciples of Aesculapius have found in it much to admire and much to appropriate for themselves. George William Lefevre, John Todhunter, and C. Fillingham Coxwell, well-known English physicians in their day, were inspired by *Faust* to such an extent that they became willing to spend many weary hours in their attempts to render the work into English.

SIR GEORGE WILLIAM LEFEVRE
(1789-1846)
Translation of *Faust I* First Printed in 1841

This English doctor was the first member of the medical profession to attempt a translation of *Faust*. Lefevre was born in 1789 at Berkhamstead, Hertfordshire. He studied medicine at Edinburgh, Guy's, and St. Thomas' Hospitals in London; received his M.D. degree at Aberdeen in 1819, and was admitted a licentiate of the Royal College of Physicians, London, in 1822.

Since, however, he was threatened with a pulmonary disease and failed to secure a position with a dispensary, Lefevre went abroad. As physician to a Polish nobleman, with whom he traveled for a period of nine years in France, Austria, Poland, and Russia, he had many interesting experiences and became intimately acquainted with the domestic life of the Polish nobility. In 1832 he took up private practice in St. Petersburg, where he was soon after appointed physician to the British Embassy. As a reward for his distinguished services while the cholera epidemic raged in the Russian capital, he was knighted.[3]

After a residence of fourteen years in St. Petersburg, Lefevre again returned home by way of Sweden, Prussia, the German baths, and Holland, and settled in London in 1842. The same year he was admitted as a fellow of the College of Physicians and three years later delivered the Lumleian lectures before this body. He died a violent death in 1846 by taking prussic acid. The necrology which appeared in the *Literary Gazette* throws additional light on Lefevre's character and life. "The flightiness," the writer says, "in nearly all these publications [a reference to the medical works and a book of travel written by Lefevre] combined with extensive travel, and peculiar talents, may be more pointedly insisted upon than would have been proper or decent at the time of their appearance. Great wit is indeed often too nearly allied to madness; and domestic unhappiness we believe, might still further be added to the cup, which in this instance proved too powerful for reason. The distressing malady of his wife, in needful retirement from the family circle and world, and the death of his two children at St. Petersburg, preyed deeply upon him; and it is with feelings of unmixed commiseration that we write a painful record of a man of no common worth and accomplishments, and much esteemed by all who knew him."[4]

As a writer on medical subjects in such volumes as *Apology for Nerves* and *Thermal Comfort,* published after 1843, Lefevre is remembered more for his whimsical style than for sound learning. His *Revelations of Russia* contain bitter attacks upon Emperor Nicholas. His most pretentious book is *The Life of a Travelling Physician* in three volumes, published in 1843. This is described by the *Literary Gazette* as consisting of "three very desultory volumes, written without art by a man of great judgment and talent, who has seen and observed much of the world, and aptly describes the countries he visited, the life in which he has mingled, and the persons with whom he was associated."[5]

We know nothing definite concerning Lefevre's relations to German literature prior to the publication of his translation of *Faust*, Part I, in 1841. It may be that the interest in *Faust* of the Anglo-German colony of St. Petersburg aroused the desire in him to try his hand at making an English version of this celebrated drama. In his Preface, he says, "Still, I have not been able to resist the temptation of trying to make my old colleague* better understood. In spite of the numerous

---

* It can be only a matter of conjecture as to why Lefevre felt at liberty to

translations, which have appeared, a correct one is still a desideratum."[6]

Since the first edition of his translation, printed for private distribution among his friends and the Anglo-German Society in St. Petersburg, was soon disposed of and received with some favor, Lefevre says he ventured to give a corrected edition to the public.[7] This appeared in 1843, dedicated to the Count Augustus Potocki, probably one of the Polish noblemen with whom he had become acquainted in his travels.

Lefevre believes that "a translation is good only, when it renders the spirit of the original as literally as the differences in the idioms of language will allow," and he feels that "with those who have not studied *Faust* in the German, this attempt will find no favor, for having no claim, or pretensions at poetry, it is only upon its presumed fidelity that it can hope for success."[8] But a cursory examination will show that Lefevre was poorly prepared to make even a literal translation. The Dedication begins:

> O ye draw near again, ye flickering forms;
> Which to the troubled sight in former times
> Before appear'd! Shall I this time essay
> To hold you fast; and does my heart still cleave
> To the same joy? O ye intrude; well, well,
> Proceed at will; as out of cloud and fog
> You play around, I feel my bosom swell
> With boyish joys before the magic breeze,
> Which as you rush along pursues your steps.

The lines above strongly remind us of Gower's well-meant but futile efforts.

The opening lines of Night I are extremely comical:

> Pshaw! physic and philosophy,
> And jurisprudence too,
> Nay, worse than both, theology,
> All I have studied through

---

call Goethe his "old colleague." No records show that he ever met, or even corresponded with, Goethe. But we know that Goethe also studied medicine and especially anatomy at Strassburg.

With pains, and am, poor silly man,
As wise as when I first began.
They call me Doctor, Master—well,
Often long years I've had a spell,
Leading my scholars by the snout,
Above, below, and round about,
And see, just after all, I trow,
That we, alas! can nothing know.
It burns my very vitals up,
Or doctor, master, scribe, or priest.

Lefevre found pleasure in the rollicking tone of Mephistopheles' Song of the Flea in the Auerbach's Cellar scene, and he has caught the spirit of it in his translation:

There once did live a king,
This king had a great big flea;
He loved the jumping thing,
As though his son were he,
The king sends for his tailor,
Who straightway to him goes,
He takes young master's measure
For jacket and for hose!

The deeply pathetic lines of Gretchen's Prayer to the Virgin are only feebly reproduced. The lines:

Wer fühlet,
Wie wühlet
Der Schmerz mir im Gebein?
Was mein armes Herz hier banget,
Was es zittert, was verlanget,
Weisst nur du, nur du allein!

Lefevre translates:

Who can feel,
Who can tell,
What fear, what smart,
Oppress the heart,
What pain in bone,
But thou alone.

Disciples of Aesculapius 123

In Lefevre's version we see a lack of all the qualities a good *Faust* translation should have. There is neither an exact rendering of the thought of the original nor even a modicum of poetry in the whole production. His knowledge of the German language and his ability to reproduce the varied metre and rhythm of the drama is entirely insufficient. At no later time has an English translation of Goethe's *Faust* reached such a low level as that of Lefevre's.

JOHN TODHUNTER
(1839-1916)
Posthumous printing of the Translation, Part I, 1924

The last among the Irishmen to translate Goethe's *Faust* was John Todhunter.* In the beginning of his career, he was a doctor of medicine, but later he took up literature and college teaching as his profession.[9] He was educated at York School and Trinity College, Dublin. From the latter institution Todhunter received the M.D. and M.Ch. (Master in Surgery) degrees. While attending Dublin University, he received the Vice Chancellor's Prize for English verse in 1864, 1865, and 1866, and was Gold Medalist of the Philosophical Society (for prose essay) in 1866. At a later date he studied in Vienna and Paris. Returning to Ireland he practiced medicine for some years in Dublin, and then became Professor of English Literature at Alexandria College, Dublin, from 1870 to 1874. After extensive travels on the continent and in Egypt, he finally settled in London, where he died in 1916.[10]

Dr. John Todhunter was active for nearly half a century as a poet, writer, and translator. The British Museum Catalogue lists seventeen titles under his name; the first paper printed, on *The Theory of the Beautiful*, was published in 1872, and the last important work which he completed was the translation of Goethe's *Faust* published in 1924. Todhunter's poetic works include *Alcestis: a Dramatic Poem*, 1879; *Forest Songs*

---

* The Irish translators of *Faust* who preceded Todhunter were John Anster, John Galvan, Thomas E. Webb, and Charles Hartpole Bowen.

and Other Poems, 1881; and *Helen in Troas*, 1886. His more important dramas are *The True Tragedy of Rienzi, Tribune of Rome*, 1881; *A Sicilian Idyll, a Pastoral Play*, 1890; and *The Black Cat, a Play in Three Acts*, 1895. Among his prose works may be mentioned *A Study of Shelley*, 1880; *Life of Patrick Sarsfield, Earl of Lucan, With a Short Narrative of the Principal Events of the Jacobite War in Ireland*, 1895; and *Extracts from the Diary of Samuel Pepys*, 1896.

To the above list must be added the work which first shows Todhunter's definite interest in German literature and which afforded him valuable preparation for the rendering of *Faust*. This was the translation of Heine's *Book of Songs* published in 1907. *Faust*, Part I, accompanied by Acknowledgments written by Mrs. Todhunter and an Introduction by Professor J. G. Robertson, of the University of London, was published in 1924. Mrs. Todhunter explains that the volume "was ready in 1914, but the war rendered the moment inopportune." She also states that the eventual publication of the volume was due to the interest shown in the translation by the late Professor Dowden, Mr. T. W. Ralleston, and Mr. J. Loewe. Professor Dowden "considered this the best translation made hitherto," and believed that it would be a "real loss to English readers" if this version were not published.[11]

"John Todhunter's aim," we are told, "was a translation preserving the original metres."[12] With this slender bit of information in regard to the translator's purposes, we must go to the version itself to ascertain the quality of the work. An examination of the conversational and meditative passages shows that at times Todhunter took no pains to reproduce the original feminine endings. Such parts are the Dedication, Prelude in the Theatre, and Forest and Cavern. In others he approximates the original more closely. In the lyric parts, such as A Rampart and Gretchen's Room, he is less consistent in this respect than in the ballad King in Thule and the numerous lyrics at the end of Scene I. The rimes are not always felicitous, and it is distinctly disturbing to come upon such combinations as "eye" and "phantasy," "done" and "on," "gander" and "wander," "one" and "alone." The metre is fairly smooth, but occasionally the logical accent is sacrificed to the requirements of metre, as in the words "itself" and "visions" in the lines from the Dedication, "My breast feels itself throb, grown young again," and, "Ye bring with you visions of happy days."

Todhunter's translation in the main is accurate in reproducing the thought of the original, but here and there we find lines that are rendered too freely. In the Prologue in Heaven the Lord says to Mephistopheles:

> Nun gut! es sei dir überlassen.
> Zieh diesen Geist von seinem Urquell ab
> Und führ ihn, kannst du ihn erfassen,
> Auf deinem Wege mit herab,
> Und steh beschämt, wenn du bekennen musst:
> Ein guter Mensch in seinem dunklen Drange
> Ist sich des rechten Weges wohl bewusst.

Todhunter translates:

> Well, from thy claws I will not snatch him,
> Draw thou that spirit from its deep source away
> And lead him, if thou canst but catch him
> Down thy own path with thee to stray,
> And stand ashamed when thou must recognize:
> A good man in his dark hour of temptation
> Knows the right way, though other paths he tries.

In the first line, Todhunter, without warrant, envisions a devil with claws, while in the next to the last we have a misinterpretation, and therefore also a mistranslation, of Goethe's words "in seinem dunklen Drange." Goethe refers here to a good man's confused striving after the higher values of life and not to any "dark hour of temptation." The expression in the last verse, "though other paths he tries," is pure padding.

Although today, when several newer translations have appeared, one must challenge Professor Dowden's statement that this version is "the best translation made hitherto," we are inclined to agree with Professor J. G. Robertson when he says, "Dr. Todhunter has certainly added materially to the number of lines and phrases in *Faust* which are more happily rendered than they have been before; he has brought us a step nearer to that perfection, unattainable as it may be, when the veil that separates tongue from tongue has become so attenuated as to be no longer a veil."[13] The best and most poetic portions in Todhunter's translation are the light, graceful, melodic lines in the Song of the Spirits toward the end of Scene 3 and in the Walpurgis Night's Dream. As a whole this version is more straightforward and its language, of course, truer to the contemporary English idiom than Bayard Taylor's, but it does not have the same fidelity to the form of the original as Taylor's version. It surpasses Van der Smissen's translation in the simplicity and naturalness of its language and approaches in this respect the style of such later versions as those of William Page Andrews and Alice Raphael. Todhunter's, therefore, must be ranked with the better translations.

C. FILLINGHAM COXWELL
(1856-1940)
TRANSLATION OF *Faust I* FIRST PRINTED IN 1932

The volume of Goethe literature published both in Europe and in America during 1932, the centennial year of Goethe's death, was remarkable. The shorter comments, newspaper and magazine articles, biographies, critical works, and translations amply demonstrated that a hundred years after the great poet closed his eyes to this earthly scene, he was still holding the world in thrall. The two nations, England and the United States, shared the honor of furnishing the *Faust* translations for this significant and memorable occasion. C. Fillingham Coxwell, a well-known English doctor of medicine, published a version of Part I, and George Madison Priest, an American university professor, rendered both parts into English.

Coxwell, born in 1856, the third in the line of the English physicians to translate *Faust*, studied at Brighton College. Then, having won an open scholarship in mathematics at Christ's College, Cambridge, he took his degree with first class honors in natural science.[14] He received his medical education at St. Thomas' Hospital, London, and in Vienna. Later he worked for six months in preparation under Sir William MacCormac for the International Medical Congress of 1881, and in 1882 was Murchison Scholar in Clinical Medicine of the Royal College of Physicians. A Doctor of Medicine of Cambridge University and a member of the Royal College of Physicians of London, he filled positions on the staff of several hospitals in that city.

Dr. Coxwell then traveled extensively and visited Australia, where for a time he practiced his profession near Melbourne. Back in London, he did research work on anthrax in collaboration with Dr. E. Klein, but again set out for Australia to investigate the effect of the Australian climate on phthisis. Returning to London, he wrote in 1905 a sketch in rimed Alexandrine verse on man's evolution and later extended this undertaking in the form of *Chronicles of Man*, published in 1915.

In this same year Dr. Coxwell traveled in Russia for four months, publishing as a result a volume called *Through Russia in War Time* in 1917. Fascinated with the Russian language, he translated Kriloff's *Fables* in the original metres, and then, after devoting the next five years to the study of folklore, his volume entitled *Siberian and other Folktales* appeared in 1926. Next followed translations of Russian poems, a satire on Bolshevism called *A Kingdom of Hate*, and a little work entitled *Pharaon and other Poems* depicting the general strike of 1926 in England.

Although Dr. Coxwell had been interested in German literature since early manhood, it was not until 1927 that he began the serious reading of German verse and Goethe in particular. In 1929 he took up *Faust* as a definite study, and this led to a translation three years later. Dr. Coxwell writes in his letter that he undertook this arduous task because of his admiration for Goethe's character and his philosophy, which elevated him and gave him supreme pleasure. He felt also that the system of versification he had in mind for the translation of *Faust* was truer to Goethe's spirit than many other efforts. "I recognized," he states, "that Goethe often wrote as a philosopher, and I avoided poor rhymes and a hard and fast system of versification which is difficult to reproduce in English. I relied on fidelity, strong rhythm, and verbal music such as lay within my power; and on a system of rhyming suited to English. The *Chorus of Disciples, Chorus of Angels* and the *Song of the Spirits*," he remarks, were particularly hard for him to translate, but "they all seemed to give way to prolonged concentration." Dr. Coxwell died in 1940, eight years after his translation appeared.*

To complete the translation of such a singular work as Goethe's *Faust* with a degree of success, even in the prime of one's life, must be accounted as no mean accomplishment. But to undertake this task and finish it when one has fully rounded out the Biblical three score and ten years, makes it an extraordinary achievement. This can be said for Dr. Coxwell's translation even though the work in itself is of no intrinsic value. We are reminded here of a similar but more successful effort by Professor William H. Van der Smissen of Canada.

The outstanding weakness of Coxwell's version is its inaccuracy in reproducing both the thought and the spirit of the original; and the success he has achieved occasionally in following Goethe's rhythmic patterns and in approximating the formal qualities of the work as a whole cannot atone for the fatal defect referred to above. A brief examination of the translation in question will make this quite clear. To start with the Dedication, let us consider a few lines taken from the first stanza where the original reads:

> Ihr naht euch wieder, schwankende Gestalten,
> Die früh sich einst dem trüben Blick gezeigt.

---

*Mrs. Coxwell, who still lives at 5 Court Downs Road, Beckenham, Kent, writes: "My husband, C. Fillingham Coxwell, died in 1940, having done no further work in translating Goethe nor the *Faust* to which you refer. Owing to our being obliged to leave our residence suddenly and its being taken over by the War Office for the duration of the war, his books, manuscripts and notes were eventually found missing."—Letter to me dated October 20, 1947.

Disciples of Aesculapius 129

> Versuch ich wohl euch diesmal festzuhalten?
> Fühl ich mein Herz noch jenem Wahn geneigt?
> Ihr drängt euch zu! nun gut, so mögt ihr walten,
> Wie ihr aus Dunst und Nebel um mich steigt;
> Mein Busen fühlt sich jugendlich erschüttert
> Vom Zauberhauch der euren Zug umwittert.

Here Dr. Coxwell translates:

> Again, O shapes! You come with hesitation,
> Who in life's morn, once filled my troubled view.
> And shall I try to hold you? feel elation
> In my attempt old fancies to renew?
> Upon me crowd! You now without vexation
> May spring from misty vapors, and pursue!
> My bosom glows again with youthful feeling
> A magic breath about my path is stealing.

Nearly every line in the translation is subject to adverse criticism. The expressions in line 3 "feel elation," line 5 "without vexation," and line 6 "and pursue," are very little else than padding and means of providing rimes for the foregoing verses. When Dr. Coxwell translates "Ihr drängt euch zu" in the fifth line as "Upon me crowd!" making an imperative of a simple statement of fact, he betrays, it would seem, his lack of knowledge of German grammar.

Similar faults may be found in practically every scene. Line 358 of Scene I, Night, "Da steh' ich nun, ich armer Tor!" is rendered, "Here I remain despite my lore." The retention of the form "Magister" for "Master" in line 360 is unnecessary and detracts from the translation. Line 2146 of Auerbach's Cellar, reading in the translation, "True happiness not rich in," is pure padding supplied to preserve the rhythmic pattern of the original and to afford a rime for "Kitchen" two lines above. If we examine his translation of such passages as the words of the Archangels in the Prologue in Heaven, in which are found, perhaps, the sublimest imagery and the grandest music contained in the whole *Faust*, we discover that Dr. Coxwell's lines remain prosy, commonplace, and uninspired.

A comparison of Dr. Coxwell's version with the one by the American Professor George Madison Priest, also completed in 1932, reveals that the latter translated more exactly, more idiomatically, and with what may be called more poetic unction than the former. Poetic passages such as the König in Thule, Gretchen at the Spinning Wheel, The Ramparts, or the more dramatic scenes such as Martha's Garden, Night, and Dungeon strongly reveal the superiority of the American's version.

It must be said, then, in conclusion, that although Dr. Coxwell's attempt to translate *Faust* is worthy of all praise as a concrete, personal testimony to the high aesthetic and moral qualities he discerned in this classic, the translation in itself is of very unequal and doubtful value. We will have to look elsewhere for the fulfillment of our dreams with respect to a perfect or nearly perfect English translation of *Faust*.

VI

Men of Letters and Faust

Part I:
> The Prologue in the Theatre.
>
> *Poet:*
> Who unifies and brings to consecration
> Parts of the whole, creating harmony?
> Who makes the tempest rage with passionate wrath?
> Who makes you feel the glowing sunset hours?
> Who scatters the fairest springtime flowers
> Over the Beloved's path?
> Who twines the laurel wreath with simple rites,
> Merit in every field to glorify?
> Who makes Olympus safe? The gods unites?
> The power of Man, which poets personify![1]

IT IS TO BE EXPECTED that there should be included among the translators of Goethe's *Faust* a large group of writers. Yet it must be said that few of these men of letters have really distinguished themselves by their literary craftsmanship. Few were inspired and creative artists; but as diligent and honest workmen, with more or less leisure on their hands, they wrote as best they could and were not afraid to compete with others more gifted in making an English version of *Faust*. Most of the members of the group will doubtless be chiefly remembered for this their one supreme literary effort. This company of translators, made up of persons of most devious backgrounds, includes Arthur Taylor, William Bell Macdonald, Jonathan Birch, John Hills, Lewis Filmore, Bayard Taylor, Frank Claudy, Alfred Henry Huth, and William Page Andrews.

Half a Hundred Thralls to Faust
ARTHUR TAYLOR
(-)
TRANSLATION OF *Faust I and II* FIRST PRINTED IN 1838

The late Mr. William A. Speck, Curator of the Collection of Goetheana at Yale University, and Professor Anton Kippenberg, of Leipzig, were the first to hold that Arthur Taylor was not only the printer of a version of *Faust* published in 1838 but also the translator. Professor Kippenberg ascribed the version to Taylor on the information obtained from Mr. Speck, who acquired two complete sets of this rare two-volume edition for his private collection. In three of these volumes Mr. Speck found the following legend printed on a strip of paper on the front cardboard cover: "Fifty copies printed. Forty only for sale."[2] In addition, one of these volumes, "No. 20," has the initials "A. T." in pen and ink below the above legend. What right had Arthur Taylor, Mr. Speck reasoned, to affix his initials to that strip in this volume, if he were merely the printer?

Lately I have been fortunate enough to uncover some additional facts which substantiate the contention for which Mr. Speck broke a lance, namely, that Arthur Taylor was the translator of this English version of *Faust*. *The Society of Antiquaries*, a periodical published in London, April 23, 1847, by the organization bearing the same name, lists among the Fellows of the Society who held life membership an "Arthur Taylor, Esq., 39 Coleman Street." We learn, further, that he was made a Fellow on December 24, 1818, and in the number of *The Society of Antiquaries* printed April 23, 1866, Arthur Taylor of 39 Coleman Street is still listed as a member.

It is also significant to find that this Arthur Taylor was the author of several books, chief among which is one entitled *The Glory of Regality*.* The complete title-page of this volume reads: "The Glory of Regality, an Historical Treatise of the Anointing and Crowning of the Kings and Queens of Eng-

---

* To this work, a copy of which is in the Sterling Library, Yale University, is appended a treatise entitled *The Queen's Claim to Coronation Examined*. This is also printed by R. and A. Taylor, but dated 1821.

land. By Arthur Taylor, Fellow of the Society of Antiquaries. London: Printed by R. and A. Taylor, Shoe Lane: Sold by Messrs. Payne and Foss, Pall Mall, and J. A. Arch, Cornhill. 1820." Taylor was the author also of another book, entitled *Papers in Relation to the Antient Topography of the Eastern Counties*,[3] published in London in 1869. To these works must be added Taylor's letters to Joseph Haslewood (1769-1833), a well-known writer and bibliophile of the time.[4]

The conclusions which may be arrived at from an examination of the above materials are as follows. First, that Arthur Taylor was both a writer and a printer. Secondly, that as a member of the Society of Antiquaries of London from 1818 to 1866 his life span would permit him to publish a translation of *Faust* in 1838. Thirdly, that his known works, especially *The Glory of Regality*, an interesting, well-planned, and well-written book of 424 pages, with pertinent quotations from over a hundred writers, both ancient and modern, reveal the author to have been an individual of broad intellectual interests who may have had a knowledge of the German language and literature and, in particular, of the greatest German classic, Goethe's *Faust*.

Although it has not been possible up to this time to find direct and absolute verification of it, yet the conclusions reached above afford reasonable proof that Arthur Taylor was the translator of the English version of both parts of *Faust*, published in London in 1838, which up to this time has been listed as an anonymous work.

A long introductory poem to Part I lauds the greatness of Goethe as an author and in the manner of a moralist recounts the story of the *Faust* drama. The whole translation, with the exception of the lyric parts, is in blank verse. It is of much the same quality as the other versions made during the first two decades after Goethe's death. An abundance of inaccuracies both in metre and in thought mar the translation. The blank verse is quite regular but, with the feminine endings few and far between, it is very monotonous. Some of the translator's best work in this type of metre is to be found in the Dedication to Part I and in the third act of Part II. The following lines from the beginning of Forest and Cavern afford an idea of Taylor's ability to render the reflective and conversational parts of the drama. The original reads:

> Und wenn der Sturm im Walde braust und knarrt,
> Die Riesenfichte stürzend Nachbaräste
> Und Nachbarstämme quetschend niederstreift,
> Und ihrem Fall dumpf hohl der Hügel donnert;
> Dann führst du mich zur sichern Höhle, zeigst
> Mich dann mir selbst, und meiner eignen Brust
> Geheime tiefe Wunder öffnen sich.

Arthur Taylor translates:

> In the forest, when the tempest howls and shrieks,
> And the swept mountain utters dirge-like moans,
> As giant pines are bearing down each other,
> With reeling stems and intertangled boughs,
> Thou lead'st me to the sheltering cave, and there
> Reveal'st to me those mysterious wonders,
> Of which my own breast is the earthly shrine.

Neither Goethe's rhythm nor his thought has been followed closely here. The following passage taken from the beginning of Act I, Part II, will illustrate with what success Taylor renders the lyric portions of the drama:

> Wenn sich lau die Lüfte füllen
> Um den grünumschränkten Plan,
> Süsse Düfte, Nebelhüllen
> Senkt die Dämmerung heran.
> Lispelt leise süssen Frieden,
> Wiegt das Herz in Kindesruh;
> Und den Augen dieses Müden
> Schliesst des Tages Pforte zu.

In Taylor's translation we read:

> Twilight, sinking o'er the scene,
> Leads the health-renewing hours;
> The soft air weaves its pearly screen
> Round the leaves and folding flowers.

> Gentle peace in soothing whispers,
> To couched mortals brings repose,
> Chaunting in the ear her vespers,
> As the gates of daylight close.

In spite of the liberties Taylor takes with the German text, it cannot be denied that he has endowed his translation of the lyric parts with a certain amount of poetic beauty. He also proves that he is able to reproduce the form of the original to a very large degree, when he chooses to do so. This translation is of considerable bibliographical interest because it is the first English rendering of both parts by the same author.

WILLIAM BELL MACDONALD
(1807-1862)
Translation of *Faust II* First Printed in 1838

Although at times anonymity may be a desirable cloak for an author to throw about himself in order to escape unfriendly and even unjust criticism, this practice does not at all times work to ultimate advantage. It did not do so in the case of William Bell Macdonald, whose real name was warped into John Macdonald Bell and was chronicled in this bizarre form by bibliographers for nearly half a century. B. Q. Morgan seems to have been the first of the *Faust* bibliographers to employ the translator's real name,[5] but the *Dictionary of Anonymous and Pseudonymous English Literature,* which was published in 1883, carries the entry: "Faust a tragedy by J. W. Goethe Part II., as completed in 1831, translated into English verse [By William Bell M'Donald, of Rammerscales]. London. 1842. Octavo Pp. VIII. 351 p. The first ed. was printed at Dumfries in 1838."[6] It is rather surprising then that this error should have persisted in bibliographical volumes for so long a time.*

William Bell Macdonald, the eldest son of Donald Macdonald and Mary, daughter of William Bell of Rammerscales,

---

*Goedeke's *Grundriss* (1912), Part III, Vol. IV, p. 633, still has John Macdonald Bell.

near Lockerbie, Dumfriesshire, Scotland, was born in 1807. He received the B.A. degree from the University of Glasgow in 1827 and afterward took up the study of medicine for a year. Then he served as surgeon on Sir Pulteney Malcom's flagship in the Mediterranean for three years and in 1831 was made a commissioner of supply. When his uncle died, Macdonald, the translator, fell heir to the Bell estate at Rammerscales; here he collected an extensive and valuable library. For some time he represented the "burgh" of Lochmaben in the general assembly of the Church of Scotland. He died at Glasgow, December 5, 1862.[7]

The *Gentleman's Magazine,* quoting from the *Dumfries Herald,* pays a glowing tribute to this Scottish linguist, scholar, and bibliophile: "By Mr. Macdonald's death a European light has been extinguished. Scarcely in the world was there such a master of languages. Mr. Macdonald was one of the most skilful collectors of books in Christendom, especially in the department of the old classics; and his library at Rammerscales is not only very large, but valuable from its many volumes of rarity. To see him, in his hall of books, with a troup of scholarly friends whom his love of learning and genial hospitality knit to him with such affectionate esteem, was a sight of which Dumfriess-shire might well be proud." Referring again to his scholastic and linguistic attainments, the writer continues: "We do not know what remains of his multifarious learning, in the shape of Notes, Prolegomena, etc., Mr. Macdonald has left behind him. As he was still advancing in his linguistic studies, he had not much time to methodize for any general publication. Every now and then he gave some short essay on the natural history of the ancients or other kindred subject, to the classical periodicals of the day; or dashed off a translation of some queer old Scotch song into German, Greek or Hebrew, as nobody else in our time could do, except perhaps the late Dr. Maginn—all in the way of nugae canorae and private circulation."[8]

The *Dictionary of National Biography,* the *Modern English Biography* by Frederic Boase, and the British Museum

Catalogue do not mention Macdonald's translation of the Second Part of *Faust*, but the last-named volume lists a number of works, practically all of which are translations: *Reports on the Progress of Zoology for the Year 1842*, translated from the German of [A. I. Wagner, F. H. Froschel, W. F. Erickson and C. T. E. von Siebold] by W. B. Macdonald, 1845; *Reports and Papers on Botany . . . On Botanical Geography*, by . . . Grisebach, translated by W. B. Macdonald and G. Busk, 1846; *Lusus Philologici.* Ex Museo Gul. B. Macdonald. [Translated in Verse, Greek, Latin, Hebrew, and German] Rammerscales, [Scotland] 1851; *Ten Scottish Songs*, rendered into German by W. B. Macdonald, Edinburgh, 1854; and finally a *Sketch of a Coptic Grammar*, adapted for self-tuition, Edinburgh, 1856.[9]

From the title-page to the first edition of this translation of *Faust II*, we learn that this version was already completed in 1831.[10] This is hardly possible, for only the larger part of Act I and the whole of Act II of the original had become available by that time. Actually, Macdonald's translation of the completed second part did not appear until seven years later. Both the 1838 edition and the second edition of 1842 are dedicated to one of Macdonald's German friends, Dr. Heinrich Nebel, of the University of Heidelberg. The reason why Macdonald translated *Faust*, Part II, into English is mentioned in the Advertisement to the second edition. Here he says: "The First Edition of this Translation was printed at Dumfries in the year 1838, and was, so far as known to the Translator, the first attempt to render this poem into any language from the original."[11] In this Macdonald was incorrect, for Arthur Taylor's version of Part II was also published in 1838. In the Advertisement the translator informs us, moreover, that his principle has been to effect "a literal transference of the drama from the German to the English, and to maintain the rhythm of the original rather than to make an attempt at elegant versification."

The few copies that "were thrown off" in 1838, Macdonald says, "received many flattering commendations . . . from German scholars, both in this country [England] and on the continent." Therefore, he offered another edition "to more public notice."[12] The first edition is marred by numerous typographical errors which have been corrected either by a reader or, what is more probable, by the translator himself.* As one of the first instances of the translation of the Second Part of *Faust* into English, this version is worthy of some further consideration.

Macdonald set out to "maintain the rhythm of the original," but he has not always succeeded in doing so. The feminine rimes, although they occur frequently, are not reproduced consistently. The translator found it especially difficult to follow Goethe's rhythmic patterns in the lyric parts. The Song of Ariel, with which Part II opens, is one of his most successful efforts, and the verse flows smoothly and gracefully. Goethe's lines here are:

> Wenn der Blüthen Frühlings-Regen
> Über alle schwebend sinkt,
> Wenn der Felder grüner Segen
> Allen Erdgebornen blinkt;
> Kleiner Elfen Geistergrösse
> Eilet wo sie helfen kann,
> Ob er heilig, ob er böse,
> Jammert sie der Unglücksmann.

Macdonald's translation reads:

> When the Floral showers of Spring
> Gently fall o'er all the fields,
> When the green earth's blossoming
> Blessing to her children yields,
> The little elves, the spirit brood
> Hurry where they aid can bring
> To the wicked as to the good,
> For misfortune sorrowing.

---

*A copy of this first edition is in the Speck Collection. Since all the revisions made in pen and ink in this particular volume are also incorporated in the second edition, it is to be concluded that this is the copy corrected by the author and that it served as the manuscript for the second edition.

Macdonald made a less successful attempt to reproduce Goethe's metre in his version of the words of the Chorus at the beginning of Act III. Here the lines:

> Verschmähe nicht, o herrliche Frau,
> Des höchsten Gutes Ehrenbesitz!
> Denn das grösste Glück ist dir einzig beschert,
> Der Schönheit Ruhm der vor allen sich hebt.
> Dem Helden tönt sein Name voran,
> Drum schreitet er stolz,
> Doch beugt sogleich hartnäckigster Mann
> Vor der allbezwingenden Schöne den Sinn.

Macdonald renders:

> Disdain not glorious Lady, thou,
> The honor-store of highest worth!
> To thee her best has fortune granted:
> Beauty's fame o'er all exalted.
> The hero's name resounds before him,
> So he strideth proudly on.
> Yet soon the stubbornest of men
> Bows himself before the sense
> Of beauty's all-constraining power.

Scarcely a single verse here follows the original metre. Both Bernays, where he translates in verse, and Gurney preserve the form of the original to a greater degree than Macdonald.

However, apart from a tendency to expand the lines of the original here and there, Macdonald has made a much more accurate translation than either the youthful Bernays or Gurney. Macdonald's version has also more passages which strike one as being tolerably good poetry than the other two. On the whole this first version of Part II is of much finer quality than the first translation of Part I made by Gower in 1823.

JONATHAN BIRCH
(1783-1847)

TRANSLATION OF *Faust I* FIRST PRINTED IN 1839;
Faust II, 1843

Jonathan Birch, who at times wrote under the anagrams Job Crithannah and John Abricht, was born in London, 1783. Although he himself had a strong desire to be a sculptor, he was apprenticed to an uncle in the city, and at the age of twenty became a member of the house of John Argelander, timber merchants, at Memel. Here in 1807 he met the three eldest sons of Frederick William III of Prussia, who fled to this place and took refuge with John Argelander during the Napoleonic invasion. For eighteen months Birch associated with these German princes, and as a result a warm, significant, and lasting friendship developed.

After five years Birch returned to London to engage in literary work. This occupation proved to be so fascinating that he continued to write throughout his life. In 1846 the King of Prussia, the former Crown Prince with whom Birch had become acquainted at Memel and who in the meantime had become an appreciative recipient of some of Birch's works, invited him to make his residence in one of the King's three palaces. Birch chose Bellvue near Berlin. At this place he died in 1847.

Birch's first works of importance were *Fifty-one Original Fables, with Morals and Ethical Index* and a translation of Plutarch's *Banquet of the Seven Sages* in 1833. These were soon followed by a volume called *Divine Emblems*, which the Prussian king valued so highly that he sent Birch a gold medal. Inspired by such a lively token of appreciation, he now set about to translate Goethe's *Faust*. Part I was finished in 1839 and Part II four years later.* Other literary efforts by Birch include translations from the German of Bishop Eylert and from the *Nibelungenlied*. In the latter task he was assisted

---

* Apparently these are the first English illustrated editions of complete translations of both parts of Goethe's *Faust*.

Mephistopheles

I am not scared by thy Commission!
I have such treasures in possession —
But my good Friend — the time comes on
For quiet joys — we delectate, anon.

Faust

If quiet on the bed of Sloth you find me!
Then, claim the Bond without delay. —
If eer with fulsome praise you blind me
So that contentment I betray —
Or eer with glad enjoyment bind me
Then — be arrived my Final day! —
Such are my terms —

Mephistopheles

Done!

Faust

——— rash be the penalty!
Or should I to the "present" say
While yet a while! thou art so sweet!
Then mayst thou me in fetters lay:
I willingly perdition meet!
Then may the passing-bell appall.*

* That appall the murderers sight
    Moves sight of the Horror

Page 106 of Jonathan Birch's manuscript copy of his translation of *Faust*, reproduced here, includes lines 1688-1705 of Part I

by the distinguished German scholars, Carl Lachmann and the Brothers Grimm. In 1841 Birch was elected "foreign honorary member of the Literary Society of Berlin," an honor accorded to only one other Englishman, Thomas Carlyle.[14]

The translator says in his Preface to Part I that he became acquainted with German literature and with *Faust* in a general way as early as 1804 and that this knowledge was broadened and deepened during his long stay in Prussia. But the serious study of *Faust* came much later. "About three years ago [1836?]," he remarks, "Faust again fell in my way,—I gave it much attention."[15] In regard to Part II, which was not published until 1843, he says: "Yet, as a few general observations elucidatory of the marvellous work may be expected, and be desirable from one who has devoted six years to the study of *Faust*, I hesitate not to fulfill such expectation."[16]

Several considerations impelled Birch to make a translation of *Faust*. One was the fact that after studying this work for some time, he discovered new beauties and delights in it, which he had missed before when he read it merely for the story and dramatic effect. "I read it again and again," he says in his Preface, "and each time with increased pleasure and wonder. I attempted some detached parts in poetry, and found that I succeeded; then did the first thought arise in my mind of making a complete translation. Not having seen any of the renderings into English, I possessed myself of two, and after having compared the parts I had done and them, and both with the German, I presumed there was room for another versified translation."[17]

A second reason was the Prussian Crown Prince's approval of hasty translations of certain parts of *Faust* and his "gracious patronage" that stimulated Birch to persevere and encouraged him to complete the translation. Coupled with this was his desire to win "the respect of the highly learned and intellectual German nation for having worthily rendered their great poet into English," as well as to induce his own countrymen "to extend their knowledge of German poetry in consequence of having placed before them Goethe's masterpiece in agreeable versification."[18] When Birch completed Part I in 1839, he presented the first published copy to the Crown Prince of Prussia, to whom the version was dedicated. The latter, upon his ascendance to the throne in 1840, reciprocated by rewarding Birch with the "great gold medal of homage."[19]

Since he had had ample opportunity "of studying and practising the German language, as written and spoken by the peer, the highly-learned, the merchant, the mechanic, and the peasant so as to become well versed in the genius of the language," Birch felt that he was fully prepared for the work of a translator.[20] But an examination of a single passage taken at random shows that he has made a translation of a very questionable character. In the Prologue in Heaven where the original reading is:

>Die Sonne tönt nach alter Weise
>In Brudersphären Wettgesang,
>Und ihre vorgeschriebne Reise
>Vollendet sie mit Donnergang.
>Ihr Anblick giebt den Engeln Stärke,
>Wenn keiner sie ergründen mag;
>Die unbegreiflich hohen Werke
>Sind herrlich wie am ersten Tag.

Birch translates:

>The Sun in soft accord, as wont of old,
>Joins in proud revelry his brother-spheres;
>And all, their fore-ordained journey hold,
>Closing in thunder sounds—their circuit years!
>The glorious sight, ennerves the angelic soul—
>Yet none may fathom the display
>Incomprehensible! the wondrous Whole
>Sparkles, as on creation's day.

One observes immediately that Birch has made several bad mistakes. "In soft accord," line one, is nothing but padding to supply the required number of accents. In the third line Birch thought "ihre" was a plural and referred to "brother-spheres" instead of the "sun." The same mistake is repeated in the next line. Line six is also a doubtful rendering of the original. Finally "sparkles" in the last line does not translate "herrlich." The metre also is reproduced in a faulty manner.

Birch improved little if any on Talbot's translation of 1834:

> The sun, along the void of space,
> Is sounding with his brother spheres,
> And rolls on his predestined race
> At thunder speed: his aspect cheers
> The Angels, though none understand
> What his mysterious music says.
> The works of the Creator's hand
> Are fresh as in creation's days.

Occasionally, as in the Dungeon scene, Birch gives us a somewhat more accurate version. Here Margaret says:

> Ich darf nicht fort; für mich ist nichts zu hoffen.
> Was hilft es fliehn? sie lauern doch mir auf.
> Es ist so elend betteln zu müssen,
> Und noch dazu mit bösem Gewissen!
> Es ist so elend in der Fremde schweifen,
> Und sie werden mich doch ergreifen!

Birch translates:

> I dare not forth; no! no hope is left for me.
> O'er all they lurk—it is in vain to flee!—
> 'Twould be a wretched thing to beg one's bread
> With a conscience over-burthened!
> 'Twould be a wretched thing to stray from place to place!
> Where'er I went, my footsteps they would trace!

Even here the translation leaves much to be desired.

However, Birch had the temerity to present a copy of his inferior translation of Part I to August Wilhelm Schlegel. Writing on January 7, 1840, from Vienna, Birch says: "Permit the honor of presenting to the 'Inimitable Translator of Shakespeare' my attempt to render the immortal Goethe's Faust into English verses. . . . It is with the utmost diffidence I place it before your eyes, conscious, that my best endeavors but imperfectly show forth its beauties of thought and diction." Then in incorrect English he complains to Schlegel of the difficulties he has encountered in making the translation: "You Sir, who know the english language thoroughly, know the difficulties I have had to encounter, especially as it determines at starting to tread as nearly as possible in your footstep, as relates to keeping closed [sic] to my Author."

He informs Schlegel also that he is already working on Part II: "I have, as you will perceive, commenced the Second Part of *Faust* and in [sic] increasing difficulties stare me in the face, yet by plan I have adopted of publishing it in portions and not binding myself down to any stated periods, I feel better able to cope with it and I have the sanguine hope that it shall succeed.... If you will honor me with your candid opinion of the Part done, I shall feel grateful—should it be favorable it will cheer me on—If unfavorable it may curb my ambition and prevent me much labors of thought and outlay of money.... Your most obedient Servant, Jonathan Birch."[21]

After having read Birch's faultily worded letter, as well as his defective translation, it seems impossible that Schlegel could have encouraged the translator to go on with Part II. Nevertheless, Birch continued his endeavors. The title-page to the fragment* published in 1840 (?), which contains the translation of the first five scenes from Part II, informs us that "Part II is in a state of great forwardness, and is intended for publication early in the year." Moreover, "Subscribers are requested to communicate their orders, stating whether they would wish to have the Translation, as it comes out in Parts, or wait until the completion, addressed to the Translator, Messrs. Black and Armstrong's Wellington Street North." Then follows the great inducement for the admirers of *Faust* to rush in their orders: "Subscribers will have an early preference in the delivery of Copies, and first impressions of the plates."[22]

* This fragment, like the complete translations of both parts of *Faust* by Birch, is embellished with engravings after Moritz Retzsch. Lillian Espy Reed in the Preface to her dissertation calls attention to the fact that English analyses of Faust to accompany illustrations by Retzsch appeared as early as 1820.—*Fragmentary English Translation of Goethe's Faust*, Yale University, 1937. The fragment referred to above is one of the rare items in the Speck Collection.

However, the "gentle readers" preferred at least not to invest their good money in Birch's partial translations, for in the Preface, finished in London, December 10, 1842, to his completed version, which was published after some delay in 1843, he states: "My project to bring out the Second Part in Numbers, was soon relinquished—being advised that such mode of publication was not acceptable, and that the public required it to come from the press a complete volume, as did my translation of the First Part. . . . That object is now accomplished, and in presenting it to the world, I beg leave to say that the present is the first time an effort has been made by the same individual to wrestle with and bring to an honourable conclusion, an English Translation of the whole* of this, the most beautiful and profound poem in the German Language."[23]

The Second Part,† like the First, is dedicated to Birch's royal German patron, Frederick William IV, King of Prussia. It is no better in quality than the version of Part I. The opening lines:

>   Wenn der Blüthen Frühlings-Regen
>   Über alle schwebend sinkt,
>   Wenn der Felder grüner Segen
>   Allen Erdgebornen blinkt;
>   Kleiner Elfen Geistergrösse
>   Eilet wo sie helfen kann,
>   Ob er heilig, ob er böse,
>   Jammert sie der Unglücksmann.

Birch translates:

>   Soon as blossom-bearing showers
>   Heavy-hovering, earthward sink;
>   Soon as fields and opening flowers
>   Give the husbandman the wink,—

---

* Birch doubtless was not acquainted with Arthur Taylor's translation of both parts which appeared in 1838, and of which fifty copies were printed and only forty offered for sale.

† In the Speck Collection is a manuscript copy of portions of Birch's translation of *Faust*, Part II. The portions included are a small part of Act II, all of Act III, and a small part of Act IV. This version differs considerably from the printed translation of 1843. It is probable that Birch revised and rewrote it once more before publishing it.

Then doth Fairies' giant spirit
Speed to help, where help it can.
Is he wicked? hath he merit?—
It bemoans the luckless man.

It would be useless to cite further passages. The quality of the translation is uniformly mediocre. All the characters speak alike; Birch has failed utterly to reproduce the style and the spirit of the original. He did not deserve the recognition given him by the King of Prussia and the Literary Society of Berlin. He lacked both the linguistic training and the talent to make a satisfactory metrical translation. The *Dublin Review* expresses its disapproval of this version in no uncertain terms: "Of the last translation of the *Faust*, by Jonathan Birch Esq. (London, 1839), the less we say the better. Had it appeared while the idea was still entertained that the *Faust* was untranslatable, it might have met some indulgence, but the success of its predecessors had cut away this ground of justification. It is incomparably the worst which has yet been attempted. As a translation, it is bad, as a poetical translation it is worse; but as a translation of *Faust* it is worst of all."[24]

JOHN HILLS
(-)

TRANSLATION OF *Faust I* FIRST PRINTED IN 1840

We are again indebted to Henry Crabb Robinson, who furnished us with a choice bit of information about Lord Leveson-Gower and his translation, for the larger share of our knowledge concerning John Hills. In his Diary for June 3, 1828, he gives the following account of the translator: "Wordsworth brought Hills to breakfast with me. I should say, mentioning Hills, that he was a great friend of John Wordsworth and a warm admirer of the poet who brought us [*sic*] acquainted. He for a time fluctuated between law and literature. Ultimately he decided in favor of a literary life—that of bookish indolence. He met on a steamboat a Quaker family and fell in love with the young lady of the party, Wordsworth's poetry being the seductive medium—a pure and idealized Galiotto. They married and lived abroad where he died also many years ago. He published a metrical translation of *Faust* which he gave me but it acquired no reputation. He was happy in his wife, but used to complain of her family, especially brothers for having overreached him in money matters. He used to speak bitterly of Quakers as a body, as if slyness and selfiishness were their characteristic qualities."[25]

In the Preface to his version of 1840, the translator corrects and supplements Robinson's statements concerning his version of *Faust*. According to Robinson's Diary,* Hills's version was published prior to June 3, 1828, but the translator himself remarks: "It is now nearly ten years since I first entertained the thought of executing a metrical version of *Faust*, and I did in fact begin it during a sojourn at Dresden in the winter of 1829. My enterprise was, however, checked almost at its outset by the intelligence I received that no less than seven different versions were then, to the knowledge of my informant, actually in the course of execution. An unfeigned distrust in my own powers led me at once to abandon all thoughts of entering into competition with a host of such appalling numbers and unknown strength; nevertheless, I did from time to time resume the work for my own amusement—fragmentarily,—and as different moods attracted me towards this or that passage in a poem so singularly variegated as the *Faust*."[26]

Then Hills goes on to explain how he came to finish the translation: "The parts thus executed were in the hands of some of my friends; and, on my return from Italy in the summer of 1838, after an absence of four years, and when, amid far different associations, my thoughts had only once been

---

* Probably Hills gave a first draft of a portion of his translation to Robinson and the latter falsely concluded that the whole had already been published. It is also possible that Hills is mistaken in regard to the time when he began his translation. The fact remains that the translation was not published until 1840. Hills's own words in the Preface (p. v) to this 1840 edition are: "I forthwith completed the translation; and, in spite of the accumulated disadvantages under which it must appear, I now risk its publication." Since Hills does not mention a prose translation in recounting the history of his metrical version it is extremely doubtful whether the 1839 prose version listed by bibliographers ever existed.

directed to this work, I was surprised to find that the favorable opinion they had in the first instance expressed of them had not been diminished by a comparision with other versions which had appeared during my absence. Thus encouraged, I did not any longer hesitate; I forthwith completed the translation; and, in spite of the accumulated disadvantages under which it must appear, I now risk its publication."[27]

In regard to the nature of translation, Hills holds that the preservation of the rhythmic character of a poem is "the essence of faithful translation, and therefore coordinate with a strict and accurrate rendering of the sense. . . . It is, then, on the ground of having attempted this combination of rhythm and verbal accuracy that I presume to claim any portion of attention or favor."[28]

Hills goes farther than his predecessor Gower and omits the whole Prologue in Heaven because he holds that it is characterized by irreverence and "seeming profanity" and because he considers it to be an unessential part of the whole work. It is, he believes, as much an afterthought as it was an after-production. "I say this, well knowing all the cant that has been canted about 'Die Idee des Ganzen'; but this we can afford to doff aside when Coleridge, perhaps the first critic that England ever produced, and A. W. Schlegel, the Coryphaeus of Germany, are of accord in repudiating all notion of the vaunted 'Einheit.' Unity it certainly has, but not of the kind which the prostrate admirers of Goethe assert."[29]

Hills's translation is of a fair quality. With the exception of the omission of many of the feminine endings, he follows the form of the original closely in such scenes as the Dedication, the Prelude at the Theatre, the Soldiers' Song, the König in Thule, and Gretchen's Prayer. However, he has recast the Chorus of the Disciples in Night I, making it a poem of three stanzas instead of one as in the original. His version reads:

> He who did lie
> In the grave for a time,
> Self-raised on high,
> Now liveth sublime!

> To Glory is near
> To the fountain of Life and Joy!
> Alas! and we still here
> To bear earth's annoy!
>
> He left us—his own—
> Here below to pine!
> Master! we groan
> For a lot like thine!

In the short Chorus of Angels preceding the above lines, he follows Goethe closely neither in thought nor in metre. It is one of the most inaccurate passages in the whole translation. The original here reads:

> Christ ist erstanden!
> Freude dem Sterblichen,
> Den die verderblichen,
> Schleichenden, erblichen
> Mängel umwanden.

Hills translates:

> Christ is arisen!
> Glory and Victory
> To Him! whom th' hereditary
> Creeping infirmity
> Of sad Humanity
> Held awhile in its prison!

The conversational passages have a certain amount of vivaciousness and freshness about them, but Hills's language lacks simplicity. Nor does he succeed in reproducing the peculiarities of speech of the various characters. Still, with respect to the faithfulness with which the thought of the original is reproduced, Hills's translation, when taken as a whole, is to be preferred to any other poetic version before Anna Swanwick's translation, which was published in 1850.

LEWIS FILMORE
(1815-1890)
TRANSLATION OF *Faust I* FIRST PRINTED IN 1841

Lewis Filmore was a newspaper reporter and journalist the greater part of his life, and essentially a self-made man. In these respects his endeavors bear a marked similarity to those of Bayard Taylor. We are indebted to the *Illustrated London News* of June 7, 1890, for the following interesting characterization: "Lewis Filmore, a quarter of a century ago, was esteemed by the few then cognisant of the interior literary management of great London daily journals, a sagacious, accomplished, and widely informed writer on various topics of political and social importance. He was also from early youth a remarkable example of the loving study and incessant exercise of purely imaginative literature, being gifted with the finest taste, the soundest critical judgment, and original powers, in no slight degree, of dramatic humor and creative fancy. That he has left no works likely to be remembered with his name, is owing to the personal temperament of a devotee of refined scholarship absolutely indifferent to worldly fame, pursuing the true, the good, and the beautiful in poetry, and in sentiment, for their own sake. No man who read and wrote so incessantly, could be more devoid of literary vanity, or care less for the external rewards of successful authorship."[30]

Professionally, Filmore's life was that of a typical, busy newspaperman. He was born in London in 1815, the son of Captain Abraham Filmore, a distinguished naval officer. A few years later, while the family was living at Plymouth, the father died. Lewis Filmore, thrown on his own resources, began his newspaper career as a reporter in early youth for the Exeter newspaper and the *Devenport Independent*. Within a short time, however, he broke off his relationships with these papers to accept a similar position with the *Sun*, published in London. Filmore gave up this position, in turn, to become permanently associated with the London *Times*.[31]

The source referred to above informs us, further, that at

first he was engaged by this paper to report on Parliamentary proceedings, but when in 1848, at the outbreak of the revolution in France, the *Times*'s Paris correspondent suddenly died, he was immediately sent to take the post. Then, at the beginning of hostilities between Germany and Denmark in 1864, on account of his knowledge of German, he was transferred from Paris to Schleswig-Holstein. Later Filmore served as special correspondent to Australia, and upon his return to Europe represented his paper in Berlin, Vienna, and other German cities. Next, toward the close of President Fillmore's administration, he was sent to the United States, only to return again a few years later to become assistant editor of the *Times*. But overwork and consequent ill health, we are told, caused Filmore to relinquish this position in 1867. He lived in Italy for two years, and then settled at Kensington, England, where he died in 1890.

As a journalist Filmore wrote articles on the war between Germany and Denmark, on the conflict between Germany and Austria, and on the dissolution of the German Confederation. He also discussed economic, commercial, industrial questions, railways, and finance. His purely literary activity, limited in scope, was confined mainly to translations from the German: Goethe's *Faust* in 1841, and poems from Schiller, Bürger, Heine, and Freiligrath in later years.* His only original work, a romantic comedy, *The Winning Suit*, written in 1863, was performed in London with some success. The *Illustrated London News* of June, 1890, reports that his attachment to belles lettres did not abate in his old age and that he continued to enjoy the pleasures of literature until the end of his life.

It appears that Filmore translated *Faust* in order that a cheap new edition might be offered to the public in the Standard Library series published by William Smith of London.[32] He proposed to sacrifice as little of the literal exactness as pos-

* The exact dates of many of these translations are not available, but the *Maid of Orleans* by Schiller appeared in 1882. The *Illustrated London News*, June, 1890, p. 708, states erroneously that Filmore made the translation of *Faust* before he was twenty years of age. As a matter of fact he was twenty-six.

sible. He tried also, he says in the Preface, to follow the author's meaning "as closely as the translator's knowledge of both languages, and the necessities of rhyme permitted him to do." But how much of a German scholar was Filmore? From the *Illustrated London News* we gather that he counted it as one of his ambitions to pick it up by himself, and he acquired not only German thus, but also Latin and French.

An examination of the translation itself reveals first and foremost that Filmore has more or less altered the form in his version. These changes are most evident in the lyric parts. The Song of the Spirits in Vor dem Tor has been changed in metre, in the length of the verse, and in the rime scheme. Gretchen's Prayer to the Mater Dolorosa has, as the following passage shows, in many respects been made into a new poem. The first two stanzas:

> Ach, neige,
> Du Schmerzenreiche,
> Dein Antlitz gnädig meiner Not!
> Das Schwert im Herzen,
> Mit tausend Schmerzen
> Blickst auf zu deines Sohnes Tod.
>
> Zum Vater blickst du,
> Und Seufzer schickst du
> Hinauf um sein, und deine Not.

Filmore has jumbled into one:

> Mother of many sorrows! deign, oh deign!
> To turn thy face with pity on my pain!
> The sword hath enter'd in thy heart,
> Thou of a thousand pangs hast part,
> Thou lookest up, thou gazest on
> The death of Him who was thy son!
> Thy gaze doth to the Father rise,
>   And to his throne;
> Thou for his grief dost breathe thy sighs,
>   And for thine own!

The same tendency is strongly evident in his rendering of the

Dedication. Most of these changes are the results of the shortening or lengthening of lines, done either deliberately or because of the translator's inability to reproduce the exact form of the original. Some passages, like lines 447-450 from the Prison scene:

> Du machst die Fesseln los,
> Nimmst wieder mich in deinen Schoss.
> Wie kommt es, dass du dich vor mir nicht scheust?
> Und weisst du denn, mein Freund, wen du befreist?

are expanded into:

> By thy hand I'm freed!
> Thou dost unlock the fetters and the chain,
> And to thy bosom foldest me again;
> How is't thou dost not shrink from me in fear?
> And dost thou know whom thou are freeing here!

The whole second verse is little more than padding. Many similar passages can be found.

For the sake of preserving the rime scheme of the original, Filmore curiously translates the word "Stich" in line 4606 as "mess":

> Meph. Come! or I'll leave you with her in this mess!
> Marg. My father! I am thine; Oh! save and bless!

Filmore is by no means an inspired translator. The great passages of the drama, Gretchen's Song at the Spinning Wheel, the meeting of Gretchen and Faust in prison, and others vibrating so strongly with emotion become tame and watery in the translation. Gretchen's touching confession:

> Wo ich ihn nicht hab'
> Ist mir das Grab,
> Die ganze Welt
> Ist mir vergällt.

is diluted to:

> Where I see him not
> Seems the grave to be,

Men of Letters and Faust

>Tuneless and harsh
>All the world to me.

Blackie's translation of these lines, although rather free, is decidedly superior:

>Where he is not
>Life is the tomb,
>The world is bitterness
>And gloom.

Much more forceful and closer to the German is **Bayard Taylor's** rendering at a later date:

>Save I have him near,
>The grave is here:
>The world is gall
>And bitterness all.

In judging Filmore's version it must not be forgotten that he enjoyed no formal training and that his translation is wholly the product of industry and perseverance. Although these qualities are greatly to be commended in a translator, they are not enough to insure a satisfactory rendering of such a difficult work as Goethe's *Faust*. It is due, no doubt, more to his connection with the publishers of the Standard Library series and to popular demand for Goethe's works than to the merit of his translation that so many editions of it were published.

BAYARD TAYLOR
(1825-1878)

TRANSLATION OF *Faust I* FIRST PRINTED IN 1870;
Faust II, 1871

>An Goethe
>Erhabener Geist, im Geisterreich verloren!
>Wo immer Deine lichte Wohnung sey,
>Zum höh'ren Schaffen bist Du neugeboren,
>Und singest dort die voll're Litanei.
>Von jenem Streben das Du auserkoren,
>Vom reinsten Aether, drin Du athmest frei,

156 *Half a Hundred Thralls to* Faust

O neige Dich zu gnädigem Erwiedern
Des letzten Wiederhalls von Deinen Liedern!*

One morning in the early spring of 1845, there sallied forth from the venerable city of Frankfurt am Main a tall, handsome youth of twenty. With a knapsack on his back and a cane from the Mammoth Cave of Kentucky in his hand, with a firm, elastic trend, his fresh, ruddy face lighted up by the early morning sun, he strode along the road leading farther on into the land of advanture: The Harz, Moravia, Vienna, and into the world beyond the Alps.

This young man was Bayard Taylor, whom the "Wanderlust" and journalistic enterprise had driven forth from his native state of Pennsylvania and the shores of the new world, back into the land of the Faust traditions and Goethe. Europe, especially Germany, was to become for him a place almost as well known and as much loved as America. No fewer than half a dozen times he left the new world for the old, where the cradles of his ancestors stood, where the people came to regard him as their adopted son, and where in later years, as the eager and brilliant student of German life and literature and as the translator of Goethe's *Faust,* signal honors were bestowed upon him.† In the little town of Gotha, nestled among the green mountains of Thuringia, he found a home and the wife‡ who

---

* The Proem to Taylor's translation of Part I, of which only the first stanza is quoted here, is perhaps the best example of Taylor's German verse. The original manuscript is in the Speck Collection.

† In 1856 Taylor wrote to his mother from Dresden: "Dresden is the literary city of Germany, and I met with all the authors living there. I was delighted to find that they all knew about me. When I called on the poet, Julius Hammer, he was at his desk translating my poem of *Steyermark.* Gutzkow the dramatist, Auerbach the novelist, Dr. Andree the geographer, and others whose names are known all over Europe, welcomed me as a friend and brother author. We had a grand dinner together the day I left. The Dresden papers spoke of me as a distinguished guest, and published translations of my poems. In fact I think I am almost as well known in Germany as in the United States."—Smyth, *Bayard Taylor,* p. 107. In 1873, when Taylor lectured at Weimar before the Gustav-Adolf Verein, the whole court was present. Among his auditors were the grandchildren of Carl August, of Herder, and of Wieland; the Baron von Stein, grandson of Frau von Stein; Baron von Gleichen-Russwurm, Schiller's grandson; and Wolfgang von Goethe.—*Ibid.,* p. 201.

‡ Taylor married Marie Hansen, niece of Mrs. August Bufleb and daugh-

to him represented all that was best in German life and culture. In the closing days of his life, his own country, well aware of his splendid personality and outstanding talents, sent him as its ambassador to the imperial court at Berlin, where, at the age of fifty-three, he passed quietly from the scenes of this life. World traveler, statesman, journalist, novelist, poet, and translator, Bayard Taylor today is still unforgotten. Through his well-known version of *Faust*, his name is linked in an enduring way with the name and fame of the great Goethe himself.

Taylor's interest in things German can be traced back to his Teutonic ancestry. His grandmother on the paternal side, Ann Bucher, was the daughter of a Swiss-German Mennonite, and the grandmother on the maternal side was also of South German or Swiss origin.[33] The translator himself gives expression to these facts in his poem "The Palm and the Pine."[34] In his early boyhood, the fountain he mentions here began "to gush again." The passing of Scott and Goethe in 1832 impresed themselves as events of great significance upon his young plastic mind.[35] Before coming to the Unionville Academy in 1840, Taylor had already acquired some knowledge of German from a study of Wieland's *Oberon*, from his grandmother, and from the Swiss servant of the Taylor family. It is also possible that the library of Kennett Square, Taylor's native town in Pennsylvania, which boasted of three hundred or more volumes, contained not only some editions of Wieland's works but also of Schiller and Goethe. When Taylor left the Academy and went to work as an apprentice to a printer in Westchester, he read Herder in German with a private tutor. Then in 1844 came his first tour of Europe and of Germany in particular. For a whole winter he lived quietly and intimately with a family at Frankfurt am Main, the boyhood home of Goethe, and at this time also he made the acquaintance of Freiligrath,

---

ter of Peter Andreas Hansen, the eminent astronomer and director of the Ducal Observatory at Gotha, October 27, 1857. August Bufleb, an honored and wealthy citizen of Gotha, with whom Taylor became intimately acquainted during a trip up the Nile in 1852, presented him with a handsome home in Gotha.—*Ibid.*, p. 111.

Gerstäcker, and Mendelssohn. From now on the author of *Faust*, side by side with Schiller, began to play an important role in Taylor's life.*

It appears that Taylor planned the translation of *Faust* long before he actually attempted it. In the Preface to Part I, written in 1870, he says: "It is twenty years since I first determined to attempt the translation of Faust in the original metres."[36] Again, in 1877, Taylor remarked to Professor Hewett, of Cornell: "When I was a young man there was a certain work I wished to achieve before I was thirty, and I could see nothing in my life beyond that date. I believed that my life would come to an end at that time. But as the time approached I gradually conceived the plan of translating Faust."[37] We can conclude, therefore, that Taylor had quite definitely decided to make the translation by 1850.

One reason why his plans were not carried out immediately was that another American, Charles T. Brooks, published his version in 1856. Taylor remarks in his Preface: "Mr. Brooks was the first to undertake the task and the publication of his translation of the First Part induced me, for a time, to give up my own design."[38] However, it appears that he began the work on his own version in September or October, 1863, and by 1866 the translation was well under way. "By the bye, while in Germany," he writes to James T. Fields at this time, "I shall go on with the translation of *Faust*. My wife is acquainted with Frau von Goethe, whom we shall visit, and I expect to gather together a deal of interesting material about Part II. I have already done nearly half of Part I. I want to do for friendship (Faust) what Petrarch (Longfellow) has done for love (Dante)."[39]

From 1866 on, the work went steadily forward, and in 1868 Taylor completed the first draft of the translation of Part I. At the beginning of the new year he started on Part II. After

---

* "*A Book of Romances, Lyrics and Songs* (1851) contains as well as echoes from Heine, distinct notes from Goethe and furnishes evidence of Taylor's first acquaintance with *Faust II*."—John T. Krumpelmann, "Bayard Taylor" (a short, factual biographical sketch, written November, 1930, and now in the Speck Collection).

considerable time spent in revising, the translator wrote to T. B. Aldrich from his country home, Cedarcroft, October, 1870: "I have been working day and night on *Faust* since I saw you, and now that the work is just about finished, I shall feel thoroughly worn out, exhausted, used up, collapsed, effete, intellectually impotent. I only hope there will be some little recognition of my labors in the end."[40]

The first edition of Part I appeared December 14, 1870, and nearly all the copies were sold on that day. In the evening a celebration took place to commemorate the completion of the work. "At the home of James T. Fields, a small but distinguished company met to congratulate the successful translator; Longfellow, Lowell, Howells, Aldrich, and Osgood sat around a bust* of Goethe which was placed upon the library table, and the night was dedicated to Goethe and Taylor."[41] It was not until March, 1871, however, that Part II was published.

Although Taylor may have done some of the translating during his frequent visits to Germany, most of it was completed at "Towered Cedarcroft," the attractive home which he built in Chester County, Pennsylvania. Here, in the land of his youth, he took up his residence in 1860. "The great entrance door opened upon a broad hall and wide oaken stairway, to the left of which, and facing south and west, was the splendid library room. Here Taylor carried forward his literary work. Here he wrote *The Poet's Journal*,† *The Picture of St. John*, and *Home Pastorals*, two of his novels, *Joseph and his Friend*, and *The Story of Kennett*, besides completing his translation of *Faust*."[42]

But what preparation did Taylor have for this work as a translator of the *Faust* drama?‡ He never attended a college or received a university degree, and it can be said of him, as it was said of a more famous author, that he knew small Latin

---

* This bust was probably that after Alexander Trippel which is now in the Speck Collection.

† *The Poet's Journal* contains the best of Taylor's original verse; his novels are of small artistic value.

‡ The Speck Collection possesses the manuscript of the translation of the entire *Faust* by Bayard Taylor.

and less Greek. Yet it was characteristic of his energy and enterprise that he took up the study of Greek when he was fifty years old.[43] Taylor was a self-made man, and his education came largely from travel and contact with people. Like Faust he knew from experience what "die kleine" as well as "die grosse Welt" was like. His journalistic exploits led him to every continent except South America. Everywhere and always his alert mind, his fine memory, and his sympathetic nature stored up rich treasures of useful information about man and his ways.

Taylor's adaptability to life in Germany and the rapidity with which he familiarized himself with the German language are surprising. In *Views Afoot* he remarks: "The winter 1844-45 I spent in Frankfort on the Main, and by May I was so good a German that I was often not suspected of being a foreigner."[44] A corroborating testimony comes from Madame von Holtzendorf, of Gotha, who writes in a letter to Taylor: "We Germans have every reason to be proud that a man like you has assimilated to himself our nature, our mode of thinking and feeling, to such a degree as to understand us perfectly."[45] All of this was good preparation, and it helped Taylor to make an intelligent translation of *Faust*.

But Taylor possessed still other qualifications which we must not pass over. Although he was no outstanding artist, he had, nevertheless, a distinct feeling for form. To one of his literary friends, J. B. Phillips, he wrote: "Really we must have a passion for symmetry, harmony, balance of thought and expression! Very likely you think I lay too much stress on what may seem minor things, but a sculptor who is satisfied if the head is good and leaves the fingers and toes half modeled is a poor artist."[46] It must be remembered, also, that Taylor had made an extensive study of German literature, especially of Goethe, and translated a considerable number of poems from Rückert, Hebbel, and other German authors before he made his version of *Faust*.* These efforts "disclosed to him his

---

* During 1870 Taylor lectured at Cornell University on German Literature. He wrote his *Studies in German Literature* about 1879, but they were not published until after his death. His *Life of Goethe and Schiller* remained a fragment.

facility in reproducing both the rhythm and the poetic sense of the original. He began with the lyrical portions; the more he tried the work, and the better acquaintance he had with previous translations, the more confidence he felt in undertaking a complete translation."[47] Taylor was also the author of a considerable collection of original poems and ballads in English,[48] and even a few in German. His skill in German verse is demonstrated in the *Jubellied eines Amerikaners* written after the German victory at Sedan. This composition aroused favorable comment throughout Germany. The proem "An Goethe" to his translation of *Faust*, conceived in German, is fresh, sincere, and melodious.

Taylor was no scholar in the ordinary sense of the term, yet he went to work in a very scholarly fashion. "He familiarized himself with the ramifications of the Faust legend in history and art. He examined a score of translations, read commentaries, compared sundry editions and compressed the labor of a lifetime into seven years."[49] He bears testimony to his own diligence and persistence in another letter to J. B. Phillips: "What would you say," he writes, "to my hunting up twenty or thirty synonyms for every chief word in a quatrain; and then spending two or three hours in making them fit in the best possible form? Then a year later, in many cases, all the work was done over again, in order to get a better combination. Nobody ever succeeded in rapid translation, not even the highest talent."[50]

Taylor believed that a translator should be adequately prepared for his task. He "should have a nearly equal knowledge of both languages, in order to get that spirit above and beyond the words which simple literalness will never give. The best condition is that in which one knows both languages so well that he does not need to break his head in the hunt for words, but keeps his strength for that part of thought which subtly expresses itself in metre and harmony."[51]

Although Taylor speaks highly of Brooks's translation, which was the first American version of *Faust* to be published, and admits that he has profited much from a study of this version, he finds in it "a lack of the lyrical fire and fluency of the original in some passages, and an occasional lowering of the tone through the use of words which are literal, but not equivalent."[52] Taylor himself endeavored to make a translation in which these faults were corrected, and which at the same time should be literal, thoroughly rhythmical, and musical. He felt that in an acceptable version even the feminine endings and the dactylic rimes of the original must be reproduced. "I intend to try to prove," he wrote to Mrs. Marie Bloede, "that no great poem can be transferred with less loss than the German of *Faust* into the English language—and to make this a part of my justification for rigidly preserving the original metres."[53]

Taylor felt that it was particularly necessary to translate the Second Part of *Faust*. To one of his friends he wrote: "I am much more delighted with the Second Part—now that I take it line by line—than I expected to be; and it makes a much better appearance in English. Bernays and Anster should have been knocked on the head before prejudicing English readers against the poem by their stupid translations. I have just obtained a third translation of the Second Part—Macdonald's—so now, I believe, I know all that have been made! And they are equally bad."[54] But Taylor himself found certain portions containing "crabbed, arbitrary constructions, words and compounds invented in defiance of all rule,"[55] to be untranslatable. "If," he remarks in his Preface, "the reader now and then falls upon an unusual compound, or a seemingly forced inversion of language, I must beg him to remember that my sins against the poetical laws of the English language are but a small percentage of Goethe's sins against the German."[56]

In the making of the translation Taylor was materially assisted by the excellent German and English scholar, Dr. William H. Furness of Philadelphia. Other friends, including E. C. Stedman, James T. Fields, and, no doubt, Mrs. Taylor—although there is little mention of it—also proved to be valuable counselors. In addition, while the translator was in Germany, he profited from the suggestions of the best scholars of that country.

The triumph of realizing, or even exceeding, our hopes is given to few of us. Although Taylor produced a translation superior to any made by his predecessors, he did not always fully achieve his objectives. Juliana Haskell in her dissertation, *Bayard Taylor's Translation of Goethe's Faust*, even concludes that "in a certain sense Bayard Taylor's *Faust* is not English. In a certain sense it is not Goethe. Taylor has given us the form of *Faust* with photographic fidelity at times. But he has Latinized, sophisticated, diluted, padded, and stripped off poetry until all vital semblance of the original has been lost. The translation inspires the reader with an unqualified admiration for the patience, zeal and industry of Bayard Taylor, but it affords him little pleasure, nor does it perform that high office of good translation, so potent to suggest the charm of the original as to win readers for Goethe in the German. In short it meets no one of the three demands which may reasonably be made upon it by the person for whom the translation was obviously intended—the English speaking person of culture who knows no German but would still make the acquaintance of *Faust*."[57]

I have quoted from Juliana Haskell at such length because her conclusions concerning Taylor's *Faust* are censorious and contrary to the favorable opinions held by many leading scholars for half a century. Earlier in her volume Miss Haskell cites the tests which she has applied to the translation: "For the purpose of this cultured English-speaking person who has no command of German, and who nevertheless desires to know *Faust*, it is essential that the translator of *Faust* shall write normal English, that he shall represent Goethe fairly, and, if he determines upon a metrical translation, that he shall invest his rendering with a modicum of poetry, of which meter and rhythm are merely the outer garb."[58] According to this critic, Taylor's translation fails to measure up to any of these tests. The best and most concise answer that can be given to these conclusions is that they are exaggerations. All who have read carefully Taylor's version will agree that certain lines, especially in Part II, are not normal English today and perhaps were not even in Taylor's time.* Still we must remember that the language of the mid-Victorian period, which is the English of Bayard Taylor's translation of *Faust*, with its greater toleration for involved constructions, inversion, ornamentation, and latinization, contrasts materially with the clarity, the simplicity, and the directness of good twentieth-century English. It may to some extent be considered a matter of taste as to whether one prefers the former or the latter.

The statements that Taylor's version does not represent Goethe, that his translation does not contain a modicum of poetry, and that he has "stripped off poetry untill all vital semblance of the original has been lost," are likewise exaggerations. Everyone is willing to admit, again, that there are lines in Taylor's version which are not Goethean and not poetical;[59] but to condemn the whole translation on account of these passages is to do it a gross injustice, particularly such portions as the Chorus of the Angels in the Prologue in Heaven, the lengthy Song of the Spirits in Study I, Faust's Soliloquy in

---

* Miss Haskell cites (pp. 62 ff.) such lines from Part II as I: 21, 31, 58, 99; II: 3, 37, 41, 139, 216, 296; and many others. Among the verses quoted are such as: "One must not so squeamish be" (I, 192); "Thou wilt my whispers like a master heed" (II, 75); "Express thyself, and 'twill a riddle be" (II, 108), which do not run contrary to English poetic usage.

A page from Bayard Taylor's manuscript of his translation of the Second Part of *Faust*, Act III, lines 9708-9734. The note below casts an interesting sidelight on the publication of Taylor's translation. However, the "sooty condition of the leaves" of which he complains is not in evidence.

"Dear Lynchie Botta:
"I meant to have sent a note with the Ms. but stupidly sealed the envelope in a hurry. The sooty condition of the leaves must be ascribed to the 'University Press' in Cambridge, not to me. Explain this when you give them away, or people will have a fearful impression of my personal habits. . . . With hearty greetings to the Professor, your old, incorrigible, inveterate friend,
"Bayard Taylor

"Kennett Square Penna.,
"April 4, 1872."

"Lynchie Botta" (Anne Charlotte Lynch Botta, 1815-1891, wife of the well-known Italian-American scholar Vincenzo Botta, 1818-1894) was an American poet of some distinction, whose home in New York became the center of the most brilliant intellectual and artistic life of the city. Here Bayard Taylor and R. H. Stoddard were introduced to the literati of New York.

Gather from the shining boy
Double bliss for hearts united:
In their union what a joy!

Euphorion.

Let me be skipping,
Let me be leaping!
To soar and circle,
Through ether sweeping,
Is now the passion
That me hath won.

Faust.

But gently! gently!
Not rashly faring;
Lest plunge and ruin
Repay thy daring,
Perchance destroy thee
Our darling son!

Euphorion.

I will not longer
Stagnate below here!
Let go my tresses,
My hands let go, here!
Let go my garments!
They all are mine.

Helena.

O think! Bethink thee
To whom thou belongest!
How it would grieve us,
And how thou wrongest
The fortune fairest,—
Mine, His and Thine!

Forest and Cavern, and many of the lyrices in the closing scene of Part II. These are not only translations but enjoyable poetry. If Taylor has not been able to impart to his translation the music, the beauty of expression which we find in the few lines done by Shelley,* his is a more faithful reproduction of the form of the original than Shelley's, and, we may add, than nearly all the other translations.

It is significant that in 1930, exactly sixty years after the first publication of Taylor's translation, during which interval no fewer than eighteen other English and American versions of *Faust* had appeared, a critic, Robert H. Fife, head of the Department of German at Columbia University, should venture the opinion that "of Taylor's translation it may be said that it is more nearly Goethe's *Faust* and at the same time more nearly poetry than any other English version."[60] Moreover, it is an unusual tribute that after the large number of editions of this translation which had previously appeared, two new ones should be published in 1930 and two others in 1932, and others still later.

> Schmerzvoll verhüllt sich die Muse, es schweigen die holden
>   Gesänge
> Die sie noch jüngst, geleitet von ihm, mit Anmuth erzählte,
> Trauer auf Erden hinieden! Doch dorten im sel'gen Elysium
> Rufen verwandte Grössen dem Staunenden jubelndes Willkomm!
> . . . .
> Ewig, wie jetzt sein Unsterbliches unter den Geistes Heroen,
> Glänze der Werth seines Thuens fort von Geschlecht zu
>   Geschlecht! †

FRANK CLAUDY
(1843-1919)
Translation of *Faust I* First Printed in 1886

> Vor deinem Throne Göttin, knie' ich nieder:
> O, leite du die ängstlich-schwachen Schritte

---

* Shelley translated the Prologue in Heaven and May Day Night.

† From a poem by Frank Claudy on the death of Bayard Taylor. The manuscript was presented to Mr. William A. Speck, July 1, 1915, and is now in the Collection of Goetheana.

Men of Letters and Faust

Auf jenen Pfad, den Er dereinst betreten!
Verhülle mir nicht deines Wesens Anmuth!
Send einen Strahl nur deiner Glorie nieder,
Begeistre mich, dass ich mit klarem Sinne
In fremder, doch verwandter Sprache Wohllaut
Sein grösstes Lied mit Ehrfurcht übertrage,
Dass es, ein Abglanz jener ew'gen Worte
In mild'rem Licht erblühe dem Verständnis
Der Neuen Welt: Ein Zeugnis Seines Schaffens.

O Blicke gnädig auf mein ernstes Wollen
Und fördere den Vorsatz zum Gelingen.*

With this ardent, beseeching prayer to the Muse, Frank Claudy, Taylor's successor in the line of the American *Faust* translators, began his version of Goethe's celebrated drama. Because he realized that the task would require great skill, and since it was to be his greatest literary effort, he felt the need of a special dispensation of poetic inspiration. Claudy was born in Mainz, Germany, January 1, 1843. After completing the elementary schools, he pursued further preparatory studies, and then attended Heidelberg University for several years. In the summer of 1864 he came to the United States and almost immediately enlisted in the Army (Company K, Coast Artillery). Soon afterward he was detailed as clerk at the Headquarters of General William F. Barry, commanding the Artillery School at Fort Monroe, Virginia. In 1874, Claudy was honorably discharged from the Army. This year also marked his marriage, the fruit of a wartime romance, to Mary Josephine Dillon Catlin of Deerfield, Massachusetts. Mrs. Claudy died in 1896, but a son, Carl Harry Claudy, author and journalist, lives in Washington, D. C., the city in which for many years his father made his home. After his discharge from the army, the translator became a government clerk in the Pension Office. This position he dignified by his beautiful handwriting, his care and neatness, and his characteristic German throughness until his death at the age of seventy-six on March 6, 1919.[61]

* This is a part of the original poem "An Goethes Muse," twenty-nine lines in length, which stands at the head of Claudy's translation.

In addition to the fine qualities as an employee, Claudy possessed a kindly, courteous, and lovable personality. He was a man with literally scores of friends and one whom everyone respected and honored for his genuineness and wide interests. For many years he served as the president and was the moving spirit of the Washington "Sängerbund," vice-president of the "Deutscher Literarischer Verein" of Washington, and an enthusiastic member of various amateur dramatic clubs.*

More than this, his cultivated tastes expressed themselves in his lectures on the music dramas of Wagner, in the acquisition of an excellent *Faust* collection,† and finally in the translation of Goethe's *Faust*. However, these attainments were but the natural developments from earlier dominant interests. Already in his student life in Germany, he showed a decided preference for folklore, history, music, and literature, and a special fondness for Goethe and Schiller.

Claudy's translation of *Faust*, the one great literary effort of his maturer years, was made in no hurried and slipshod way. Begun in 1870, it was not completed until fifteen years later. As an introductory effort there appeared in 1883 a small volume with the translation of the Dedication, the Prologue in Heaven, and Under a Gateway.[62] In 1886 the complete translation of the First Part of *Faust* in the original metres was published.

The translator seems to have been attracted in a peculiar way by the *Faust* drama. He "might have been a spiritualist or an astrologer if his sound, German, common sense and his education had not prevented such outlets for the vein of mysti-

---

* Miss Anita Schade, reader and actress of Washington, D. C., who knew Mr. Claudy intimately, states in a letter, December, 1930, that Mr. Claudy played the part of the King in Hertz's *König Renée's Tochter*; in *Jane Eyre*, the part of Rochester; and in scenes from Goethe's *Faust*, the part of Mephistopheles, while Miss Schade played the role of Gretchen. These plays were staged by the Deutscher Literarischer Verein in Washington, D. C., of which Miss Schade was founder and president.

† This collection, finally totaling some 1,500 volumes, contains nearly all the English and American translations of *Faust*, besides many of the extremely rare books on Goethe and Schiller. After Mr. Claudy's death, the whole collection was acquired by the Library of the Supreme Council of the Scottish Rite of Freemasonry for the Southern Jurisdiction of the United States, and is now in the House of the Temple at 16th and S streets, Washington, D. C.

cism which was in him. The supernatural passages in *Faust* were his favorites."⁶³ Other reasons for imposing upon himself the difficult task of translating *Faust* are found in his Introduction to the original edition. There he says: "I began the following translation of the First Part of Goethe's *Faust* sometime before the publication of Bayard Taylor's masterly rendition of the poem, and before I had any knowledge of the fact that such a work was then in progress. No thought of publication dwelt at that time in my mind. My life-long enjoyment of the beauties of the original, and the desire to render them accessible to the friends whom I have gathered around me in this my adopted country, by producing a translation at once more metrical and more literal than any then known to me, were the only motives that led to the beginning and urged the continuance of the present work."

Corroborating in part the statement made above about the peculiar attraction *Faust* had for him, he goes on to say in his Introduction: "A strange fascination, experienced only by those who enter deeply into the study of Goethe's master-work, urged me onward even in the very midst of the discouragement caused by the appearance of Mr. Taylor's version* Far from intending to place my work on the same level, I offer it simply as a tribute to Goethe's genius, as an illustration of this fascination which would not allow me to relinquish my self-appointed task even after I had become partially convinced that its accomplish-

---

* It does not appear that Claudy ever met or even corresponded with Taylor. However, after the latter's death, Claudy had occasion to write to Mrs. Taylor. In a letter to Mr. William A. Speck, Yale University, dated July 1, 1915, he says: "I myself had a short correspondence, years ago with Mrs. Taylor. I wished to translate her husband's *Deukalion* into German, and asked her opinion. I gave it up, after a time, having found it too difficult; nor do I know whether any German translation was ever made of the poem." Claudy also knew and corresponded with William Page Andrews, another American translator of *Faust*. But this version, begun in the eighties, did not appear until 1929, and then only in a revised form. Concerning Andrews, Claudy wrote to Mr. Speck, November 11, 1915: "Before I forget it—Are you acquainted with Professor W. P. Andrews, formerly of Salem, Mass., and now in Capri, Italy, and do you know what has become of him? We had quite a lengthy correspondence about my translation, and he took dinner with us once, when my dear wife was still living. Once he wrote me from Capri that his translation of *Faust*, first and second part, was now complete." (These letters to Mr. Speck are in the Yale University Library.)

ment was no longer a necessity as regarded [*sic*] the execution of my original purpose." Finally, he adds: "As far as I have been able to ascertain, this is the first time that one of Goethe's own countrymen has attempted to translate *Faust* into the English language. May the American people kindly receive his rendition of the greatest work of the greatest of German poets."*

We find, then, that there were several reasons why Claudy made the translation: his particular interest in Goethe and in *Faust;* the attraction which the drama held for him, coupled with the personal pleasure it afforded him; the desire to produce a more satisfactory version than had been made thus far; and, finally, the belief that he was the first of Goethe's countrymen to attempt an English translation.

As far as Claudy's linguistic qualifications for this work are concerned, it may be said that in view of the fact that he grew to manhood in Germany and attended the University of Heidelberg, his technical knowledge of German, as well as his "Sprachgefühl" for that language, was superior to that of most of the other translators. However, the same can hardly be said of Claudy's knowledge of English. All of it was learned by "exposure," his son writes, and by reading and conversation after coming to America at the age of twenty-two. Still "he wrote beautiful English; his written grammar was faultless. He spoke with a decided accent, and occasionally with Teutonisms creeping in; thus, he invariably said 'on the table,' when he meant 'at the table' . . . [but] he never wrote 'on' for 'at.' "[64] In this connection, it is also to be remembered that Mrs. Claudy, the person from whom he learned the most, was a cultured woman and had a full command of idiomatic English.

Then, too, Claudy acquired a certain command of the language in translating many shorter poems and German essays and in writing a considerable number of poems, lectures, and essays of his own on musical subjects. Little of this work has ever been published, but the poem "An Goethes Muse," a part

---

* Although no direct evidence is at hand that v. Beresford, whose translation of *Faust*, Part I, was published in 1862, was Goethe's countryman, there exists a possibility that such was the case.

of which is given above, shows that Claudy was not entirely uninspired, particularly when writing in his native tongue. In the field of translation his creditable rendering of Bayard Taylor's "An Goethe" from the German into the English was one of the last of his literary efforts.* An example of Claudy's ability to render the English into German is to be found in his translation of Gilbert's *Pygmalion and Galatea*.†

Carl H. Claudy, the son of the translator, describes the manner in which *Faust* was actually translated in the Claudy home so realistically and sympathetically that his words are worth quoting here: "He [the translator] often said it was as much my mother's and my aunt's work as his. Picture to yourself two sweet faced, keen minded New England women; one stout, enthusiastic German; a little room, a student lamp, a table covered with books and papers and dictionaries and books of synonyms, a rich voice reads aloud the German (he had a fine baritone voice for singing), then renders the phrases into rough English; all of them write down the rough [translation], and then begins the process of refinement, of discussion, and of looking up."

In the same interesting way he continues: "They worked in perfect harmony, those three; Aunt Carrie would be sewing or embroidering (I never saw her clever hands empty), and she would listen while they discussed; then she would put in the one word which might clarify the whole situation. Dad would jump up to give her a resounding German kiss for her help, or pat her on the back. . . . How do I know? I have heard . . . all my life I have heard of those beautiful years when *The Book* was in the making and I can remember, when I was six or seven, seeing the joy and pride and delight they had in it,

---

* In a letter written from Washington, D. C., June 15, 1915, to William A. Speck, Claudy says: "In reply to your request for an autograph, I enclose you my translation of Bayard Taylor's beautiful *An Goethe*, prefixed to his translation of *Faust*."

† Miss Anita Schade wrote me in a letter dated December, 1930: "Frank Claudy translated also Gilbert's Pygmalion and Galatea for me and gave me the manuscript which I have preserved faithfully. As far as I know there is no other German translation of this mythological comedy, which was played with so great success by Mary Anderson and Julia Marlowe."

just for its own sake; just because it was a world shut in from a reality not always happy, without; a little world love ruled; culture surrounded; music permeated . . . a bit of the best of Germany brought and mingled with a little of the best of old New England."

Such is the romance of Claudy's translation of Goethe's *Faust*. No doubt, if one could know the complete story of all the translations of Faust, other very interesting instances would be discovered, showing how this "greatest work of the greatest of German poets" has fascinated all types and classes of people.

Claudy's translation has not escaped the fate of all the others. Like these his version has been praised by some; condemned by others. A reviewer in the *Menorah* finds that Claudy has brought to his work "a critical knowledge of the German language, and a remarkable understanding and use of English. Such qualifications, added to a poetic gift of his own, and a sympathetic and loving appreciation of the spirit of the immortal work, could hardly fail to produce a noble result. . . . Perhaps the weakest parts of Claudy's translation are the scenes in Auerbach's Cellar and in the Witches' Kitchen. The rendering of the text is fluent and clear, but there is a lack of that poetic flow of language which is so prominently noticeable throughout the other parts of the work."[65] The *New York Times* remarks on the Song of Margaret at the Spinning Wheel that "Mr. Claudy gives a very good translation of this scene; in fact his whole work shows that it was undertaken and carried out con amore."[66]

Distinctly less favorable are the comments in the *Nation:* "It has, however, a peculiar interest, as being the work of a native German, and this after fifteen years of labor. We cannot agree with the glowing circular of the publishers announcing it as 'a splendid translation': but while it is far inferior both in ease and literalness to that of Charles T. Brooks, it has merits of its own. It would be curious to point out, had we the space to give it, some passages in which the translator gains by his native intimacy with the German, and others where he loses again by his want of the same kind of knowledge of the

Reproduction of a page of manuscript from Frank Claudy's translation of Faust I, Study II, lines 1714-1735

English."67 The *Westminster Review* calls the language of this version "German-English, readable German-English, pleasant German-English," but holds "that it will succeed in bringing Goethe home to English readers as few translations have hitherto done," and that "the merit of this translation is its faithfulness to the original."68 To the above assertion that the language is German-English may be added the less severe statement from the *Menorah* that "In a few instances the foreigner is betrayed through some idiom, or some want of comprehension of the inflection of the English." But, the same reviewer feels, "these are minor faults and do not avail to injure in any great degree the beauty of this remarkable translation but rather by their insignificance serve to emphasize its worth."[69]

Just how much truth is there in the charge that Claudy's language is marred by Germanisms? This can be said: There are in this version a number of constructions which betray the fact that the translator's mother tongue was German. The following are examples. Claudy translates the line:

"Und mich ergreift ein längst entwöhntes Sehnen."

rather awkwardly as:

"And grasps me now a long unwonted yearning."

Another too literal rendering is that of the line:

"Wie anders wirkt dies Zeichen auf mich ein!"

as:

"How differently affects my soul this sign."

We have a clear case of a Germanism when Claudy translates the line, "Was wettet ihr?" as: "What bet you?" Again he has Margaret say to Faust: "Dearest man, I love thee tenderly." We do not feel that if Margaret had spoken English she would have said "dearest man." It would have been "sweetheart" or "darling" or some other term of endearment, for "dearest man" does not connote the same idea as "bester Mann."

But, after all, the inversions, the too literal passages, the peculiarly German turns of expression are relatively few; indeed far fewer than one might expect in the work of a translator who did not know a single word of English six years before beginning his translation. This is explained, first, by the fact that Frank Claudy possessed an unusually alert mind, a good memory, an acutely sensitive and musical ear which enabled him in a very short time to master the vocabulary, the swing, and the rhythm of what was to him a foreign tongue; secondly, by the circumstance that during the whole translation Mrs. Claudy, as well as her sister, Miss Caroline Catlin, with their superior knowledge of English, passed judgment on every line before it was finally accepted.

There is no question that this version as a whole is superior in literal faithfulness and in metrical accuracy to all of the translations completed before 1850, and even to a large number after that date. But this does not mean that Claudy's translation does not have inaccuracies of metre and a considerable amount of padding for the sake of supplying the proper number of metrical feet to the line as well as the needed rimes. This is the case in the second stanza of Gretchen's prayer to the Virgin:

> Das Schwert im Herzen,
> Mit tausend Schmerzen
> Blickst auf zu deines Sohnes Tod.

Claudy translates:

> Sword-pierced heart-broken,
> With pangs unspoken,
> Thou gazest at thy son, dead but divine.

Still Claudy's version is to be preferred here to Bayard Taylor's awkward and unmusical rendering:

> The sword thy heart in
> With anguish smarting
> Thou lookest up to where Thy Son is slain.

The feminine endings have been followed rather closely throughout the lyrical portions of the play, but in the more sustained reflective and conversational passages, the correspondence to the original is not so evident. Here and there, also, impure rimes are to be found. The metre, although not especially musical, is fairly smooth throughout.

That Claudy wrestled long and hard to reproduce the exact meaning of the original is evident from a passage in a letter written to Mr. William A. Speck, July 1, 1915, in which he remarks: "Speaking about changes, I will say that I am entirely dissatisfied with my own and with most translators' (even Bayard Taylor's) rendering of 'Das Werdende,' in the Prologue in Heaven." Then he asks: "Did not Goethe have Evolution in his mind, the *Cosmos*, the *Universe*, when he wrote this? And would it not be better to say:

> That which to Being grows and
> Works and lives for aye, etc."

It seems to me that this is an excellent and perhaps the best rendering of the passage yet made.

This translation, as we have observed, has its shortcomings; it lacks that final stamp of poetic genius, that melodiousness, that choiceness of expression, which make great poetry even of a translation. Yet it will stand as a worthy and lasting monument to the love, the deep admiration, and the profound devotion which Frank Claudy felt for his great master and ideal, Goethe.

ALFRED HENRY HUTH
(1850-1910)
TRANSLATION OF *Faust I* FIRST PRINTED IN 1889

Alfred Henry Huth, English bibliophile, writer, and translator of Goethe's *Faust*, born in London in 1850, was the son of Henry Huth, the famous English merchant banker and book collector.[70] At the age of eleven, Alfred, together with his older brother, accompanied the well-known historian, Henry Thomas Buckle, who was a close friend of the Huth family, on an educational tour through Egypt and Palestine. This trip, which began in the autumn of 1861, came to a close with Buckle's death in the East the following year.[71] In 1864 Huth was enrolled at the Rugby school, where he remained for three years. Thereupon he attended lectures at London University for another year, and then concluded his studies by spending two years (1869-1871) at the University of Berlin.[72]

Since Henry Huth died about this time, his son Alfred

now came into the possession of an ample fortune and the father's splendid library of over ten thousand choice volumes gleaned from the fields of early English, Spanish, and German literature. Under the circumstances nothing was more natural for the younger Huth than to follow in his father's footsteps as a writer and bibliophile. One of the first things he did was to complete and publish his father's unfinished catalogue of this great collection. The care and augmentation of the library formed one of his chief interests up to the end of his life in 1910. He was a member of the Roxburghe Club and at different times served as its treasurer and vice-president. In 1892 Huth was largely responsible for the founding of the Bibliographical Society, acting first as its treasurer and then as its president. He urged in a paper before this organization a general catalogue of British works, but the project proved to be too extensive to be carried out at that time.[73]

A glance at the bibliography of Alfred Henry Huth reveals that only two of his works are purely literary in character. He began his career as an author with the volume *The Marriage of Near Kin considered with Respect to the Laws of Nations, the Results of Experience*, etc., London, 1875. This was followed by a volume called *Speculum Humanae Salvationis*, privately printed for the Roxburghe Club. Then he published a third book, bibliographical in character, *An Index to Books and Papers on Marriage between Near Kin*, London, 1879. Two of Huth's later works are of much greater interest to the student of literature. Supplementing available records largely with his own personal recollections of the man, he wrote a biography, *The Life and Writings of Henry Thomas Buckle*, London, 1880. Finally, climaxing his career as a writer, he translated Goethe's *Faust*.[74]

Since we are mainly concerned with Huth as a translator of *Faust*, we shall have to consider just what preparation he had for this important and most difficult piece of work. Concerning his father, we are informed that during his travels and longer periods of residence at Hamburg and Magdeburg, he learned to speak German perfectly; also that he could converse in Persian, Arabic, and Hindustani. The son must have acquired at an early age some of his father's facility to master foreign languages and in a special way the German tongue. Huth finished his translation in 1889, after two years of study at the University of Berlin.

Huth believed it necessary to give an explanation of why he should inflict another translation of *Faust* upon the English reading public. He remarks in the Preface: "The addition of one more to the forty odd translations of *Faust* already before the public may perhaps be a compliment to Goethe, but requires an apology to the reader. I began it in my boyhood, while yet ignorant of what had already been done, and without any design of publication; other work caused me to lay it aside, and only the accident of leisure in a country house induced me to take it up again. But with succeeding years the difficulty of adding anything worthwhile to the mature work of our predecessors becomes increasingly apparent, and he must be a bold man who thinks he has entirely superseded what has been done before him, nevertheless I trust this translation will have a certain value of its own." He then goes on to say that it is perhaps impossible to make a satisfactory English version if one allows himself to be fettered by rime and metre, and he admits that the difficulty of rime has often compelled him to resort to paraphrase.

In spite of Huth's previous training in German, an examination of his version shows that the "certain value of its own" which it possesses is small indeed. German still was essentially a foreign language to him, and the translation is very amateurish, with errors of all kinds abounding. Line 3 of the Dedication, "Versuch' ich wohl euch diesmal festzuhalten?" Huth renders with very awkward inversions as, "This time to hold ye fast essay shall I?" He has employed this word order in his translation because he needed a rime for "nigh" in the first line. Line 4, "Fühl ich mein Herz noch jenem Wahn geneigt," he translates equally badly as, "Feel I my heart is bent upon the craze." Huth has missed the mark widely again when he translates almost unintelligibly lines 13 and 14,

Men of Letters and Faust

> Der Schmerz wird neu, es wiederholt die Klage
> Des Lebens labyrinthisch irren Lauf,

As

> The pain's recalled, and we plain us anew
> Of life's devious and labyrinthine guise.

If we compare such lines with passages chosen from scenes nearer the close of the drama, one is led to believe that the former are the earliest parts translated by Huth and that the latter represent the work of his maturer years. His rendering of A Forest and Cavern, although in many ways lacking the charm of the original blank verse, is at least an intelligible translation. The opening lines of this scene,

> Erhabner Geist, du gabst mir, gabst mir alles,
> Warum ich bat. Du hast mir nicht umsonst
> Dein Angesicht im feuer zugewendet.
> Gabst mir die herrliche Natur zum Königreich,
> Kraft sie zu fühlen, zu geniessen. Nicht
> Kalt staunenden Besuch erlaubst du nur,
> Vergönnest mir in ihre tiefe Brust
> Wie in den Busen eines Freunds zu schauen.

Huth renders:

> Spirit sublime! Thou gavest me, gavest me all
> That I did ask. Thou didst me not for nought
> Thy countenance in fiery flame reveal.
> Thou gavest unto me glorious Nature for my realm,
> With power to feel it, and enjoy it. Not
> Mere crude acquaintance, cold and wondering Thou
> Didst grant me in her inmost heart to see,
> As in the bosom of a friend it were.

In this passage the translator also had the advantage of not being "fettered by rime," and it must be regarded as one of his best.

Huth's contention, that it is necessary to use a partly "Jacobean" vocabulary in order to render properly such a drama as *Faust* because of mediaeval features, can hardly be taken seriously. It is foolish to say that we cannot talk of supernatural beings as if we believed in them in modern English. Certainly no German reader feels that Goethe's modern German stands in the way of a full appreciation of the old Faust legends, and to the modern English reader the use of such unusual and archaic words as "rede," "ken," "wight," "enscorcel," "wis," "yore," "eyen," etc. is distinctly disturbing. As a result, the translation, instead of being made more effective, becomes less intelligible and, therefore, less effective. This tendency to use archaic words in certain parts of the drama is evident in many of the translations, including Anna Swanwick's, Theodore Martin's, and even Bayard Taylor's, but Huth alone makes it a definite principle which he follows consistently.

It must be said then, that Huth's translation is distinctly a third-rate piece of work. It lacks the verbal accuracy and intelligibility, the simple style, the spiritual atmosphere, and the entrancing melody of the original. It stands on a level with such versions as those of Galvan and Colquhoun.

WILLIAM PAGE ANDREWS
(1848-1916)
Translation of *Faust I* First Printed in 1929

The noted American Goethe scholar and translator of *Faust*, William Page Andrews, son of Samuel Andrews, a Unitarian clergyman, and Rebecca Scudder Andrews, a relative of Horace E. Scudder, editor of the *Atlantic Monthly*, was born November, 1848, at Framingham, Massachusetts. When still quite young, he moved with his parents to Salem, the old home of the Andrews family, where he attended the public schools, and then continued his studies under private tutors. On account of poor health, he could not complete his education at Harvard as many of his relatives before him had done.

In early manhood Andrews for some years held the office of clerk of the Essex County Court. However, even during this period his chief interest was in literature, which reflected itself in the fact that his most intimate associates were writers and students. During this time also he first took up the study of German with private teachers and as a result became deeply interested in German literature and the works of Goethe. Soon after his marriage in 1889, Andrews, on account of the precarious condition of his health, removed to Italy, where he lived on the island of Capri in a state of semi-invalidism until his death in 1916. Professor Karl E. Weston says of him: "He was scholarly rather than a scholar in the strict meaning of the term. His knowledge of the literature of European countries and of America was extensive. He was one of the most cultured men I have known."[75]

Andrews' literary career began in 1890, with the publication of his paper "On the Translation of Faust" in the *Atlantic Monthly*.[76] This he followed in the next year with three essays on "Goethe's Key to Faust."[77] Also about this time he published *Jones Very, a Memoir*, and a collection of Very's poems. For some time afterward he continued to contribute verse and prose to such magazines and papers as the *Nation, Forum, Boston Transcript*, and the *Christian Register*, and then, in 1913, he republished "Goethe's Key to Faust." Finally, to climax his literary endeavors, Andrews completed his translation of *Faust* in 1915.

His interest in *Faust* developed in the early eighties, soon after he began to study German, and from this time on he applied himself diligently to the works of Goethe, always noting carefully all the references and illusions which might shed light on difficult passages in the *Faust* drama. These references together with his own deductions therefrom make up the contents of the essays comprising "Goethe's Key to Faust." "Where are we to look for the key to Faust?" Andrews asks in the first of these on "The Prologues." His answer is: "We are to go to the poet's life, to the poet's thought, and there we may read, by the light thrown on the poem, from the varying epochs of his earthly career, and find the answer to our enigma in the poem itself, and in the many thoughts and experiences of the poet whose life and thought are reflected in it."[78]

There is no question that the translation of *Faust* was for

Andrews the dominating interest of his life. Because it was done wholly for his own pleasure and satisfaction, the work had a great attraction for him, and he had no other ends in view, except, as Professor Weston states, "to publish his theories and to make a literal translation of the drama." In this endeavor he was encouraged by "his American, English, and German literary friends in Capri, and earlier by such friends as Horace Scudder and professor George Herbert Palmer of Harvard." Professor Weston writes also that "the translation must have been begun in the eighties" and "completed in 1915"; and that "practically the entire work was accomplished during his residence in Capri." Frank Claudy wrote Mr. Speck, of Yale University, June 15, 1915, that he was acquainted with Andrews and that "once he [Andrews] wrote me from Capri that his translation of *Faust*, first and second part, was now completed."[79] This seeming disagreement between Professor Weston and Claudy as to the time when Andrews' translation was completed is satisfactorily explained by another passage from Professor Weston's letter to me in which he says: "During the years he was engaged in the work, several versions were made of the work, but were replaced by revisions." We conclude, therefore, that in Andrews' letter to Claudy he referred to one of the versions of both parts which was again revised at a later date.

However, Andrews did not live to see his translation in print. After his death in 1916, Professor Weston, his literary executor, in collaboration with Professor George M. Priest, of Princeton University, subjected Andrews' version of the First Part to a thorough revision before publishing it in 1929. Of this revision Professor Weston says: "On receiving the manuscript I made a partial revision and, later, together with Professor Priest, went through the translation in great detail. In many cases Mr. Andrews' desire for strict literalness was carried too far and these over-literal passages had to be recast into equivalent but less awkward English. In some cases the translation was not quite accurate and again the versification was careless, especially in the conversational passages. This required considerable revision of the versification. During his last year, Mr. Andrews' health was failing which I feel accounts for many of the inaccuracies that we had to correct."

As may be seen from Andrews' excellent article "On the Translation of Faust," his theory of translation is based entirely on Goethe's own ideas. As indicative of the translator's office, he cites Goethe's words in the notes to the *West Easterly Divan:* "The translator is a person who introduces you to a veiled beauty; he makes you long for the loveliness behind the veil." He also refers to Goethe's discussion of the various types of translation, in which the author of *Faust* rejects the prose translation as well as the free version which recreates the original into a new poem, in favor of "the highest and last, where one strives to make the translation identical with the original; so that one is not instead of the other, but in the place of the other.... This sort of translation," continues the quotation from the *West Easterly Divan,* "approaches the interlinear version, and makes the understanding of the original a much easier task; thus we are led into the original,—yes, even driven in." This third and "highest" kind, Andrews asserts, requires "the reproduction of both word and style, with movements of the original verse," which "has not been attempted in any of the yet known versions."[80]

Professor Weston's explanation of Andrews' theory gives us still more light on this point: "His ambition was to produce an absolutely literal translation that would enable a person with very little knowledge of German to follow Goethe's text, which he hoped could be printed with the translation in parallel. The literalness of the translation, he thought, should not be hampered by a slavish following of Goethe's rimes which he felt to be the defect of some translations. He tried to follow the structure of Goethe's verse which varied with the person speaking or the mood to be expressed. This he felt to be most important, the actual sequence of [the] rime of the original being secondary in his opinion."

Since Andrews' work was thoroughly revised prior to its publication in 1929, one cannot be sure of the nature of the original version. Professor Weston says that he and Professor Priest revised the translation in three ways: they corrected its over-literalness, its verbal inaccuracies, and careless versification, especially in the conversational passages. However, in the Foreword to the translation, the editors add that they "have attempted to carry out Mr. Andrews' ideal of suitable and expressive prosody with literalness of translation."

In its present form the faults named above have been largely eliminated. There are very few passages which one can call over-literal. The following lines, which represent one of the most literal portions in this version, do not prove objectionable. Line 6 of the Dedication, "Wie ihr aus Dunst und Nebel um mich steigt," is translated by Andrews, "When ye from mist and vapor round me rise." Lines 5 and 6 from the Prologue in Heaven:

> Ihr Anblick giebt den Engeln Stärke,
> Wenn keiner sie ergründen mag,

read in Andrews' version:

> Its aspect gives the angels power,
> Though none can fathom e'er its ways.

There are numerous passages that have been translated rather freely and some quite erroneously. An example of this may be found in the Dedication. The lines:

> Es schwebet nun in unbestimmten Tönen
> Mein lispelnd Lied, der Äolsharfe gleich;

Andrews renders:

> My plaintive songs uncertain tones are turning
> To harps aeolian murmuring at will.

The metres in the Andrews' translation, as published in 1929, follow the original closely, and in many instances more faithfully than Bayard Taylor's. Let us take for an example a part of Valentine's first speech. Where the German reads:

> Und nun!—ums Haar sich auszuraufen
> Und an den Wänden hinauf zu laufen!—

> Mit stichelreden, Naserümpfen
> Soll jeder Schurke mich beschimpfen!
> Soll wie ein böser Schuldner sitzen,
> Bei jedem Zufallswörtchen schwitzen!
> Und möcht ich sie zusammenschmeissen,
> Könnt ich sie doch nicht Lügner heissen.

Andrews translates:

> And now!—I could tear out my hair
> And try to run up a wall!
> With stinging speeches, nose in air,
> Now any scamp may at me swear!
> Like some bad debtor I'm to sit,
> And at each casual word I'll sweat!
> I'd like to smash their heads together
> Yet could not call them liars either.

Taylor starts off with a ragged halting metre which becomes smoother later on:

> And now, I could tear my hair with vexation,
> And dash out my brains in desperation!
> With turned up nose each scamp may face me,
> With sneers and stinging taunts disgrace me,
> And, like a bankrupt debtor sitting,
> A chance-dropped word may set me sweating!
> Yet though I thresh them all together,
> I cannot call them liars either.

If the verse of the Andrews translation compares favorably as a whole with Taylor's and often even exceeds it in smoothness, Taylor is more faithful in the reproduction of the feminine endings. In the last passage quoted above, Taylor has followed Goethe in every line, whereas Andrews has done so only in the last two. This may be explained, at least as far as Andrews himself is concerned, by what he says in his essay "On the Translation of Faust" referred to above: "In the recitative portions of the First Part of *Faust*, the principal aim is simplicity, the directness of colloquial speech; the rhyme is of secondary importance, and used, or even at times omitted with entire freedom." Nevertheless, taking all the longer sustained and conversational passages of this translation into consideration, the number of feminine rimes in proportion is greater than in the lines quoted above. In the lyric passages this version follows the original very closely in this respect.

To compare Andrews' translation still further with Taylor's it may be said that the language of the former is simpler and more direct and hence closer to Goethe's than that of Taylor. Inversions are avoided with great care. Andrews' translation also reproduces the varying moods of the original with greater success. The style used is appropriate for the character speaking, and Mephistopheles, Faust, the citizens, the students, Gretchen, and Martha all speak naturally. Goethe has the student say in Before the City Gate:

> Blitz, wie die wackern Dirnen schreiten!
> Herr Bruder komm! Wir müssen sie begleiten.
> Ein starkes Bier, ein beizender Toback,
> Und eine Magd im Putz, das ist nun mein Geschmack.

Andrews' translation of this passage, although somewhat inaccurate, strikes the right note:

> By thunder! how the whacking wenches stride!
> We must go with them, brother, come along.
> Strong beer, tobacco with a bite, and, on the side,
> A servant-maid decked out, for these I long.

Taylor's version of this passage is even looser than Andrews', and does not succeed so well in reproducing the student slang:

> Deuce! how they step, the buxom wenches!
> Come Brother! we must see them to the benches.
> A strong, old beer, a pipe that stings and bites,
> A girl in Sunday clothes,—these three are my delight.

Alice Raphael's version of this passage is superior to those of Andrews and Taylor in that it combines greater verbal accuracy with characteristic student language:

> Hell! how those husky creatures step along!
> Here, boy, lets join them! Come, make haste!

Biting tobacco, some beer good and strong,
And a servant-girl dressed up, h'm that's my taste.

Perhaps the finest passage in Andrews' translation is Gretchen's prayer to the Mater Dolorosa. The first two stanzas read:

> Thou, ever grieving,
> Bend down, relieving
> With face benign my agony
>
> The sword is tearing
> Thy heart; Thou, bearing
> A thousand pangs, Thy dying Son dost see.

Here we have felicitous, yet simple, poetic language combined with unusual harmony of metre and rime. The feminine endings of the original, which have all been reproduced, add much to the beautiful cadences of the lines.

As a whole this translation, as it now appears, must be considered an improvement over most of the previous attempts. One would like to see still greater accuracy, but the style and the spirit of the translation are faithful to the German. Georg Witkowski remarks in *Die Literatur*:[81] "What the two editors have added of their own, we do not know; but as the work appears in the fine print of the Princeton University Press, in regard to its language and its metre, it is, among all the English translations of *Faust*, the closest to the German. In this respect it is also superior to the widely known version of Bayard Taylor."*

---

* I have translated this passage from the German.

VII

The Manse and Faust

Faust:
Do not misunderstand me, blessed one!
Who dares to name Him?
Who can acclaim Him,
Saying, "Yes, I believe in Him"?
Experiencing Him everywhere,
Who would dare
To say, "I do not believe in Him"?
The All-enfolding,
The All-sustaining,
Does He not enfold and uphold
You—me—Himself?
Does not the earth lie firm beneath?
Do not the heavens arch above?
Do not eternal stars ascend,
Nodding with friendly light and love?
. . . .
Then call it what you will!
Call it Happiness! Heart! Love! God!
I have no name for it!
Feeling is all!
The name is only sound and smoke
Which fogs the glow of Heaven.[1]

MANY OF THE most eminent servants of the Church, steeped in its sacred writings, have, at the same time, manifested a keen interest in the masterpieces of world literature. Of course, there is nothing incongruous in this, for literature, whether sacred or secular, is primarily concerned with God, with man, and his behavior. Hence, a knowledge of secular literature leads to a clearer understanding of sacred literature. Little wonder, then, that Goethe's *Faust*, one of the great international classics, was eagerly read, carefully studied, and even laboriously translated in the Manse. For a more interesting and a more representatively human figure—admirable in his ideal striving but deeply repugnant in his baser designs—than the hero of *Faust* can hardly be found elsewhere. Five British churchmen, Warburton Davies, Leopold J. Bernays, Archer Thompson Gurney, Charles Keegan Paul, William Dalton Scoones, and one American, Charles Timothy Brooks, have made English versions of *Faust*. To the credit of the majority of them, it may be said that their translations are not without considerable merit.

WARBURTON DAVIES
(1790-1870)
TRANSLATION OF *Faust I* FIRST PRINTED IN 1834

All *Faust* bibliographers since William Heinemann, whose catalogue *A Bibliographical List of the English Translations and Annotated Editions of Goethe's Faust* appeared in 1882, have listed in their works an anonymous English version published in London in 1834 by Simpkin and Marshall.[2] The following story of how the veil of anonymity was lifted from this translation is probably one of the most interesting yet recorded in the annals of bibliographical science.

To begin with, it must be recalled that the German-American *Faust* translator, Frank Claudy, acquired for his private collection of English *Faust* translations a copy of the volume in question, bearing what purported to be the translator's name.* On the front end-paper cover of this volume, there is to be found a book plate with the name T. W. Downes, Esq., and the second fly-leaf bears the inscription in pen and ink: "To the Rev. James Johnson, from his old and much attached Friend, the Translator." Then follows in not too legible a handwriting,

---

* This volume was a part of the Library of the Supreme Council of the Scottish Rite of Freemasonry, Washington, D. C., where the Claudy Collection of Goetheana is housed. In 1935 the Curator of the Speck Collection prevailed upon the Supreme Council to transfer this interesting item to the Yale Library.

probably that of the translator himself, a signature which for some years was considered by Professor Schreiber and myself to read "By Barburton Devies." At the bottom of the title-page are given the place of publication, the name of the publishing firm, and the date: "London: Published by Simpkin and Marshall, Stationer's Hall Court. MDCCCXXXIV."

Corroborating evidence to the effect that "Barbuton Devies" was the name of the translator seemed to come from another quarter, namely, from the library of the late Professor Priebsch of the University of London where a second copy of this 1834 translation was found, apparently bearing the same signature.[3] However, Professor Schreiber, feeling that the name Barbuton Devies, and especially the given name "Barbuton," was a very unusual one, and that we could, therefore, still be in error, subjected the signature to further close study. It was this persistent and shrewd follow-up by Professor Schreiber which brought the definitive answer to our puzzling question as to the real identity of the translator.

In all justice to Professor Schreiber we will let him inform us how he metamorphosed one airy Barbuton Devies into a real flesh-and-blood Warburton Davies. I quote from his letter to me dated January 9, 1948: "I have just settled the matter of the anonymous 1834 edition of the *Faust*. Some weeks ago I sent a photostat copy of the title page to Closs at Bristol University. He married Priebsch's daughter. Through all the Bristol bombings, he tells me, the library of his father-in-law came through unscathed. He has compared our inscribed title-page with one in his possession. You will remember that we read the name as Barbuton Devies. By subjecting our title-page to careful scrutiny through a magnifying glass, I came to the conclusion that the B is really a W, and that the r is omitted. Closs now assures me that the omission of the r was a *Flüchtigkeitsfehler* and that the name of the translator is Warburton Davies."

However, Professor Schreiber went still further in his quest for certainty as to the identity of the translator. In a more recent letter dated January 17, 1948, he informs me that,

> # FAUSTUS,
>
> ## 𝔄 𝔗𝔯𝔞𝔤𝔢𝔡𝔶.
>
> TRANSLATED FROM THE GERMAN OF GOETHE.
>
> *by*
> *Warburton Davies*.
>
> LONDON:
> PUBLISHED BY SIMPKIN AND MARSHALL,
> STATIONERS' HALL COURT.
>
> MDCCCXXXIV.

Reproduction of the title-page to a copy of the translation of *Faust*, Part I, by Warburton Davies

although Davies still remains a shadowy figure, "he does have some body now," and then Professor Schreiber submits convincing documentary evidence as to the historicity of Warburton Davies.* First of all, in Burke's *Landed Gentry* under "Davies of Elmley" is to be found the following entry: "Son of Thomas Henry Davies of New House, County Hereford, Advocate-General, Calcutta (1751-1792). Married Anna Baillie Davies.

---

* Miss Barbara Simison of the Yale Library Reference Department was most helpful in bringing Davies back from the shadows.

Children 1) Thomas Henry Hastings; 2) *Warburton of Woodgate, Sussex, born 29 January 1790; married 29 December 1821 Sophia Anne, daughter of Sir James Bland Burges of Beauport and died 23 Sept., 1870. Son James Henry 1822-1866.*"[4] In the second place, in Joseph Foster's *Alumni Oxoniensis* a notation on Warburton Davies runs as follows: "St. John's College matriculated 26 November 1808 aged 18: Worcester College, B.A. 1812."[5] Finally, to check the name, if possible, also from any existing records of Davies' wife's family, Professor Schreiber consulted a volume entitled *Selections from the Letters and Correspondence of Sir James Bland Burges*[6] and found the following notation: "*Sophia Anne married in 1821 Rev. Warburton Davies, died without issue in 1858.*"

Now that we have been able to establish that Warburton Davies is the translator of the English version of *Faust* published by Simpkin and Marshall, London, 1834, let us briefly recapitulate here the available facts relative to his life and literary activity. Born in 1790 in Hereford County, England, the son of Thomas Henry Davies and Anna Baillie Davies, a family which enjoyed the distinction of belonging to the English landed aristocracy, the translator was matriculated at St. Johns College, Oxford, at the age of eighteen and was awarded the degree of B.A. by Worcester College, Oxford, four years later (1812).

Another interesting point to be gleaned from the records cited above is that Davies held the title of "Rev." and was, therefore, a clergyman. As such he became the first of a group of six to translate Goethe's *Faust* into English. Moreover, his ministerial character ties in naturally with the inscription on the second fly-leaf of the translation, namely, "To the Rev. James Johnson, from his old and much attached Friend, the Translator." It was, then, a case of a gentleman of the cloth remembering his fellow clergyman and life-long friend with his *magnum opus* as a convincing proof of the genuineness of their friendship.

Beyond this we cannot go at present as far as the life and work of Warburton Davies are concerned, and, therefore, we shall turn to his translation of *Faust* which appeared in 1834 and for which he will perhaps be remembered the longest.

Davies remarks in his Preface that it had long been a subject of astonishment and regret to him that the English people possessed "no complete version of a work of such acknowledged excellence as Goethe's *Faust*." "It is true," he continues, "the English reader had been made acquainted with very considerable portions of it, but still he had never been able to enjoy it as a whole. In attempting to procure him this gratification," he says, "I was well aware I exposed myself to the charge, that *Faustus* had been published above forty years when I commenced this translation."*[7]

The translator says further that he had completed the first draft of his version and was in the act of revising it when Hayward's prose version appeared. This discouraged him so much that his first impulse was to throw his work aside, as no longer necessary. He remarks: "I was only deterred from so doing by the reflection that a prose translation of a poem, however well executed, can scarcely quite satisfy the great mass of readers, whose chief object is amusement. I, therefore, determined to proceed; and it is with pleasure I embrace this opportunity of acknowledging the obligations I am under to Mr. Hayward's valuable work. It afforded me the greatest assistance in passages of doubt and obscurity, and from the notes I derived much important information."[8]

Davies says that his aim has been to make "as faithful and literal a transcript of the original, as the nature of the metre and difference of idiom would allow.... The original is written in a variety of metres; but I have confined myself to blank verse, except in the lyrical parts, as better adapted, in my opinion, than any other measure, to convey a true conception of the author."[9]

Moreover, Davies, like Francis Leveson-Gower before him, especially since he was a clergyman, is still prejudiced against the Prologue in Heaven because of the "tone of levity with

---

* Is Davies referring here to the Faust fragment published by Goethe in 1790? *Faust*, Part I, as we know, did not apear until 1808.

which it treats matters of the most sacred nature," and, therefore, he feels that it "must be repugnant to English feelings."[10] He also omits the Prologue on the Stage and the Intermezzo because they seem to have "no necessary connection with the piece" and possess, he believes, no particular interest for the reader.[11]

Although Davies, like Arthur Taylor and James Adey Birds some time later, was unable to give an adequate idea of the metrical variety and charm of the original by employing blank verse in the translation of the larger parts of the drama, still many of his lines have a smooth flowing quality, and his diction is simple and pleasing. But the use of blank verse, with the same number of metrical feet to each line, forced the translator to decrease or increase slightly the number of verses for the various parts. For the same reason also, he has expanded and at times condensed the thought of the original. A passage from the scene Before the Town Gate will give an idea of Davies' ability as a writer of blank verse. As he walks along with Wagner, Faust, lost in contemplation, says:

> Du bist dir nur des einen Triebs bewusst;
> O lerne nie den andern kennen!
> Zwei Seelen wohnen, ach! in meiner Brust,
> Die eine will sich von der andern trennen:
> Die eine hält in derber Liebeslust
> Sich an die Welt mit klammernden Organen;
> Die andre hebt gewaltsam sich vom Dust
> An den Gefilden hoher Ahnen.
> O, giebt es Geister in der Luft,
> Die zwischen Erd' und Himmel herrschend weben,
> So steiget nieder aus dem goldnen Duft
> Und führt mich weg zu neuem bunten Leben!

In Davies' translation these lines read:

> As yet one impulse only dost thou know,
> Oh, never form acquaintance with the other.
> Two souls, alas, dwell in my bosom; one
> Would from the other separate itself.
> The one, with stubborn fondness for the world,

Clings to it with fixed organs; while aloft,
Spurning this misty state, the other soars
To regions where our great forefathers dwell.
Oh! if there be now hovering in the air
Spirits which empire hold 'twixt earth and heaven,
Swift from your golden atmosphere descend,
And bear me hence to new and varied life.

Davies has more difficulty in reproducing the short lyric lines in such parts as the songs at the end of Night I. He alters the metre, expands the thought, and practically makes new poems of them. His translations of the ballad König in Thule and of Gretchen's Prayer in the Zwinger scene, while approximating the form and the spirit of the originals, still leave much to be desired as far as fidelity to the originals is concerned. Davies evidently found it much easier to compose in long lines than in short ones. His translation as a whole, however, compares favorably with the metrical versions up to 1835.

LEOPOLD J. BERNAYS
(1820-1882)
Translation of *Faust II* First Printed in 1839

Leopold J. Bernays, born in London, December 28, 1820, translated *Faust* at an astonishingly youthful age. He was educated at the Merchant Taylor's School and St. John's College, Oxford. At the latter institution he was a Fellow, received from it the B.A. degree in 1843 and the M.A. in 1846. After having been Headmaster of Elstow School in Essex from 1847-1860, Bernays entered the ministry and died as the Rector of Great Stanmore, Middlesex, 1882. Besides the translation of *Faust*, Part II, and *Other Poems*, he published a *Manual of Family Prayers and Meditations*, and *The Church in the Schoolroom*.[12]

Dr. Adolph Bernays, father of the translator, in a letter written to Johann Peter Eckermann, Goethe's private secretary, November 28, 1839, gives us some valuable information as to the date and the conditions under which his son translated

Faust.[13] He says: "To you, as a friend of the immortalized Goethe under whose eyes the greatest work of the greatest poet came to its completion, I take the pleasure of sending a copy of the translation of the second part of *Faust* by my oldest son. It appeared, as you probably know, at first in the *Monthly Magazine*, and for its coming into being, it is indebted alone to the encouragement [offered] by J. A. Heraud, the present editor of that periodical, who is a friend of our family, and to the willingness of a young man, at the time seventeen years of age, a scholar in the upper class of the local Merchant Taylor's High School, to take upon himself, besides his arduous studies, this gigantic task."*

There were two specific reasons why Bernays should translate *Faust*. In the first place, he was urged on by the belief that he was the first one to attempt an English version of Part II. This is clear from several sentences in the above letter to Eckermann, in which Bernays' father writes: "Moreover, while we have eight or nine of the *First Part*, his translation is the first of the *Second Part* which has ever appeared in English; a second, however, which has just been announced by Mr. Birch, if judged by the translation of the *First Part* by this man, is of little consequence." Of course, we know now that two earlier translations had already been published, those of William Bell Macdonald and Arthur Taylor, both in London in 1838.

The second reason for the publication of this translation was to give the English readers an opportunity to become fully acquainted with the merits and demerits of the much decried Second Part. Heraud, editor of the *Monthly Magazine*, who, contrary to the great mass of public opinion, thought highly of the Second Part, puts it in these words: "That these points may be settled to the satisfaction of the English readers, we have caused a prose, literal version of it to be made . . . on which as a faithful translation, implicit confidence may be placed."[14]

Bernays himself felt that he was amply prepared to undertake this task. He dedicated the volume to the Reverend J. W.

---

* For the sake of convenience I have translated the larger part of this letter from the German.

Bellamy, Headmaster of Merchant Taylor's School, "as a poor memorial but a grateful acknowledgment of the excellent instruction, perservering attention and unvarying kindness which produced and fostered the taste for literature of which the following translations and poetical essays are a result."[15] His words in the Preface to the translation ring with the sureness and confidence of youth: "Indeed, had I not thought that I possessed in some measure, the power of executing that which I had undertaken, it would have been in the highest degree presumptuous, I had almost said criminal in me, to have undertaken it at all."[16] Heraud, himself, feels that Bernays is "a translator whose happy position precludes the possibility of erroneous interpretations."[17]

For an explanation of the peculiar nature of the translation, namely, that it is done partly in prose and partly in verse, we turn once more to the Preface and to Adolph Bernays' letter to Eckermann. In the former the translator explains that he has done all those parts in prose where the accuracy of the translation would be imperiled by rendering in verse. He has thought it right to sacrifice the seductive attractions of rime and smoothness of language to the higher duty of presenting a faithful mirror, as far as may be done, of the ideas of the original.[18] A slightly different explanation for the varied form of the version is given in the above-mentioned letter, in which the father writes to Goethe's former secretary: "Probably you will object to the form of the translation. The story concerning it is essentially this: Mr. Heraud thought that a prose translation would cost my son less time and effort than a metrical one, and that at the most he should render the lyrical parts in the metre of the original, but without rime; a plan in which Hayward's translation of the *First Part* was kept in mind, and which in addition had this advantage that thus much space was saved. The youth, however, slowly became so tired of breaking up the glorious metrical structure into ordinary, even if melodious prose, that he preserved more and more the poetic form, with the result that the last two acts no longer contain any prose."

Upon its publication, Bernays' version was highly praised.

The *Literary Gazette* says of it: "Mr. Bernays, an idolater of the poet, has rendered his extraordinary production partly into prose and partly into the original metres: in both he has displayed a knowledge of his principle, and a command of the two languages."[19] The *Foreign Quarterly Review* states that Bernays' "thorough acquaintance with both languages has enabled him to do for the Second Part of *Faust*, at once and once for all, what the First Part wanted long in vain, a correct prose version."[20]

This high praise is only justified, however, when we limit the comparison of Bernays' translation to those of his contemporaries and to Anster's version. He renders the thought of the original with fully as much literal exactness as Arthur Taylor and with greater veracity than Macdonald, Birch, Gurney, or Anster. The following excerpts, arranged in the order of the publication of the translations, show the relative merits of these versions in this respect. The last eight lines of the drama:

> Alles Vergängliche
> Ist nur ein Gleichnis;
> Das Unzulängliche,
> Hier wird's Ereignis;
> Das Unbeschreibliche,
> Hier ist's gethan;
> Das Ewig-Weibliche
> Zieht uns hinan.

are made to read in the various translations as follows: William Bell Macdonald (1838):

> All is of this earth's sphere
> Seeming alone;
> The insufficient here
> Being has grown.
> The indescribable,
> Here is it done;
> The Virgin Eternal
> Leadeth us on.

Arthur Taylor (1838):

> What passeth away
> Is but similitude;
> Abortive essay,
> Here, as Event, is viewed;
> Here mysteries shine
> In achievement's clear guise;
> The Ever-Feminine
> Wills that we rise.

Leopold Bernays (1839):

> All that doth pass away
> Is but a symbol;
> The insufficient here
> Grows to existence;
> The indescribable
> Here is it done;
> The ever feminine
> Draweth us on.

Jonathan Birch (1840):

> All that passeth away
> Is but typical display:
> The insufficient
> Is here—adequate;
> The indescribable
> Is here done;
> The Ever-Feminine
> Draweth us on.

Archer Thompson Gurney (1842):

> All earthly Joy and Woe
> Like visions vanish;
> Here heavenly starbeams glow
> No shades can banish;
> The nameless goal divine
> Here is it won.
> The Ever-Feminine
> Draweth us on.

John Anster (1864):

> Here what thought could never reach to
> Is by semblance made known;
> What man's words may never utter,
> Done in act—in symbol shown.
> Love, whose perfect type is Woman,
> The divine and human blending,
> Love for ever and for ever
> Wins us onward, still ascending.

The prose portions of Bernays' translation often render the thought of the original more exactly than the parts in verse, but, taken as a whole, there is not much that we admire in it today. The frequent change in form is disturbing; the prose is bald, and the verse lacks the vitality, the beauty, and the music of the original. Still, considering the youthfulness of the translator, the work is an unusual performance.* That he ranked high as a German scholar in the estimation of his contemporaries, is indicated by the fact that the list of subscribers to the original edition includes such names as Sir Walter Scott, Robert Southey, William Wordsworth, Henry Hallam, H. C. Robinson, and two of the later translators of Part II, Jonathan Birch and John Anster.†

ARCHER THOMPSON GURNEY
(1820-1887)
Translation of *Faust II* First Printed in 1842

Archer Thompson Gurney, who was the third clergyman in this group and the fourth translator to make an English version of the Second Part of *Faust*, was born at Tregony in Cornwall, July 15, 1820. He enrolled in 1842 as student of the Middle Temple to prepare for the career of a barrister, and was called

---

* Bernays' father denies specifically that he helped his son in the translation: "All I did was that I went through the work with him and assured myself that he understood it at least as well as I. All the rest is his own."

† Bernays, besides writing a number of original poems, also translated some poems by Uhland, Schiller, Immermann, Hebbel, and Goethe. His translation of "Mignon" is perhaps the best of these.

to the bar in 1846.[21] However, he altered his views within the next few years, and in 1849 he exchanged the legal profession for the ministry. The most famous of his long list of charges include the English Court Chapel at Paris from 1858-1871, and the lectureship at Trinity Church, Westminster, after his return to London.[22] He died at Bath, England, in his sixty-seventh year.[23]

Besides being a famous preacher of the Church of England, Gurney gained some note as author and translator. The British Museum Catalogue, 1888, mentions sixteen titles, whereas the *Bibliotheca Cornubiensis*[24] lists twenty. Among these works are translations and original poems of an historical, sacred, and secular nature, theological writings in prose, etc. To the last class belongs his most popular book, *Words of Faith and Cheer*, published in 1874.

Works that show Gurney's interest in German literature and life are: *Turnadot, Princess of China*, a Drama from the German of Schiller with Alterations, 1836; translation of *Faust*, Part II, 1842; "The German Mind," published in the *English Review*, 1848;[25] *Go not to the Rhine*, Rhine warning song by Howard Glover, the English version by A. Gurney, 1861; and *Parables and Meditations for Sundays and Holy Days*, translated from the German, 1874.

We are unable to say just when Gurney's interest in German literature, and, especially, in Goethe and *Faust*, began. Since it is known that the translator's father died in Bonn, Germany, 1843, we might be tempted to assume that the Gurney family, like so many other Englishmen, resided in Germany for some time, and that Archer Gurney, the translator, born in 1820, had thus gained a firsthand knowledge of the German language. On the other hand, since Gurney's father was an educated man and author himself and had traveled in Germany, it is not at all impossible that the son acquired his knowledge of the German language under his father's tutorship. However the case may be, the fact that Gurney had translated and redacted the drama called *Turnadot, Princess of China*, from the German of Schiller, early in 1836, at the age of sixteen, and completed his translation of *Faust*, Part II, in 1842, when he was twenty-two, presupposes diligent study of German at an early age.

Among the *Faust* translators, Gurney is one of the first to understand the importance of the Second Part and to approach it with an unbiased mind. Having made clear the general character of both parts, he lays special stress in his Preface upon the fact that Part II is absolutely essential for a satisfactory understanding of Part I. "The first Part," he says, "concludes, leaving us in the greatest doubt and uncertainty as to whether the will of Faust will ever be reconciled with that of Heaven, and the erring sinner seek and find salvation. The second part solves our doubts, and shows by what means this great result was obtained—namely by true benevolence and love."[26]

Gurney's theory of translation is interesting because it approaches a compromise between the ideas so far held that a translator must slight either the thought or the form of the original. He remarks about his translation in his Notes: "It is not always literal, but I have ever striven to produce an effect in English that should correspond with that produced in German by the author. I considered it particularly necessary, as far as in me lay, to employ the same fill of words, the same melodious harmony, which I found in the original. Unless this is done, it is altogether impossible to produce a corresponding effect: if a mere verbal translation be sought for, it should be made in prose."[27]

An examination of Gurney's translation shows that he has been successful in imitating the rhythmical effects of the original. His verse is smooth and flowing, with a pleasing variation of vowel sounds. The opening lines of Act V, Scene I:

> Ja sie sind's, die dunkeln Linden
> Dort in ihres Alters Kraft,
> Und ich soll sie wiederfinden
> Nach so langer Wanderschaft!
> Ist es doch die alte Stelle,
> Jene Hütte die mich barg,
> Als die sturmerregte Welle
> Mich an jene Dünen warf!

The Manse and Faust

Gurney translates:

> Yes, 'tis they, those lime trees, smiling,
> Still in green old age they stand,
> Here once more my heart beguiling,
> As when first their forms I scanned.
> Still the ancient spot doth greet me,
> That old hut, which saved my life.
> Where the billows bore me fleetly,
> On that night on ocean strife!—

However, in many instances, Gurney's version is marked by grave errors in translation which reveal a definite lack of understanding for the German text and, perhaps, the inability to translate it. Act I, lines 4679-4682:

> Des Lebens Pulse schlagen frisch lebendig,
> Äther'sche Dämmrung milde zu begrüssen,
> Du, Erde, warst auch diese Nacht beständig,
> Und atmest neu erquickt zu meinen Füssen.

he renders:

> Life's pulse all freshly beats yet once again
> The incense of the morning breeze to greet;
> Thou earth, like me, tonight hast softly lain,
> A mother slumb'ring at her offspring's feet.

It is evident from the following passage, and an examination of the translation will reveal many passages like it, that his equally young predecessor Leopold Bernays is a more exact German scholar than Gurney. Lines 5201-5207 from Act I:

> Nur Platz! nur Blösse!
> Wir brauchen Räume,
> Wir fällen Bäume,
> Die krachend schlagen;
> Und wenn wir tragen,
> Da giebt es Stösse.

Gurney translates:

> Room!—void disasters!
> Hence with your clatter!

> Forests we shatter,
> Which crash like thunder
> Over and under.

Bernays' version reads:

> Room! room! make room here!
> Room! room! we want here.
> We fell the tall trees
> Which crashing fall down,
> And when we bear them
> Roughly we jostle.

Thus we see that while Gurney has succeeded fairly well in reproducing the metre, the varying rhythmical effects of the original, he did not possess a sufficient knowledge of German to make an accurate translation.

CHARLES TIMOTHY BROOKS
(1813-1883)

Translation of *Faust I* First Printed in 1856

> Dear Poet Soul! whose gentle, tuneful lyre
> Has soothed with music many another's woe;
> How shall we sing of thee, now, sweet and low,
> Thou hear'st thy welcome from the perfect choir?
> How shall we sing of thee? our loves aspire
> To voice thy worth, that all the world may know;
> The full heart falters; ah! no more!—but so—
>
> Half Lamb, half Cowper! All thy pure heart's strings
> Trembled in music with the breath of heaven;
> And like a quiet brook that laughs and sings,
> Thy glad life glided from clear pools above
> And in those mirrored deeps bright stars of even
> Smiled a still benison of peace and love.*

The American pioneer in the art of translating *Faust* was Charles Timothy Brooks. His birth in 1813 and childhood

---

* A poem, appearing on a fly-leaf to Brooks's *Poems, Original and Translated*, which William Page Andrews, who later also translated *Faust*, wrote and dedicated to Brooks.

at Salem, Massachusetts, his student life at Harvard, several trips to the South, a more distant one to Europe and Germany, another to India, his pastorate of nearly two score years at the Newport, Rhode Island, Unitarian Church, and his death there in 1883—these are the salient events of his outward life. The inscription on the bronze tablet affixed to the Brooks Memorial in the Channing Memorial Church, Newport, Rhode Island, summarizes the spiritual qualities of the man: "A persuasive preacher, and eminent as a scholar and poet, he was still more distinguished for the simplicity and purity of his character, his child-like faith in God, and never-failing charity towards his fellowman."[28]

Brooks's main interest was always in language and literature. Even in the preparatory school before entering Harvard, he excelled in language study, and at Harvard (1828-1832) he laid special stress on the study of modern languages: French, Spanish, Portuguese, Italian, and German. The interest in the last tongue and its literature was called forth especially by his inspiring teachers of German, Dr. Karl Follen and Professor Charles Beck.[29] From his diary of August 17, 1831, we learn that his "geliebtes Deutsch" gave him more enjoyment than anything else. Jean Paul, whom he was reading industriously, he calls "der Einzige." In his senior year he took up the study of *Faust*, and he remained not unaffected by the death of its author, whom he referred to as a "universal genius."

After Brooks graduated from the Harvard Divinity School and had been installed as Unitarian minister at Newport, his interest in German literature continued. "A class for the study of German literature, which met under his direction, included many of the brightest young people of his parish and community, and was of great interest and value in their higher culture—He maintained a lively correspondence with certain of the friends already named, as well as with J. T. Fields, Dr. Beck, the Rev. William R. Alger, George Bancroft, Charles Eliot Norton, with Count von Auersperg (Anastasius Grün), Ferdinand Freiligrath, and other German and American men of literature."[30]

The records fail to give us the exact date when Brooks began his translation of *Faust*, but we know that in the latter half of his senior year at Harvard he became acquainted with this work, and since he tried his hand at translating from the German at an early date, he may have attempted portions of it soon after 1832. Shortly after 1838 his diary has the following entry: "Scribbled into doggerel a little of 'Faust,' in the midst of which I was called down; and there stood Theodore Parker, large as life, with spectacles and pouting look,— the genius of an antique book. How glad I was to grasp the hand of my quondam fellow student, hallmate, brother linguist, punster, German scholar, and general wag! I forgot the present at once, and lived over again the old hall hours. He's just left town,—went off in the carryall with his basket of books. He gave me a most tantalizing glimpse of Tieck."[31]

Charles W. Wendte, his biographer, records that in 1853 Brooks revised his first volume of translated poems and called it *German Lyrics*, and that he was hard at work, in the intervals of parish duty, on his version of Goethe's *Faust*, begun long before, and also on Richter's *Titan*. On account of a throat affection, he was compelled to suspend his pulpit duties for some time in 1854, and as a result of that "he gave himself to his German studies with especial zeal at this time, completing his versions of *Faust* and *Titan*, and beginning a rendering of Rückert's *Wisdom of the Brahmin*, besides translating many lesser poems from the language."[32] Two years afterward Brooks's complete translation of *Faust*, Part I, appeared. Unless the translator labored on this version while on his ten months' trip to India in 1854, the entire translation was made at Newport.

A comparison of the German work with the available translations seems to have convinced Brooks that no rendering of this "wonderful poem into the exact and everchanging metre of the original, has until now been so much as attempted. To name only one defect, the very best of versions, which he has seen, neglect to follow the exquisite artist in the evidently planned and orderly intermixing of male and female rhymes—

The Manse and Faust

A similar criticism might be made of their liberty in neglecting Goethe's method of alternating different measures with each other."[33] In a letter to Bayard Taylor in response to the latter's gift of his translation of Part II, Brooks says among other things that "after all, I am very weak in the Faustian literature, my work upon Part First having been a simple labor of poetic love."[34]

Here, then, we have Brooks's explanation of why he translated *Faust*, namely, to make, as a labor of love, a better translation than had been made up to that time. This is characteristic of the man's whole attitude toward German literature, and it explains all the rest of his translations, such as those from Rückert, Uhland, Freiligrath, and many others. To make the English-speaking world acquainted with the German men of letters and the products of their pen came to be the passion of his life. To Jean Paul, to Rückert, to Schiller, and to Goethe, he was drawn in a special way because the same freedom from the restraints of tradition, the same broad, forward-looking attitude on life, characterized them as well as himself.

We have seen how diligently Brooks pursued the study of German while in college. Almost at the same time "he tries his skill at translating German ballads, and attending for the first time a concert of German music, and is quite carried away with the new world of harmony it reveals to him. We soon find him scribbling poetry on every occasion and subject, and acquiring a dangerous facility in rime."[35] Before 1856, the year in which his translation of *Faust* was published, this facility had given rise to a large number of original poems in English* and many translations from the German. Among the latter group we have such titles as Friedrich Schiller's *William Tell*, 1837; *German Lyrics*, 1838; *German Lyric Poetry*, 1842; Friedrich Schiller's *Homage of the Arts*, 1846; and *German Lyrics*, 1853.† Therefore, it appears that Brooks was far from

---

* *Phi Beta Kappa Poem*, 1845; *Aquidneck, and Other Poems*, 1848.

† Brooks continued to translate all his life. In 1862 appeared Jean Paul Richter's *Titan*; Kortum's *The Jobsiad* (First Part), 1863; Leopold Schefer's *Breviary*, 1867; Berthold Auerbach's *Aloys*, and *Poet and Merchant*, 1877; Friedrich Rückert's *The Wisdom of the Brahmin* (Books I-VI), 1882; and

being a novice when he attempted to translate *Faust*.*

Soon after Brooks had finished his translation, one of the greatest American scholars of German literature, Henry Wadsworth Longfellow, wrote the translator concerning his version saying that it "gives the reader a better and more complete idea of it [*Faust* in the original] than any other translation."[36] This opinion is representative of that held by the majority of the contemporary scholars, who appreciated Brooks's serious attempt to follow the original in its rhythmical patterns. And, as a whole, it is safe to say that this version compares very favorably with Bayard Taylor's translation published in 1870.

To me it appears that Brooks translates the comic scenes, such as the Auerbach's Cellar episode, if with somewhat less fidelity to the meaning of the original than Taylor, still with more spirit and gusto. This was because of Brooks's natural endowment, his keen sense of the ludicrous, and his powers of lively repartee. Mephistopheles' Song of the Flea reads in Brooks's translation:

> There was a king, right stately,
> Who had a great big flea,
> And loved him very greatly,
> As if his own son were he.
> He called the knight of stitches;
> The tailor came straightway:
> Ho! measure the youngster for breeches,
> And make him a coat today!

Taylor puts it thus:

> There was a king once reigning,
> Who had a big black flea,
> And loved him past explaining,
> As his own son were he.

Jean Paul Richter's *Invisible Lodge*, 1883. This is only an incomplete list. His translations of lyric poems include such an array of names as Grün, Rückert, Kerner, Nathusius, Geibel, Platen, Lenau, Claudius, Uhland, Freiligrath, Wilhelm Müller, Langbein, Chamisso, Gellert, Seidl, and others.

* In addition to *Faust*, Part I, it appears that he only translated a few other short selections from Goethe, the opening scene of *Faust*, Part II, being the most important.

> He called his man of stitches;
> The tailor came straightway:
> Here, measure his coat, I say!

Taylor's metre is usually no improvement over that of Brooks, and he follows the latter's wording very closely in some instances. The rendering of the last two lines of the Dedication:

> Was ich besitze seh' ich wie im Weiten
> Und was verschwand wird mir zu Wirklichkeiten,

which Brooks translates:

> What I possess I see afar off lying,
> And what I lost is real and undying,

Taylor renders as:

> What I possess, I see far distant lying,
> And what I lost, grows real and undying.

In poetic power, however, in nobility of expression, and in beauty of phrase, Taylor's translation is often superior to that of Brooks. Brooks, for instance, renders Michael's part in the Song of the Archangels thus:

> And tempests roar, glad warfare waging,
> From sea to land, from land to sea,
> And bind round all, amidst their raging,
> A chain of giant energy.
> There, lurid, desolation blazing,
> Foreruns the volleyed thunder's way:
> Yet, Lord thy messengers are praising
> The mild procession of thy day.

Taylor translates this passage with somewhat more dignity and poetic beauty as:

> Rival storms abroad are surging
> From sea to land, from land to sea.
> A chain of deepest action forging
> Round all, in wrathful energy.
> There flames a desolation, blazing
> Before the thunder's crashing way!

Yet Lord, Thy messengers are praising
The gentle movement of Thy Day.

From a study of Brooks's translation, one gains the impression that it is uniformly of a high quality. Bayard Taylor recognized this in a concrete way by accepting Brooks's theory of translation and by following his predecessor's phraseology and diction very closely at times. In fact, the first American translation, published by Charles Timothy Brooks, is so superior to the first English version by Lord Leveson-Gower that the progress made during the intervening time toward an acceptable translation of *Faust* is truly remarkable.

Probably the hours of highest triumph for Brooks came on his trip to Germany in 1865, when the literati of Stuttgart gave a banquet in his honor. His biographer describes the event thus: "On the 27th of August occurred 'the memorable evening' in Mr. Brooks's literary career, when a company of authors and poets assembled to show their regard for the amiable and accomplished translator of *Faust* and *Titan*. Among those present were Dr. Gerok, the renowned preacher and poet; Jacob Corvinus; also a son of the poet Gustav Schwab; Dr. Edward Hoefer, a favorite poet; his friend Platinius, and others. He is introduced at the close of the social meal as one to whom Germany is much indebted, whereupon the whole company rise and drink his health with great enthusiasm."[37] For nearly a score more years after this, Charles T. Brooks was to continue his ministry of love to his people at home and his chosen work as translator and interpreter of German literature to the English-speaking world.

CHARLES KEGAN PAUL
(1828-1902)

Translation of *Faust I* First Printed in 1873

Charles Kegan Paul, churchman, proponent of the labor movement in England, publisher and translator of Goethe's *Faust*, was the son of Reverend Charles Paul, curate of White Lackington, near Ilminster, Somersetshire. Born there in 1828, he was first educated at the Ilminster grammar school, then at Eton, and in 1846 he matriculated at Exeter College, Oxford, from where he received the A.B. degree in 1849. At Exeter, Paul met Charles Kingsley, who brought him into association with F. D. Maurice, Tom Hughes, and other leaders of the Co-operative and Christian Socialist movements of the time.[38]

Upon his graduation Paul took Holy Orders, and, for the next two years, he served as curate of Great Tew, but having been ordained to the priesthood in 1852, he accepted a charge at Bloxham near Banburg. In the following year, however, Paul gave up this position to travel with some pupils in Germany. After his return to England in 1853, he was given a chaplaincy at Eton College and advanced to the place of Assistant Master the next year. In this capacity he served his Alma Mater until 1862, when he was presented with the vicarage of Sturminster in Dorsetshire.[39]

At this place, where Paul remained until 1874, he took great interest in the Agricultural Laborers' Movement of which Joseph Arch was the chief exponent. Paul thus became an iconoclast in that he was the only beneficed clergyman in Dorsetshire who gave the movement any support. He attended the workingmen's meetings, gave public addresses, and suffered ridicule and public abuse for their cause. Moreover, during his last years at Sturminster, Paul changed his views regarding the position and importance of the Church and religion as a whole. He drifted from Anglicanism to Unitarianism and Agnosticism, then to Positivism, and, finally, late in life, he embraced Roman Catholicism.[40]

In 1875 he came to London to take a position as "reader" to the firm of H. S. King, publishers, where soon he was made a partner in the business and relieved King of his responsibilities as head of the firm. When fire later destroyed a large portion of the publishing house, Paul associated himself with the Hansard Printing and Publishing Company. But since this venture also ended disastrously, he reduced the scope of the activities of the H. S. King Company and then finally retired from the position of manager. However, misfortune still dogged his steps, for not long afterward he was run over by an omnibus and as a result remained an invalid until his death in 1902.[41]

During his years of residence in London he was very active as a publisher and writer, being especially attracted to the young authors of the day, whose works he published in preference to those of better known writers. The British Museum Catalogue of 1893 lists sixteen works by Paul. Among them those of a religious and theological nature predominate; a few are biographical, and a few are translations. Works with some literary importance today are *Faust*, Part I, translated from the German of Goethe, 1873; *William Godwin: His Friends and Contemporaries*, 1876; *A Philological Introduction to Greek and Latin, for Students*, 1876, translated from the German of Ferdinand Bauer; a translation of *Thoughts of Blaise Pascal*, 1884; a volume of autobiography called *Memories*, 1892; and a small volume of original verse.

Very little can be gathered from available records as to when Paul first became interested in German literature and Goethe in particular. But the Dedication of his translation of *Faust* to the Reverend Charles Old Goodfield, Provost of Eton, informs us that it was the latter who "first and more than any other taught the translator to value Literature and to strive after mental culture." Paul was at Eton for nearly a decade before coming to Sturminster in 1862.

The translation of *Faust* was completed at the vicarage of Sturminster exactly ten years after Paul's arrival there. No doubt, the leisure time he had there did much also to widen his literary interests which now definitely came to include Goethe. He regarded his translation of *Faust* in the nature of an experiment. In the Preface he says: "The present translation of the First Part of *Faust* may seem to need a few words of preface. It is one more attempt to show that poems in languages so intimately related as German and English may be rendered very closely each into the sister tongue; that the form perhaps even more than the spirit may be in great measure preserved. Since my own translation was completed, I have read all other versions I could find and see that none of them follows precisely the same rules I have laid down for myself; it seems, therefore, still worth while to send forth my own experiment."[42]

Paul then goes on to state the rules he has tried to observe in his rendition of *Faust:* To follow the same order in the rimes as in the original; to translate each speech, paragraph, and song in the same number of lines as are found in the German; to attempt no slavish or exact reproduction of quantity or accent in the same metres; and to use double rimes but sparingly, since they occur only sparingly in good English poetry. However, he attempts to make, as far as the English language permits, a strictly literal version.

A translation made after this pattern should possess a high degree of verbal accuracy, higher indeed than is present in Paul's version. It is possible to read on for pages in this work without finding any grave errors, and then again passages will occur where there are many inaccuracies. The Dedication is particularly full of errors. Line 4: "Fühl ich mein Herz noch jenem Wahn geneigt?" he translates: "Feel my heart bent to each delusive show." He has left out the important word "noch," and translates "jenem" as if it were "jedem." In line 7, "youthful tremors" is hardly an acceptable way of rendering "jugendlich erschüttert." In line 9, "froher Tage" is translated as "happier time," "froher" being considered an adjective in the comparative degree. A number of instances of padding occur: line 12, "you," line 14, "prime," and in line 28, "as a hand." In line 22 "sad" is no equivalent for "bang." We see that Kegan Paul's knowledge of German and his skill as a translator are not equal to the task.

Similar inaccuracies are found in the scene Night I. The translator renders too loosely lines 690, 691:

> Ich grüsse dich, du einzige Phiole!
> Die ich mit Andacht nun herunterhole.

as:

> I greet thee, Phial, like no other there,
> And lift thee from thy shelf with care!

Paul has also failed to bring out sufficiently the distinctive character, the spirit, and the varying moods of different parts of the drama. We miss much of the elegiac note in the Dedication, the rollicking, carefree abandon in Auerbach's Cellar, as well as the deep undertone in the Zwinger Scene, while Valentine's fiery denunciation of Margaret becomes pale and enervated.

As a whole, Paul has reproduced the form of the original to a fuller degree than the spirit. It seems that the translator has worked at his task rather slavishly and without inspiration. He lacks also the thorough knowledge of German necessary to make an acceptable translation. This version is somewhat inferior to that of Sir Theodore Martin published a few years earlier, not so much because of verbal inaccuracies, of which Martin's also has a considerable number, but because it gives us still less of the spirit of Goethe's drama than Martin's version.

WILLIAM DALTON SCOONES
(1821-1891)
TRANSLATION OF *Faust I* FIRST PRINTED IN 1879

William Dalton Scoones was the oldest son of William Scoones, a prominent lawyer of Tonbridge (Tunbridge), Kent, England.[43] The father, himself an old Tonbridgian, duly registered the nine-year-old boy, born in 1821, at the town school, which he attended from 1830 to 1838. In October, 1838, young Scoones matriculated at Trinity College, Oxford. He studied at Lincoln's Inn in 1842, but returned to Oxford in time to receive his B.A. from Trinity College in 1843.[44]

Although, during his student days, Scoones is reported to have excelled rather in cricket and in swimming than in theology, he later took Holy Orders and became successively curate of Thurloxton, Somerset; Greenfield and Turckenham, Middlesex. In 1856 he was advanced to the position of vicar of Langley Marish, near Slough, Bucks, where he served in this capacity until his death in 1891. Further details about his life and literary activities are not available, except that he

The Manse and Faust 215

was the author of a metrical translation of *Faust* which was published in 1879 and of various other translations.[45]

Scoones's version of Faust, the last of those by a group of six clergymen, is of uneven quality. The metre is surprisingly accurate, and the rimes and even the feminine endings are reproduced with a good deal of skill. But there are unfortunate lapses in the rendering of the thought. In the following passage from Study II which Scoones has divided into two stanzas, he gives the sense of Goethe's lines but does not always translate accurately:

> Verlassen hab' ich Feld und Auen,
> Die eine tiefe Nacht bedeckt,
> Mit ahnungsvollem, heil'gem Grauen
> In uns die bessere Seele weckt.
> Entschlafen sind nun wilde Triebe
> Mit jedem ungestümen Thun;
> Es reget sich die Menschenliebe,
> Die Liebe Gottes regt sich nun.

> Now that o'er meadow, vale and plain
> The shades of night a mantle draw,
> My better soul awakes again
> To tender, deep, foreboding awe.

> Now hushed is every wild desire,
> With every rash unhallowed deed,
> The love of man now rises higher,
> The love of God is felt indeed.

The same desire to go his own way characterizes Scoones's rendering of the lyrics in Before the Gate, Gretchen's Prayer to the Virgin, and the lyrics in the Walpurgis Night's Dream. Scoones is at his best in the ballad König in Thule and the Song of the Spirits at the end of Study I.

The lines written in iambic pentameter in Wald und Höhle have been reproduced with a fair degree of accuracy. One of the best conversational passages is from the scene Martha's Garden in which Margaret catechizes Faust. In reply to her questions about his belief in God, Faust says:

> Angelic creature! Do not misconceive!
> Who dare give Him a name?
> And who proclaim,
> "Him I believe"?
> Who can so certain be,
> That boldly he
> Will say, "I disbelieve"?
> The All-Embracer,
> The All-Sustainer,
> Thee—me—Himself?

The language in this whole scene is simple and natural; here Scoones reproduces with a certain degree of success the spirit of the original.

Taken as a whole this translation contrasts rather strongly with that of Birds, whose version of Part I appeared in 1880. On the formal side, where Birds's version is weak, Scoones's is strong; but Birds's translation is characterized by greater verbal accuracy. It may be said, finally, that Scoones's version compares favorably with most of the translations in the particular group in which it appears here.

VIII

Soldiers and Faust

Soldiers (singing):
Castles with battlement,
Turret and tower,
Maidens with arrogant
Notions of power,
I would obtain!
Bold is the struggle,
Mighty the gain!
Let trumpets be sounding
As we go by,
Whether to pleasure,
Or whether to die.
O what a tempest!
O what a life!
Castles and women
Must yield in such strife.
Bold is the struggle,
Mighty the gain,
As all the soldiers
Go marching amain.[1]

THE AUTHOR of *Faust* has not forgotten the role of the soldier in his dramatic portrayal of life. In few places can one find a more lively and a more realistic interpretation of the traditional warrior's life than in the original German of the lines quoted above. In Valentine, the returned veteran, with his love of good fellowship, with his deep affection for his sister Margaret who for him is the embodiment of all womanly virtues, and with his self-effacing bravery, Goethe has apotheosized the martial spirit. Many pages in Part II, also, resound with the clash of arms and the echoing tread of soldiers' feet. There is, then, in *Faust*, with its abundance of adventure, with its pathos, and with its tragedy, that also which appeals to the man-at-arms. Two soldiers, Captain Charles Henry Knox and Geoffrey Montagu Cookson, have immortalized themselves more, perhaps, by their attempts to translate *Faust* than by the excellence of the service which they rendered to their country in their chosen profession.

CAPTAIN CHARLES HENRY KNOX
(-1855)
TRANSLATION OF *Faust I* FIRST PRINTED IN 1847

Lord Francis Leveson-Gower and Captain Charles Henry Knox are the only English translators of *Faust* who had a personal acquaintance with Goethe. With respect to Knox's early life we know nothing, but it appears that he was in Weimar in 1816. R. G. Alford, in an article entitled "Englishmen at Weimar," writes: "Through the kindness of Dr. Ruland of Weimar, I am enabled to give the names and all that is at present known with regard to the persons whose portraits were painted [for Goethe]. The sitters' names are in all cases recorded at the back of the portraits. In many cases, as will be seen, nothing is known beyond the mere name."[2] Following Gough's (Goff's)* name on this list we find "Knox—Englishman," with the annotation: "Was at Weimar 1816." This means, then, that Knox had already met Goethe at this time and that the latter had requested him to have his portrait sketched for Goethe's private gallery.†

Direct testimony as to Knox's acquaintance with Goethe

---

* William Goff (or Gough), born 1799, visited Weimar, 1825, where he was introduced to Goethe by Count Vandreuil, the French minister. He died at Weimar while on a visit there in 1849.—*Publications of the English Goethe Society*, V., 191. He translated the Dedication from *Faust* into English.—*Goethes Werke*, XIII, entries for Sept. 4 and Oct. 16, 1831.

† Henry Crabb Robinson, whose name is also included in this list, says: "I have already mentioned Goethe's fondness for keeping portrait memorials, and can only consider it as an extreme instance of this that I was desired to go to one Schmeller to have my portrait taken—a head in crayons, frightfully ugly, and very like. The artist told me that he had within a few years done for Goethe more than three hundred. It is the kind of *Andenken* he preferred. They are all done in the same style—full faced."—*Diary, Reminiscences and Correspondence of Henry Crabb Robinson* (ed. Sadler), II, 110.

comes from Knox himself. In the Preface to the 1847 edition of his translation of *Faust*, he writes. "I also admit some personal motives of my own [for translating *Faust*], namely that many years ago, during a residence at Weimar, it was my good fortune that some effusions of mine, printed for private circulation in an ephemeral publication called *Chaos*,* attracted the notice of Goethe, who did me the honor of having my portrait taken for his private collection."[3] Further evidence of Knox's personal contact with Goethe is to be found in Goethe's *Tagebücher*. For February 13, 1827, we find this notation: "Mr. and Mrs. Count Marschall and Miss Mellish. After that the Englishmen Knox and Richardson." Somewhat over a year later, March 27, 1828, Goethe made the following entry: "Ten o'clock in the morning young Sartorious and Eckermann. Mr. Knox, to say farewell."[4]

There seems to be a conflict in our sources in regard to the time when Knox first met Goethe and when he had his portrait made. Dr. Ruland furnished Alford the information that Knox's portrait was completed in 1816. The earliest reference to Knox, however, in Goethe's *Tagebücher* is February 13, 1827. Moreover, as we have already noted, Knox himself says, in the Preface to his translation (1847), that an article published by him in *Chaos*, which was not started until 1829, attracted Goethe's attention to him. As a result, a friendship sprang up between the two which led to Goethe's request for Knox's portrait. On the other hand, as we learned above, Knox visited with Goethe as early as February, 1827. Whatever the real facts are, it must be assumed that Knox was a frequent visitor at Weimar, or, better, that he lived there for a number of years.

From a different source we learn of another side of Knox's life—his connection with the English army. In December, 1826, he held the position of an ensign in the "95 foot"; in 1829 he became "lieut. 85 foot"; in 1836 he was made a "cap-

* This periodical was started by Ottilie von Goethe. It served as a mirror to reflect the intellectual and social life of Weimar and of the Goethe circle in particular. The Speck Collection possesses Sorets' incomplete file of this publication.

tain 94 foot"; and in 1853 he became "lieut. Col. Royal Glamorgan militia."⁵ This rank he held until his death in 1855. From the above, then, it becomes clear why he should first sign himself Captain and later Colonel Knox.

According to the British Museum Catalogue of 1890, Knox was an industrious writer. Besides the translation of *Faust*, it lists twelve other titles, most of them of works of a narrative and historical character. Some of these are: *Traditions of Western Germany*, three volumes, 1841; *Hardness: or the Uncle*, three volumes, 1841; *Softness: A Novel by the Author of Hardness*, three volumes, 1842; *Rittmeister's Budget*, three volumes, 1842; *The Old River: or a Chronicle of the Rhine*, 1842; *Daydreams, Poems*, 1843; and *Harry Mowbray, a Tale*, 1843.

The translator's knowledge of German and his interest in *Faust* may be assumed to date back to his years at Weimar when he was in personal contact with Goethe and a member of Weimar society circles, but we have no information as to when he began to translate the drama. The first edition of Part I of which we have definite knowledge was completed and published at London, 1847.* In his Preface the translator cites two reasons for undertaking the task. The first, which seems rather pointless, is "a confession of faith in the power of the English language"; the second is the fact that he was quite flattered by Goethe's recognition, and felt that "not an unnatural anxiety to justify this preference may be considered a sufficient apology for the present attempt."⁶

As is the case with so many other translators, Knox is worthy of all praise for his good will toward Goethe and for his industry in the attempt to make a more acceptable English version than his numerous predecessors. But as far as a thorough understanding of the drama itself, as far as an adequate scholarship, including an expert knowledge of both German and English, and a keen appreciation of poetic qualities are concerned, we find few traces of all this in his translation. His notes,

---

* See Bibliographical Note, pp. 302-3.

voluminous, often farfetched, and wooden in character, are of a piece with the translation itself.

Like Blackie and Anster, Knox expresses great fear lest his translation should become too literal: "I can safely affirm that I have slurred nothing; and whilst I have, as far as possible, avoided any circuitous paraphrase, I have in no case availed myself of the inglorious expedient of rendering a passage literally but unintelligibly, and then sheltering myself behind the dictionary."[7]

An idea of how inaccurately Knox proceeded in the translating of *Faust* may be gained from the following passage, taken from Study I, in which Mephistopheles says to Faust:

> Du wirst, mein Freund, für deine Sinnen,
> In dieser Stunde mehr gewinnen,
> Als in des Jahres Einerlei.
> Was dir die zarten Geister singen,
> Die schönen Bilder, die sie bringen,
> Sind nicht ein leeres Zauberspiel.
> Auch dein Geruch wird sich ergetzen,
> Dann wirst du deinen Gaumen letzen,
> Und dann entzückt sich dein Gefühl.
> Bereitung braucht es nicht voran,
> Beisammen sind wir, fanget an!

Knox translates:

> More in this house, I promise thee,
> Enjoyment shall thy senses gain,
> Then a year's sameness would attain.
> The songs these tender spirits sing,
> The lovely images they bring,
> No empty fancy spectacle;
> Delight it yields the sense of smell,
> Thy palate also will they please;
> No preparation do we need,
> All are assembled, now proceed.

It will be noticed that Knox translates "Stunde" as "house." "Fancy spectacle" is hardly an acceptable rendering of "leeres Zauberspiel." The verse reading "Und dann entzückt sich dein

Gefühl" has been left out altogether. One gets the impression that Knox could not have made an accurate literal translation even if he had set out with this idea expressly in mind. In the Song of the Spirits which follows the above passage, Goethe has fifty-nine verses while Knox has only forty-seven. This is due not to omitted portions, but rather to the longer rimeless lines which Knox clumsily employs every now and then. He has failed utterly to reproduce the lilt, the metre, the colorful vowels, and the feminine rimes of the original, as the following example shows:

> Schwindet, ihr dunkeln
> Wölbungen droben!
> Reizender schaue
> Freundlich der blaue
> Äther herein!

Knox translates:

> Vanish thou gloomy vault,
> And let the azure sky
> Look in with its enchanting friendliness.

Poetically this translation compares favorably neither with Blackie's nor with Anster's, but it avoids Anster's glaring fault of expanding so enormously upon the original. However, as we have seen, Knox has the contrary failing of occasionally leaving out lines and decreasing the number of verses appreciably. As a whole Knox's translation stands on a level with those of Talbot and Lefevre.

GEOFFREY MONTAGU COOKSON
(1867-)

TRANSLATION OF *Faust I* FIRST PRINTED IN 1925

Geoffrey Montagu Cookson was born at the Dallington Vicarage, Northamptonshire, England, November 14, 1867, and received his education at Clifton College and Balliol. In 1891, Cookson entered the Ceylon Civil Service, but at the outbreak of the World War he entered the army and served with the Dorsetshire Territorials in India from 1914 to 1916. After three years spent in the Intelligence Department of the army, he made his home at 51 Victoria Grove, Bridport, Dorset, England.[8]

The translator has to his credit a number of published works: *Denys of Auxerne*, a drama in verse, 1912; numerous poems contributed to current magazines, 1914 to 1916; a verse translation of Aeschylus, 1923; a paper on *The Prometheus* read before the Classical Association; and a verse translation of *Faust*, 1925.

In a letter to me Cookson says that he had no special preparation in German, and that he had made no translations from that language before attempting his version of *Faust*. However, because of a particular interest in this classic and in the personality of Goethe, and at his brother-in-law's request, he undertook the task. Once started, Cookson carried on the work with great zeal and enthusiasm, for, although the version was begun in August, 1924, it was already completed in October, just two months afterward. The drama is prefaced with an historical introduction by J. G. Robertson.

The publishers state on the paper wrapper to the volume that it is "a new, thoroughly modern translation." However, when applied to a translation such as Cookson's, the term *modern* is synonymous with *jazz*, and, therefore, connotes much that is undesirable in this version. There are strong indications that the work was dashed off in a hurry by one inadequately prepared for the task. Many passages are translated too freely and inaccurately, while the metre at times is rough and shoddy. The lines from the Choir of the Women in Night I:

> Mit Spezereien
> Hatten wir ihn gepflegt;
> Wir, seine Treuen,
> Hatten ihn hingelegt;
> Tücher und Binden
> Reinlich umwanden wir,
> Ach, und wir finden
> Christ ist nicht hier.

Cookson translates very loosely as:

> Faithful and tender
> We laid him so fair,
> With sandal and cedar,
> With spikenard and myrrh,
> Wrapped in white linen,
> Borne on the bier
> Here we entombed him—
> But Christ is not here.

He has altered the metre and also the thought somewhat in the last stanza of Gretchen's Prayer to Mater Dolorosa:

> Hilf! rette mich von Schmach und Tod!
> Ach neige,
> Du Schmerzenreiche,
> Dein Antlitz gnädig meiner Not!

Cookson translates:

> Help me! Save me! Shield me
> From shame and misery!
> Queen of sorrows, yield me
> Thy comfort or I die!

These faults are fully as accentuated in the recitative portions. If we take the passage containing Faust's Curse, for example, we find that he has changed the original metre of four stresses to one with five. Moreover, while Goethe has varied the rhythm with constantly recurring feminine rimes, Cookson omits them all, and, as a result, the masculine rimes become very monotonous in this sustained passage. Throughout the drama the translator uses the feminine endings very sparingly in both the conversational and in the lyric passages.

Cookson has done his best work in the spirited portions of the drama. He has caught and reproduced the cynicism of Mephistopheles, the gayety and bravado of students and soldiers, the carefree mood of the peasants under the lime tree, the uncouth, unrestrained manner of the motley band on the Blocksberg, with success. Mephistopheles says to the Lord in the Prologue in Heaven:

> Excellent: but I fear, too short a run.
> As for my bet, I count the wager won.
> But in my triumph you must not protest
> If you should see me puffing out my chest.
> Dust he shall eat as greedy as hot cake,
> As did my cousin, the distinguished snake.

While Cookson has made of the Soldiers' Song practically a new poem, its vigor, its dashing, martial manner in words and metre, are close to the spirit of the original. In a passage, however, like the following, from Before the City Gate:

> The shepherd he has made himself smart for the ball
> With jacket and ribbon and nosegay and all;
> As spruce as a sprat on a griddle.
> Round the linden there wasn't a place to be had,
> And all of them danced as if they were mad;
> > With a snicker-snee
> > And a tweedle-dee-dee,
> > Merrily scraped the fiddle,

Cookson's language becomes dangerously slangy. In Auerbach's Cellar and the Witches' Kitchen this tendency is carried to such an extreme that it becomes offensive.

Although the translator has reproduced with some success the parts where the dominant notes are those of gayety, revelry, and lack of restraint, he does not render satisfactorily the sublime, the solemn, the tragic moods of the drama. His versions of the Song of the Archangels, of Faust's meditations in Night I, and in Forest and Cavern, have no appeal. His rendering of Gretchen's Song at the Spinning Wheel, her Prayer to the Virgin, and the Dungeon Scene are weak and ineffective, and fail to grip the reader with the deep pathos, the poignant grief, and the despair that animate these scenes in the original. Taken as a whole, the undesirable qualities of this translation far outweigh its good points.

IX

Scientists and Faust

> Why grin, you hollow skull, except to say
> That once your brain, perplexed like mine,
> Yearning for Truth, pursued the light of day,
> Then in the dusk went wretchedly astray?
> Ye instruments, ye jeer at me, I feel,
> Cog and circle, cylinder and wheel!
> I stood at the door, ye should have been the key;
> Though fashioned well, ye raised no latch for me.
> Unfathomable by light of day,
> Nature will permit no one to steal
> Her veil; what to your spirit she will not reveal,
> With lever and screw you cannot wrest away.[1]

FAUST IS NO MORE a handbook of science than a textbook of Christian theology or a prepared guide to moral conduct. Still, one would have to search diligently to find profounder utterances about God or more telling examples of the devastating consequences of moral transgression than in this classic, in which, at the same time, statements, ideas, and propositions with scientific implications are legion. Each of these in turn reflects the author's deep interest in such fields as chemistry, geology, architecture, aviation, optics, meteorology, medicine, evolution, and spontaneous generation. In this work Goethe the scientist challenges step by step the superiority of Goethe the poet.

Previously, the English translators of *Faust* whose interests were centered primarily in the practice of medicine have been discussed. In this section there are presented three scientists, for the most part, men of obscure origins and personal histories who became so fascinated by *Faust* that they decided, for better or for worse, to bequeath to the world their own English versions of this great work. John Galvan, William Barnard Clarke, and James Adey Birds compose this group.

JOHN GALVAN
(1816-   )

TRANSLATION OF *Faust I* FIRST PRINTED IN 1860

The few facts available at present concerning John Galvan (Galvin) do not permit any extensive and definite deductions concerning his life and his personal interests. From the volume *Alumni Dublinensis* we learn that he was the son of a merchant, Bartholomew Galvan, and born in 1816. He is listed as being a sizar at Trinity College, Dublin University, on May 29, 1839, of Catholic faith, and aged twenty-three.[2] Since Todd's list of Dublin graduates does not include the name of the translator, he was probably only an undergraduate at Trinity College. The introductory pages to Galvan's translation, published in 1860, inform us that when he made his version of *Faust*[3] he was an ex-scholar of Trinity College, and that he resided in Dublin. According to *The Poets of Ireland*[4] Galvan was not only a translator of *Faust* but also the author of a work entitled *Crustula Pueris* or *Iambic Crumbs for Junior Grecians*. The fact that Galvan at the time of publication dedicated his *Faust* translation to Charles A. Cameron* M.D., Ph.D., Professor of Chemistry at Trinity College, may be of some significance as to his vocational interests. In view of the foregoing facts, which have been gleaned from various sources, it is probably safe to say that Galvan was an Irishman, that his major interest was of a scientific nature, and that he cultivated literature as a hobby.

The "translation was made," Galvan says, "to gratify private literary tastes, and with very slight expectation of it ever appearing in print."[5] He has grave fears that it will be regarded as a failure, and, therefore, pleads the arduous nature of the task as an apology for the inadequacy of its execution. "I have done my best," he says. "To have succeeded, even in a

---

* Sir Charles Alexander Cameron, Ph.D., F.R.C.S.I., was Vice-President of the Institute of Chemistry, Medical Officer of Health, Dublin, and a member of many scientific societies. Besides being the author of numerous scientific books, he was the translator of *Short Poems: from the German*, published in London, 1876.—Kirk, *Supplement to Allibone's Dictionary of Authors*, I, 276.

partial degree, were worthy of the highest literary ambition; while failure, where so many have failed, can prove no great disparagement to one who has never before ventured to court the public favor."[6] Galvan acknowledges the great help he has received from Hayward's prose translation. In his attempt to make this English version of *Faust* he has "endeavored to be faithful to the original, conceiving, as I do, that no passage, however beautiful or suggestive, should be expanded beyond the modest limits of legitimate translation."[7]

After an examination of this version, one feels that Galvan's apologetic and humble attitude is fully warranted. His translation is another of those dilettante efforts which are bound to reflect little credit on the translator himself and to deflect from Goethe a reputation among English readers. The style of this translation is almost as prosy as that of Colquhoun's, which appeared eighteen years later. A comparison of Galvan's rendering of the first stanza of the Prologue in Heaven with the original shows that the translator was able to impart to his work only a modicum of poetic grace. The passage:

> Die Sonne tönt nach alter Weise
> In Brudersphären Wettgesang,
> Und ihre vorgeschriebne Reise
> Vollendet sie mit Donnergang.
> Ihr Anblick gibt den Engeln Stärke,
> Wenn keiner sie ergründen mag;
> Die unbegreiflich hohen Werke
> Sind herrlich wie am ersten Tag,

Galvan translates:

> The sun chimes on, in the olden mode,
> In the emulous song of his brother spheres,
> And o'er his predetermined road
> In the might of his thunder-speed careers.
> His presence gives strength to the angel band,
> Though none may fathom his awful power;
> Thy works tower out, as great and as grand
> As once in the light of Time's dawning hour.

This stanza shows also that Galvan either could not or did not care to follow Goethe's metre. The original is wholly in iambics, but Galvan's lines are a mixture of iambics and anapests. Galvan makes no consistent attempt to reproduce Goethe's feminine endings; neither does he succeed in following Goethe's complicated rime pattern.

The best and most enjoyable portions of this translation are the lighter, gayer scenes in Before the Gate, Auerbach's Cellar, and Walpurgis Night's Dream. Here Galvan has caught the spirit of the original more closely than in any other part, and these portions remind one strongly of Cookson's version published some sixty years later. The unrestrained, fresh manner in which Galvan makes Mephistopheles speak is both interesting and amusing. He says to Faust at the beginning of Study II:

> That's the ticket, lad
> I hope we shall like one another;
> I come to chase thy fancies brother;
> Like youth of blood, behold me clad
> In scarlet coat, all gold belaced,
> With mantle of stiff silk, too, graced.
> A cock's plume in my beaver stuck;
> At every step a long sword clashing
> In short, take my advice, my brick,
> Then unrestrained come on with me,
> And something of the world see.

In a similar strain Valentine says to Mephistopheles in Night:

> Whom are you coaxing here! Hell-fire!
> You curs'd, infernal, old rat-catcher!
> To the devil I first pitch the lyre!
> Then to the devil the vile gut-scratcher.

The second edition published in 1862 is in all respects the same as the first; hence it would probably be more correct to call it a reprint (*Titelauflage*) than another edition. The printer, John M. O'Toole and Son, was probably persuaded by the author to supply the many unsold copies of the translation with a new title-page in an attempt to stimulate the sales. William Barnard Clarke, whose translation of both parts appeared in 1865, remarks in his Preface: "Galvan's book is not positively bad, but incorrect, not true to the original, and full of paraphrases; like all his colleagues too free, so that he loses the distinctness of the original work."[8] B. Q. Morgan calls Galvan's version a "travesty of Goethe's Faust."[9]

WILLIAM BARNARD CLARKE
(-)
TRANSLATION OF *Faust I and II* FIRST PRINTED IN 1865

According to the publication *The Royal Academy of Arts*[10] William Barnard Clarke was by profession an architect. In 1835 he was instrumental in the restoration of Waltham Cross, with scenery as it probably appeared in the reign of Edward I, and in 1862 he exhibited his plans for the proposed Botanical Garden on Primrose Hill. His address is given as 9 Chapel Street, Bedford Row.*

The title-page to Clarke's translation as well as the British Museum Catalogue[11] inform us further that he was a "fellow of the former Architectural Society of London, founded in 1832, and of the Helvetian Architectural Society." The latter source referred to above lists not only his translation of both parts of *Faust* but also a volume entitled *The Guide to Hayling . . . With . . . Engravings from Sketches* by W. B. C., 1836. Moreover, the fact that he wrote the Preface[12] to his translation at Littenweiler, Germany, in 1865, the year in which his version was made public, and also the circumstance that it was published in Freiburg as well as in London, may indicate that the translator was an Englishman, who for some time had been living in Germany, probably following his profession as an architect in that country.

---

* The title-page of the copy in the William A. Speck Collection of Goetheana has inscribed on it in pen and ink the following name and address: "Fredk. Clarke, 10 Chapel Street, Bedford Row." It seems plausible that this was the translator's brother, and since Frederick Clarke lived next door to where this version was published, he was probably the translator's English agent.

In his Preface Clarke criticizes the more important translators, who have preceded him, for the manifold errors in their versions, and concludes that "there is very little to be praised in any one of them."[13] He then goes on to say concerning the history of his own effort: "I here repeat that the translation of both parts, with a few original notes has been the result, with little interruption, of twenty years study." He next calls attention to the fact that his English version has practically the same number of verses as the German. "This arose," Clarke continues, "from the circumstance which I discovered during my long study, that the closer a translator kept to the original, the greater the facility he obtained both in metre and rhyme, and the sense of two Iambics were with facility and of necessity embodied in one line." In regard to the form, he adds: "I have adopted the same metre with all its changes, not even omitting these varieties in the numerous songs, which Goethe has happily dispersed through his original work."[14]

After he had made such a long and thorough study of both *Faust* and its English versions, one would naturally expect from Clarke's hand a translation of the better sort, but in this we are again disappointed. He found it comparatively easy to lay his finger on the vulnerable points in the versions of his predecessors; however, his own translation is, if anything, worse than these. There are abundant examples of over-literalness and many cases of clumsy, unidiomatic, un-English diction and inelegant sentence structure. The last two verses of Part II in their awkward translation read:

> The feminine ever will
> Draw us high on.

The initial lines from Lynceus' Song in Act V make unpleasant reading:

> To gaze far created,
> Plac'd here to behold.
> Tower-dedicated,
> I joy in the world.

That Clarke was a poor English scholar is evident from such

a line as the following taken from the speech of Plutus in Part II, Act I: "Courageous steps together have you ran!" The fourth line of Act II: "Der kommt so leicht nicht zu Verstande," is rendered unintelligibly by Clarke as: "Comes not so light to reason's stand."

The following more extended passage, from Ariel's Song at the beginning of Act I, shows clearly the limited ability Clarke had to reproduce the marvelous beauty of Goethe's lyrics. The lines:

> Horchet! horcht! dem Sturm der Horen
> Tönend wird für Geistesohren
> Schon der neue Tag geboren.
> Felsenthore knarren rasselnd,
> Phöbus Räder rollen prasselnd,
> Welch Getöse bringt das Licht!
> Es drommetet, es posaunet,
> Auge blinzt und Ohr erstaunet;
> Unerhörtes hört sich nicht.

Clarke translates:

> Heark! heark! how, the hours storm away,
> Tuning for spirits ears their lay,
> Already comes the new born day.
> Rocky portals creak them clattering,
> Apollo's wheelworks roll on shattering;
> What a noise the light brings out!
> Trumpets burst loud, blasts are sounded,
> Eyes twinkle and the ear's astounded,
> List not to the astounding shout.

The deficiencies in Clarke's knowledge of both English and German as well as in poetic inspiration are all too evident. Consequently he has been able to reproduce Goethe's metre in fewer than half the lines and his ideas in hardly a single verse, while the music, the flowing rhythm, and the connotive diction of the original are wholly lacking. This version gives but a very distorted notion of the real *Faust*.

JAMES ADEY BIRDS
(1831-1894)

TRANSLATION OF *Faust I* FIRST PRINTED IN 1880;
Faust II, 1889

James Adey Birds, the only son of Reverend William Taylor Birds, was born November 9, 1831, at the rectory of Preston-on-the-Wildmoors, Shropshire. He was educated at Rugby and at Exeter College, Oxford, received the B.A. degree from Oxford, 1855, and was made a F.G.S. in 1878.[15] From the scanty records available, the dominating interest in Birds's life appears to have been natural science.[16] At his death in 1894, he bequeathed his geological and mineralogical collections to the Natural History Museum at Derby.[17]

The only literary achievement of Birds seems to have been his translation of *Faust*, Part I, published in 1880, and Part II, in 1889. Since so many others have labored in the same field before him, he deems it necessary to offer an explanation for making another version. He remarks in the Preface to Part I: "My own reasons for attempting a new one are probably the same that have influenced each successive translator, namely, that former translations, excellent as in many respects they have been, have failed to satisfy myself, and that I felt there was still room for a further effort, with the aid of former endeavors and all the advantages of the present time, to lay before the reader unacquainted with German, in a new or hitherto almost unattempted form 'this greatest of modern poems.' "[18] In regard to his use of blank verse in the longer part of his version, Birds remarks: "Blank verse, indeed, appears to me to be the practicable mean between prose and an imitation of the original metres, both of which, though from opposite causes, are inadequate instruments to reproduce the poetry. A translation in prose does not allow full scope to the powers of the language; while one in the original, perhaps in any rhymed metres—exceeds them."[19] After declaring that Shelley was led by his poetic instinct to actually adopt blank verse in the specimens which he gives from the Walpurgis-Night, he reminds us that the two best translations of Dante's *Divina Commedia* and Tennyson's specimens from Homer are in blank verse.

While Birds has employed blank verse in the rendering of the larger portions of Part I, he has used rime in translating the Dedication, the two Prologues, the songs, and a few other short passages "where that was obviously the natural form."[20] His translation is a fairly successful effort as far as an intelligent reproduction of the thought of the original is concerned. But Birds is no poet, and, especially in the lyrical parts, the charm of the original is lacking. One of the best passages in Part I is the Song of the Spirit in Night I:

> In the flood of life
> Up and down I go,
> In the storms of strife
> Whirl I to and fro!
> Birth and death,
> An eternal ocean,
> Life's glowing breath,
> And its changeful motion,
> So at Time's whizzing loom I ply,
> And weave the life-garment of Deity.

During the nine years that intervened between the publications of Part I and Part II, Birds's theory of translation changed somewhat. Part II is entirely in rime. The translator offers this explanation for the change in technique: "As to the form of translation suitable for this Second Part, we may remark that since, as Mr. Taylor says, it has a higher intellectual, though less passionate, interest than Part I, it lends itself more readily to translation into rhyme; and therefore we have attempted it in that form, although not always in the original metre."[21] It would seem, however, that just the reverse is true, for if the intellectual content of Part II were greater than that of Part I the rimes would be less essential, since the aim then would be to portray truth rather than beauty in form and expression. Although the translator does not always follow the metrical pattern of the original, Birds's version of Part II shows greater metrical skill than that of Part I.

Finally it must be added that the diction of both parts is far from simple and natural. The translator displays a fondness for archaic terms like "certes," "coz," "sooth," "yclept," "enringing," etc., which today are out of place in rendering the more modern German of Goethe. Both parts are equipped with extensive explanatory and illustrative notes taken largely from Goethe's own life and writings.

X

Women as Translators of Faust

Helena:
I hear and witness marvels manifold;
Amazement takes me, much would I inquire.
Yet now instruct me wherefore spake the man
With strangely-sounding speech, friendly and strange:
Each sound appeared as yielding to the next,
And, when a word gave pleasure to the ear,
Another came, caressing then the first.

Faust:
If thee our people's mode of speech delight,
O thou shalt be enraptured with our song,
Which wholly satisfies both ear and mind![1]

OF THE NEARLY half a hundred translators of *Faust* here considered, only two were women, one English and the other American. This does not indicate, however, that *Faust* is a man's book only. On the contrary, there is every reason why, from the standpoints of sheer human interest and dramatic power, its appeal to the feminine mind and heart should be quite as deep and as genuine as to the masculine. In Margaret, one of the central characters of the play, Goethe has created one of the outstanding and genuinely tragic figures of all literature. Symbolically she represents that trusting, suffering, and redeeming love without which man retrogresses to the level of a brute. With profound insight the poet has indicated the immortal quality of this deepest and purest of all human attributes by extending the period of Faust's character development under Margaret's guidance into the regions beyond.

Perhaps it is because of their intuitive insight into the motivating forces of the play and their deep understanding of the fundamental issues of life itself that Anna Swanwick and Alice

Raphael have recaptured the spirit of the original to such a remarkable degree in their English translations of Goethe's *Faust*. We shall, therefore, bring our cogitations on the long array of English *Faust* translators to a close with a chapter in which the art of translation stands on an unusually high level.

ANNA SWANWICK
(1813-1899)
Translation of *Faust I* First Printed in 1850; *Faust II*, 1879

With Anna Swanwick we ascend to the high places of translation as an art. She, as the first woman to make an English version of Goethe's *Faust*, imparted to her work a new high standard of excellence which proved to be a definite challenge to all translators who came after her.

Born in 1813, in Liverpool, Miss Swanwick grew up in a home in which religious devotion, serious thinking, and studious habits were encouraged at an early age.[2] As a child, she astonished her elders with her mental alertness, and she readily committed to memory the more important poems of the best English authors of that time and earlier times. Together with her oldest sister Mary, with whom she enjoyed the most intimate companionship until the latter's marriage, she enrolled at the age of sixteen in a school for girls in Liverpool, where both studied for several years.[3] Then in 1831, Mary L. Bruce tells us in *Anna Swanwick, a Memoir*, prompted by the desire to study German and Greek, Miss Swanwick spent eight months in Berlin with Professor Zumpt, the director of the Kriegschule at that place. At the end of this short but very stimulating period of intense study, she returned home to begin her long career as a translator.[4]

In addition to her literary labors, she distinguished herself as a champion of the rights of women. As a leader in social and educational reform, she took great interest in the founding and maintaining of Queens and Bedford colleges for women.

For some time she also assisted in Girton College, Cambridge, and Sommerville Hall, Oxford.

The large and distinguished circle of friends Miss Swanwick gathered about herself bears ample testimony to the high esteem in which she was generally held. Her broad sympathies as well as her high degree of intelligence enabled her to associate with the great men of England and other lands. With Professor Max Mueller she discussed the science of religion, with Professor Adams, the latest news of distant planets, with James Russell Lowell, the literature of America, and with Gladstone, as an oft-repeated breakfast guest, she talked about the affairs of state. Miss Swanwick was the first woman to be elected to the scientific society known as the Royal Institution. Toward the close of her long life, the University of Aberdeen granted her the degree of LL.D. Miss Swanwick was a charter member and vice-president of the English Goethe Society when she died in 1899.[5]

During her stay in Berlin, Miss Swanwick made rapid progress in mastering the German language. Her instructor, to quote from Bruce, cited above, "was a very clever man, an authority on grammar, and it was very gratifying to the young student from England to find that he took a great interest in helping her improve her knowledge of German, encouraging her in the kindest way to join in the conversation." Professor Zumpt also directed her reading, and at this time she became acquainted with the works of some of the outstanding German philosophers and literary men. She read extensively in Kant, Schleiermacher, Fichte, Lessing, Herder, Heine, Jean Paul Richter, and, no doubt, Goethe also. In later years Miss Swanwick enthusiastically remarked that during these eight months in Berlin under Dr. Zumpt's guidance, she had gained a more thorough knowledge of Greek, German, and mathematics in a few months than she would have done at school or college with a far longer period of class teaching.[6]

Although Miss Swanwick did not regard Goethe as one of the world's greatest poets, she devoted a considerable portion of her life to the study and the translation of his works. In

1835 her sister's marriage deprived her of a fellowship for which Miss Swanwick endeavored to compensate herself by losing herself in Goethe. "Anna Swanwick felt the parting from her beloved companion so keenly that life seemed to have lost its interest for her, and to occupy her thoughts, she took to the study of Goethe's *Iphigenia*. She used to describe herself as sitting under the shade of the trees in the botanical gardens at Glasneven, near Dublin, with her Goethe and dictionary pondering over the translation of difficult passages, and she worked so hard, that in three weeks she had completed the translation of the play, as well as her imperfect knowledge of the language permitted. She then attempted the *Torquato Tasso*, and Schiller's *Jungfrau von Orleans*. No thought of publication ever crossed her mind at this time—she worked purely as a mental distraction—but it so happened that this first attempt at translation proved the index which pointed the way to her life-work as translator some years later."[7]

The source just quoted furnishes us the following additional facts concerning Miss Swanwick's translation activity. In 1843 she published a volume called *Selections from Dramas of Goethe and Schiller*, Translated with Introductory Remarks.* Although this volume created no great stir, it did attract the attention of Mr. Henry G. Bohn, the publisher, who was putting on sale a number of translations of classical works under the Standard Library Series. He at once asked Miss Swanwick, then a relatively unknown author, to translate Schiller's *Jungfrau von Orleans* and Goethe's *Egmont*. The two translations appeared in 1850. Soon after the publication of the English version of the *Maid of Orleans*, Miss Swanwick received a letter from Mr. Bohn asking her to translate also Goethe's *Faust*, Part I. Unwearied by the tasks just performed, Miss Swanwick started to work on this venture immediately, and the translation was published in the same year, 1850, together with her English versions of *Iphigenia in Tauris*, *Torquato Tasso*, *Egmont*, and Sir Walter Scott's version of *Goetz von*

---

* This volume contains Goethe's *Iphigenia*, the first act of *Tasso*, and a part of Schiller's *The Maid of Orleans*.

Berlichingen in a volume called *Dramatic Works of Goethe*.

Miss Swanwick did not translate *Faust* primarily for monetary considerations, however. "To reproduce Goethe's master work," states Mary Bruce, "in a way that Goethe himself would have approved, was her sole ambition."[8] The translator says in the Preface to her *Dramatic Works of Goethe:* "The endeavor to render into English verse the finer passages of *Faust*, has been to me a source of the highest enjoyment, and if others derive any pleasure from the perusal of my translation, I shall feel amply rewarded for the labor attending the less inviting portions of my task."[9] After a lapse of almost thirty years during which time she had translated the dramas of Aeschylus and the complete works of Schiller, and traveled on the continent, Miss Swanwick revised her version of *Faust*, Part I, and finished the translation of Part II. Again this was done at the request of Bohn, her publisher, and like the original translation of Part I, the complete work was published in 1879 in Bohn's Standard Library.

Miss Swanwick attacked the problem of her translation of Part I in an interesting manner. "First, she made the original so thoroughly her own that she could repeat it passage by passage, and thus carry it in her mind wherever she went, all the time endeavoring to find English words to express the meaning of each German word as accurately as possible—having done this she wrote it down, and put the passage into metre as nearly resembling the original as the difference of language would permit."[10] From the above source we learn also that when Bohn offered to send her all the translations that had already appeared, she refused the offer, because she desired her work to be entirely original. She worked *con amore* and with great concentration.

Anna Swanwick's theory of translation is strongly at variance with that of Abraham Hayward. While the latter emphasized literal exactness and the reproduction of the thought of the original at the expense of everything else, Miss Swanwick felt that "as poetry ought always to be beautiful, the charm of the original must never be sacrificed to the endeavor to be literal."[11]

In the Translator's Preface to the complete edition of 1879, she elaborates on this theory still more: "I cannot subscribe to the opinion which has recently found several powerful advocates, namely, 'that verse translations of good poetry are a mistake,' and consequently that prose is the appropriate medium for its reproduction." She holds that "the poetic thought can only find adequate expression in tones which harmonize with the music of the original verse."[12] In other words, a translation should reproduce the original as nearly as possible in form, content, and spirit.

Miss Swanwick's translation of Part I was not received with any great degree of enthusiasm. Hauhart attributes this, and probably correctly, to the fact that the translation was not published separately, but in a rather thick volume containing four other works, and to the fact that the public appetite was sated by the large number of verse translations that had already been published.[13] To this might be added that her sex militated against the success of the undertaking. Miss Swanwick was a pioneer among women in this type of work and obliged to overcome public prejudice. With the passing of the years, however, her version came into its own. By 1880 no fewer than five editions had been published, and, even after the turn of the century, new editions have continued to appear; the last in 1914.

One of the earliest reviews of Miss Swanwick's translation was published in the *Literary Gazette* for 1851. After claiming that her translation of the Dedication is marked by vagueness and inability to express Goethe's deep feeling in the simple language and the perfect cadence of the original, the writer questions whether a woman is at all capable of translating *Faust*. He says: "As we advance into the play itself, it does not appear that Miss Swanwick is more fortunate. It may, indeed, be questioned whether any woman, however gifted, could do justice to the *Faust*. It abounds in passages which a woman can hardly be expected thoroughly to understand, and there is a terrible force and closeness in style which are to be found in no female writer that we know. . . . Clever and graceful as Miss Swanwick often is, when she comes to passages of concentrated power, she is sure to fail; indeed she seems not to feel how indispensable in such passages it is to preserve the very cadence and measure of the original."[14]

Although this criticism of Miss Swanwick's translation is partly just, we must bear in mind that it applies equally well to all earlier versions, and its shortcomings are not peculiar to her sex. No one, we may assert, has been able, nor indeed will be able, to reproduce *fully* the power, the feeling, the simplicity of language, the "very cadence and measure of the original." But in Miss Swanwick's translation we notice a decided advance in the type of poetic technique displayed, while her reproduction of the thought of the original is certainly more faithful than that by any of her predecessors except Hayward.

Miss Swanwick's rendering of Faust's Curse in Study II, a test passage for any translator, is a commendable effort to reproduce the original in its powerful diction, its rhythm, and its spirited tone. But she is at her best in such a passage as Margaret's Prayer to the Mater Dolorosa. Here we have a woman's soul in deep distress laid bare and interpreted by a pitying, sympathetic, kindred spirit, with the result that the passage in the translation conveys the deep pathos of the original to a remarkable degree. There is also a graceful flowing quality in the lines which further enhances the beauty of the passage as a translation. We quote it here only in part:

> Ah, who can know
> The torturing woe,
> That harrows me, and racks me to the bone?
> How my poor heart, without relief,
> Trembles and throbs, its yearning grief
> Thou knowest, thou alone!
>
> Ah, wheresoe'er I go.
> With woe, with woe, with woe,
> My anguished breast is aching!
> Wretched, alone I keep,
> I weep, I weep, I weep.
> Alas! my heart is breaking!

Women as Translators of Faust

In Miss Swanwick's revised version of Part I, 1879, she endeavors to approximate the metre and rime of the original more closely by reproducing the feminine rimes, but it has been done with only a fair degree of success. There are also in this edition minor improvements in the verbal accuracy of the translation.

The Second Part of *Faust* by Miss Swanwick, not translated until 1879, is fully on a level with her version of Part I. It is an incomparably better rendering than that of Arthur Taylor, Bernays, Gurney, Birch, or Anster. It is not too much to say that it compares favorably with the version by Bayard Taylor. Part II opens with the Song of Ariel:

> Wenn der Blüthen Frühlingsregen
> Über alle schwebend sinkt,
> Wenn der Felder grüner Segen
> Allen Erdgebornen blinkt:
> Kleiner Elfen Geistergrösse
> Eilet wo sie helfen kann;
> Ob er heilig, ob er böse,
> Jammert sie der Unglücksmann.

Taylor's version reads:

> When the spring returns serener,
> Raining blossoms over all:
> When the fields with blessing greener
> On the earth-born children call;
> Then the craft of elves propitious
> Hastes to help where help it can:
> Be he holy, be he vicious,
> Pity they the luckless man.

Miss Swanwick translates:

> When in vernal showers descending
> Blossoms gently veil the earth,
> When the field's green wealth up-tending,
> Gleams on all of mortal birth:
> Tiny elves, where help availeth,
> Large of heart, there fly apace;

> Pity they whom grief assaileth,
> Be he holy, be he base.

Both translators have attempted to reproduce exactly the metre and rime of the original, but in this they have done violence to the German text. Taylor, in order to get a feminine ending to rime with "serener," line one, has construed the German strong adjective "grüner" as if it were in the comparative degree. Miss Swanwick has appropriated the word "uptending," which reminds us strongly of a passage in Anster's translation of Part I, to agree with "descending." There is, of course, no justification in the German text for such a procedure, but these are good examples and show to what lengths translators feel themselves compelled to go to render the German feminine endings into English.

Sir Theodore Martin, who finished his translation of *Faust*, Part II, somewhat later, wrote to Miss Swanwick: "Accept my best thanks for your *Faust*. I have been rapidly through the *Second Part*, and congratulate you on the way you have accomplished your most difficult task. I may speak, for I know by hard adventure how difficult it is."[15] Professor Dowden's criticism of Miss Swanwick's translation of both parts is eminently just when he says: "The fidelity of the translation I think most admirable. In meditative and reflective passages very little is lost, in passages which tend to the lyrical, or where without being lyrical, Goethe shows his power of wing, inevitably, the loss is somewhat greater. In *Faust* I think there is more that cannot be perfectly rendered than in some other of Goethe's plays, such as *Tasso* and *Iphigenia*."[16]

ALICE RAPHAEL
(1887-   )

Translation of *Faust I* First Printed in 1930

> One lesson, Nature, let me learn of thee,
> One lesson which in every wind is blown,
> One lesson of two duties kept at one
> Though the loud world proclaim their enmity—

Of toil unsever'd from tranquillity!
Of Labor, that in lasting fruit outgrows
Far noisier schemes, accomplished in repose,
Too great for haste, too high for rivalry!*

Alice Raphael, the second woman to publish an English version of Goethe's *Faust*, was born on June 22, 1887, at Brownsville, Texas. Her mother, of French-Jewish extraction, was reared in Scotland, and her father, Gabriel Matthews Raphael, was an American of German-Jewish descent. Although Brownsville in 1887 was no longer a mere pioneer outpost but a cultivated little town on the Mexican border, it was still largely under Spanish influence; consequently Alice spoke Spanish before she entered the public school. Her home, however, contributed more toward her intellectual and spiritual development in these youthful days than the school; for, encouraged by her parents, Alice became deeply interested in drawing and music, and to these subjects she added the study of Hebrew before she was ten years old.[17]

Gabriel Matthews Raphael, a businessman, died when his daughter Alice had just reached the age of eleven. Mrs. Raphael with her children moved to New York City, and subsequently, in accordance with the educational plans conceived by the father before his death, she took the children, of whom there were two besides Alice, to France for two years.

By the time Alice was fourteen, the Raphaels were back in New York, where she entered the school of Dr. Julius Sachs and, among other studies, showed a particular liking for psychology. In 1904 she entered Barnard College, but because of inadequate preparation and ill health her college days were

---

* These lines, from the sonnet "Quiet Work" by Matthew Arnold, stand at the beginning of the translator's Foreword. Alice Raphael explains their presence in the following words: "During the many years in which *Faust* has been my companion, this sonnet of Matthew Arnold's has become more and more closely associated with it. For, the poem expresses the temper in which the translation has slowly evolved and also the spirit in which Goethe toiled to understand nature, but to which he gave expression only in the second part of *Faust*. The significance of Goethe's labor, which in lasting fruit outgrows far noisier schemes, can be more clearly understood as we approach the hundredth year following his death than during his lifetime."

short. Once more Mrs. Raphael took her children to Europe for a year, a large part of which was spent in Germany. During the winter Alice stayed in Berlin, where she studied music, primarily, and here it was that she first heard German spoken. At this time she made a number of attempts to express herself in literary form, some of which bore fruit later.

Alice Raphael was married in 1912 to Mr. Henry J. Eckstein of New York. Shortly after the birth of a second daughter, the family moved to Greenwich, Connecticut, where the Ecksteins resided for the next ten years, and where, following some sporadic publications of short stories, her translation of *Faust* was begun. In 1918 she was asked to write the Introductory Essay for *Twenty Drawings*, a volume by Kahlil Gibran, the poet-painter. But except for this, she concentrated wholly on the translation of *Faust* until 1928.

In the above-mentioned year the Eckstein family returned to New York. After having read extensively in analytical psychology under the guidance of Dr. Beatrice M. Hinkle and Dr. Carl G. Jung, and after taking a course of medical lectures at the New School directed by Dr. Fritz Wittels, she qualified as a lay analyst. In this capacity she served as assistant to Dr. Hinkle for a number of years, and it may be said that Alice Raphael's interest in analytical psychology and in literature are still predominant in her life today. A book entitled *Goethe and the Philosopher's Stone* will be published soon. *Goethe the Challenger*, an earlier volume, appeared in 1932, two years after the publication of her translation of *Faust*, Part I. The latter in a considerably revised form should soon be ready for republication. Alice Raphael now lives in Washington and Old Lyme, Connecticut.

The Raphael version of *Faust*, then, is very intimately bound up with the translator's own intellectual and spiritual development. By her mother she was endowed with the vivacious and the artistic sides of her nature, and from her father she inherited the more serious, the philosophical outlook on life. Since Alice Raphael had been passing through what she herself calls an "intellectual Sturm und Drang" for some time, she corresponded with William James in regard to the problem of the divided self which so concerned her, and James replied: "I cannot answer this question—nor do I believe that anyone can today; but what with one man's peppercorn of light upon another, we are gradually closing in upon this subject."

This question, Alice Raphael writes, was to be re-solved many years later through the findings of analytical psychology and the working out of the Faustian problem. William James suggested to her: "Shut up James; get out into the open air, and you will come back to psychology as tough as India Rubber." Consequently, although she continued her musical studies, behind which the urge to creative activity continued unabated, she gave herself over to the social life which now opened up. Encouraged by Dr. Hinkle and Dr. Jung, she once more resumed her interest in psychological problems, and thus Alice Raphael was led back to the *Faust* drama with which she had first become acquainted when she was seventeen.

But it was also to some extent the suggestion made by James Oppenheim, a leader in the free verse movement in 1918, that Alice Raphael should translate portions of *Faust* to cultivate her sense of form, which led her to make an English version of this drama. She first attempted some of the Angels' Choruses and the Dungeon scene in free verse. When Dr. Hinkle saw these parts, she encouraged her to make an entire version of *Faust*, and thereupon she set to work in earnest. "I went home," she writes, "and that night translated the entire scene beginning Forest and Cavern. I was astonished at the ease with which I swung into the task, and in six weeks I had completed the first draft. This was in free verse and met with the approval of James Oppenheim, who always felt that I was opening a new world to him." During the next two years she worked on the translation of the Second Part, and by 1920 she "was ready for some outside assistance."

In the course of the next decade, fifteen revisions of the translation were made, and each time it emerged resembling more closely in both spirit and form its matchless original. It should be mentioned here that several other contemporary students of *Faust* have left their imprint on the Raphael translation. One of these was Mr. Richard Bloch, who insisted very strongly that the form, which was now partly free verse and partly blank verse with some of the lyrics in rimed stanzas, "would never be acceptable. He brought me Schlegel and Tieck," Alice Raphael writes, "and read to me passages in German which I compared with the original. He urged me to attempt the task in its original metres, and little by little I began to recast the *Faust*."

By a happy coincidence, in 1922, it was suggested to Alice Raphael that she consult with Mr. William A. Speck, the well-known bibliophile and ardent student of *Faust*, who, through the acquisition of his collection of Goetheana by Yale, was already identified with that university. Her first meeting with him in New Haven proved to be a very interesting occasion. "I spent an hour with Mr. Speck and left him a duplicate copy," writes Alice Raphael. "He was enormously interested in the idea and said to me, 'You know that I must be very critical.' 'I would expect nothing else,' I replied. 'What college did you graduate from?' he asked. 'I'm not a college graduate,' I answered; 'I approached this from the point of view of the artist, and not the scholar.' 'Thank God for that,' he said. 'How many of the translations have you read?' 'How many,' I answered, 'are there many? I only know of four.' 'Well thank God for *that*.' We both laughed and the ice was broken." From this time on until his death, Mr. Speck stood *in loco parentis* to this translatioin. By his kindly persuasion he completely removed Alice Raphael's prejudice against making a translation in the metres and rimes of the original, and again the rimed draft of Part I was completed in six weeks. During the ensuing years Mr. Speck went over the translation with the

Walpurgis Night
Faust, Mephistopheles, Will-o'-the-Wisp
(in alternating song)

Since it seems we've been admitted
To these dream-like magic spaces,
Guide us nicely through these places,
So that soon we be permitted
In the vast and desolate regions.

Watch the trees like forest legions
Passing by and swift descending,
While the cliffs keep bowing, bending,
And the rocks' long snouted fellows—
How each snorts and how each bellows!

Over stones, through meadows growing,
Down rush brook and brooklet flowing;
Do I hear rustling? Do I hear singing?
Songs in which the heart rejoices
Like those truly heavenly voices
Which we love and loving hail,
While faint Echo, like a tale
Of olden, golden days, is ringing?

Tu-whit! Tu-whoo! Not far away
Cry plover, screech-owl and the jay.
Did they remain awake to-day?

From Alice Raphael's translation of *Faust*, Part I, revised but as yet unpublished version, Walpurgis Night, lines 3871-3891

author line by line for correctness of thought and expression. Finally, a different type of revision, from the standpoint of English prosody, was begun in 1925 and completed in 1930.

When Alice Raphael first consulted Mr. Speck about her translation, it was he who saw in it a possibility "that it could be a version which would give pleasure to the general reader and open up *Faust* to a public which would not be interested in one which would otherwise satisfy the scholar." That this translation possesses these qualities cannot be denied. Its most striking and pleasing characteristic is its simple and natural and yet idiomatically correct English. This is true of the more philosophical and exalted passages as well as those in which conversation predominates. To illustrate the first type, let us take some lines from Faust's meditation in Forest and Cavern:

> Then thou dost lead me into a sheltering cave
> And revealest me to myself and layest bare
> The deep mysterious miracle of my nature.
> And when the pure moon rises into sight,
> Soothing above me, then about me hover,
> Creeping from rocky walls and dewy thickets,
> Silver shadows, phantoms of a bygone world,
> Which allay the austere joy of meditation.

The following passage from Valentine's speech in Night II is a good example of straightforward, modern, everyday English:

> When I'd be drinking with the men,
> Where many fellows like to boast
> About their pick of girls, and then,
> Filling their glasses, drink a toast,
> I'd sit in quiet unconcern,
> Leaning on my elbows, attend
> To all their bunkum to the end,
> Then smiling, stroke my beard and turn,
> A brimming goblet in my hand,
> And say, "Each to his taste! But where,
> I ask you this, throughout the land
> Is there a girl who can compare
> With my own Gretchen? Out with it—say!"

Women as Translators of Faust

No higher tribute can be paid to a translated drama than to say that it is successful where most others have failed in reproducing the variety, the styles within the style, of the original. It follows from this that the characters: the poet, the archangels, God, Faust, Mephistopheles, Gretchen, Valentine, and all the rest, being rightly differentiated, emerge in proper contrast as vital beings with ideals, with towering passions, with ambitions, and with overwhelming griefs. The spirit of the original lives and moves in this translation. A definitive proof of this can be supplied. When Max Reinhardt cast about for a translation of Part I, he asked his advisers to find for him the most actable version for a *Faust* production in English. They chose Alice Raphael's translation, and Goethe's *Faust* went over the boards in Los Angeles and San Francisco in a memorable production.*

Another laudable quality in this version is the fidelity and clearness with which it reproduces the thought of the original, in which respect it stands almost without a peer. Both Bayard Taylor's and William Page Andrews' versions have more inaccuracies, and neither preserves the proper balance between a too literal and a too free rendering so well. Perhaps the most difficult passage to translate in the whole *Faust* drama is the last Chorus of the Angels in Night I. Here Alice Raphael's skill as a translator is seen to good advantage. The original reads:

>Christ ist erstanden
>Aus der Verwesung Schoss!
>Reisset von Banden
>Freudig euch los!
>Thätig ihn Preisenden,
>Liebe Beweisenden,
>Brüderlich Speisenden,
>Predigend Reisenden,
>Wonne Verheissenden,
>Euch ist der Meister nah,
>Euch ist er da!

* The Speck collection possesses a complete scrapbook on this venture.

Taylor translates:

> Christ is arisen,
> Out of corruption's womb;
> Burst ye the prison,
> Break from your gloom!
> Praising and pleading him,
> Lovingly needing Him,
> Brotherly feeding Him,
> Preaching and speeding Him,
> Blessing, succeeding Him,
> Thus is the Master near,—
> Thus is he here.

Andrews' version, which follows Taylor's closely in phraseology, reads:

> Christ is arisen
> Out of corruption's womb!
> Burst bonds that prison,
> Joyfully come!
> Actively pleading Him,
> Showing love, heeding Him,
> Preaching, far speeding Him,
> Rapture succeeding Him,
> To you the Master's near,
> To you is here.

Alice Raphael's translation reads:

> Christ has transcended
> The womb of corruption!
> Let the bond of destruction
> Be joyfully rended!
> To those serving through deeds,
> Spreading love by their teaching,
> Sustaining men in their needs,
> Bearing tidings and preaching,
> He not only is near,
> He is verily here.

In Alice Raphael's lines the thought is most clearly rendered; next in excellence comes Andrews', and last Taylor's.

From an examination of many passages in Alice Raphael's translation, it appears that the most vulnerable point in her version is its external form. She does not succeed as well as Bayard Taylor and does not surpass Andrews in reproducing the metre and the rime of the original. The above passage is a case in point. Here Taylor excels, Andrews follows, and Raphael stands last. In the passage in Night I beginning with line 430, where Faust gazes upon the sign of the Macrocosm, Andrews observes Goethe's feminine rimes closely while Alice Raphael neglects them altogether. Similarly, in the lines following the Soldiers' Song in Before the Gate, we look for the feminine rimes in vain in Alice Raphael's version. But it is usually superior to Taylor's version and compares favorably with Andrews' translation in its melodious lines and its felicitous language. One marked exception is the second and third stanzas of Gretchen's Prayer to the Mater Dolorosa, where the diction is distinctly prosaic. Here Anna Swanwick's translation, which is inferior in most respects to Alice Raphael's, contains more pleasing, more poetic lines. Andrews' rendering also comes closer to being real poetry and preserves to a greater degree the original form of this exquisite lyric.

Taken as a whole, however, Alice Raphael's version is perhaps the most acceptable that has yet been made. Its shortcomings with respect to external form are more than counterbalanced by its other excellencies: its simple, natural, and straightforward diction, its faithful reproduction of the spirit and the thought of the original, and its poetic qualities. In many ways it is the most readable version yet published.

Contemporary criticism has, for the most part, been favorable to this new contribution to the art of translating *Faust*. Professor George M. Priest of the Department of German, Princeton University, writes in a letter: "I admire the translation greatly. It is a long stride in advance of Taylor in many respects, especially in clarity, in accuracy, and in smoothness.... The translation of the First Part has, above all, reproduced the spirit of the original to an amazing degree. I do miss Goethe's variation of rime-sequence and his varying masculine and feminine rimes. English possesses far more possibilities of feminine rimes, I think, than the translator grants. . . . Goethe's masculine rimes hit all the harder because they so frequently follow feminine rimes."[18]

The well-known American literary critic, Mark Van Doren, asserts in the Introduction to Alice Raphael's translation that by means of this version "the reader may be assured that he hears the poem as Goethe, standing on the other side of his interpreter, wanted him to hear it."[19] Finally, we may cite the enthusiastic testimony of Professor Carl F. Schreiber, Curator of the William A. Speck Collection of Goetheana at Yale University: "Alice Raphael has the mark of Faust upon her, for she felt her way into the spirit of the immortal poem, before she resorted to scholarship to convince herself that what she had felt was not her creation, but a faithful reproduction of the original."[20] The popularity of this translation is attested to by the fact that the first edition of one thousand copies was exhausted within a few weeks after its publication. A second printing was found necessary in the same month, and several new editions have appeared since that time.

Epilogue

William Taylor of Norwich, a little more than a century ago, said concerning *Faust:* "Everyone forbids it to be read, yet each in his turn reads it; and if one does not rise the better, one rises at least the wiser, from its perusal."* In these words one of the earliest English students of German literature strikingly reveals the contradictory attitude of Englishmen toward *Faust* in the first two or three decades after its publication. But Taylor does more. When he says that everyone forbids it to be read, yet each in his turn reads it, he gives signal testimony to the magnetic qualities of *Faust*.

Abraham Hayward, who in 1833, three years after these words were written, published the first English prose version of Goethe's great drama, enlarged more definitely in his Preface on its universal appeal: "As the sun beam breaks itself differently in every eye, and the starred heaven and nature are different for every soul mirror, so it is with this immeasurable and exhaustless poem. We have seen illustrators and continuers of *Faust*, who, captivated by the practical wisdom which pervades it, considered the whole poem as one great collection of maxims of life; we have met with others who saw nothing else in it but a fantastic solution of the enigma of existence; others again, more alive to the genius of poetry, admired only the poetical clothing of the ideas, which otherwise seemed to them to have little significance; and others again saw nothing peculiar but the felicitous exposition of a philosophical theory, and the specification of practical life." This manifold appeal of Goethe's *Faust*, referred to by William Taylor of Norwich and by Hayward, offers, perhaps, the best explanation of why so many scholars and would-be scholars have attempted to translate this work into English.

* W. Taylor, *Historic Survey of German Poetry* . . . (London: Treutel and Würtz, Treutel jun. and Richter, 1830), III, 323.

Assuming for a little while the role of Faust, the conjurer, let us command this numerous company of translators to pass before us in review. What a motley group it is, composed of Englishmen, Irishmen, Scotsmen, Americans, and one Canadian! They represent many different callings, conditions, and stations in life; we find here the educated and the ignorant, the rich and the poor, the socially and politically prominent as well as the plain citizens and the commoners. In this company are the wealthy timber merchant, Jonathan Birch; the journalists and writers, Lewis Filmore, Bayard Taylor, Anna Swanwick, and Alice Raphael; the bibliophile, Alfred Henry Huth; the police captain, Thomas J. Arnold; the architect, W. B. Clarke; members of the civil service and soldiers like Charles Henry Knox, G. M. Cookson; and the pension clerk, Frank Claudy. There are scientists like James Adey Birds and John Galvan. The law contributes outstanding men like Abraham Hayward, Sir Theodore Martin, and Thomas E. Webb. The university professors and educators include John Stuart Blackie, Albert G. Latham, John Shawcross, G. M. Priest, F. G. G. Schmidt, Carlyle Ferren MacIntyre, and John F. L. Raschen. The physicians in this group are William Bell Macdonald, Sir George William Lefevre, John Todhunter, and C. Fillingham Coxwell, and the clergy is represented by such names, among others, as Archer Thompson Gurney, Charles Timothy Brooks, and Charles Kegan Paul. Finally we must mention the Honorable Robert Talbot, a nobleman, Lord Francis Leveson-Gower, Member of Parliament, and Sir George Buchanan, who stood for two score years before the kings and queens of Europe as representatives of the highest social and political strata among the translators of *Faust*.

Several groups stand out from the rest for still other reasons. Lord Francis Leveson-Gower and Captain Charles Henry Knox were the only English translators who could boast of having met Goethe, while Abraham Hayward, Jonathan Birch, and Robert Talbot corresponded concerning their translations with the renowned German writer and literary critic, August Wilhelm Schlegel. Finally, in the comparison of the English with the American translators, it is an interesting fact that among the former were an appreciable number of such obscure personages that not even their dates are available, whereas the American translators, almost without exception, were individuals standing high in their particular lines of endeavor and well known in public life.

It is interesting also to note the various motives which led the different translators to take up their work. Lord Francis Leveson-Gower and Sir George Buchanan seem to have completed their versions as tasks that they set for themselves. John Stuart Blackie, Charles Timothy Brooks, Frank Claudy, and Alice Raphael felt that their lives had been singularly uplifted and benefited by their study of *Faust*, and, therefore, they attempted to give this great drama to the English-speaking world as a sort of evangel. On the other hand, Lewis Filmore and Anna Swanwick completed their versions as the result of solicitations from publishers who were anxious to acquire a translation of *Faust* for their series of publications.

By far the largest group, however, undertook the task in a distinct spirit of rivalry. Having read the versions already made, they found them to be of "such poor quality" that they thought there was ample room for another and better one. There were a few like John Anster, Jonathan Birch, John Hills, v. Beresford, G. M. Cookson, and Carlyle Ferren MacIntyre, who were spurred on to complete their translations by the encouragement given them by publishers, friends, and even princes. Finally, there were several, like Sir George Lefevre, John Galvan, and William Dalton Scoones, who undertook the task merely to occupy their time.

During the first two decades after the publication of *Faust*, Part I, in 1808, this masterpiece made slow progress in capturing the imagination and the hearts of the English-speaking peoples. Only one virtually complete translation, that of Lord Francis Leveson-Gower, came off the press during this time. But the interest that such eminent literary leaders as Percy Bysshe Shelley, Lord Byron, Samuel Taylor Coleridge, Sir Walter Scott, and Thomas Carlyle manifested in the works of

Goethe, and their active encouragement of those attempting to translate *Faust*, were largely responsible for the increased number of translations in the first decade after Goethe's death. If we consider the two parts separately, sixteen versions were published during this interval. However, when this first great wave of enthusiasm had spent itself, the next ten years brought forth only two new versions. During the succeeding period (1852-1862) only three were added.

But after this temporary numerical decline, there came a permanent revival of interest so that four or five new translations were published in practically every succeeding decade until the turn of the century. Professor Carl F. Schreiber, Curator of the William A. Speck Collection of Goetheana at Yale University, in his pamphlet, *A Note on Faust Translations*, sums up succinctly the history of the publication of the *Faust* translations in the following words: "The fashion and the passion to English the *Faust* has continued down through the decades with great persistence. To put it baldly, an English *Faust* translation has appeared on the average every second year." No fewer than forty-eight persons have competed in this venture. Thirty-four have published translations of Part I; three of Part II; and eleven of both parts of *Faust*. Part I, therefore, has been translated into English and published forty-five times and Part II fourteen times. Several more versions of both parts are under way.* It is safe to assert that no other single work, be it ancient, modern, or contemporary, has been translated as many times into English as Goethe's *Faust*.

It is inevitable that the individuals composing this large company of *Faust* translators would treat their subject with varying degrees of skill, with the result that the translations

---

* Among these may be mentioned a revised version of Part I and a new translation of Part II by Alice Raphael; a completed but unpublished translation of Part II by John Shawcross, who has already published a version of Part I; a similarly completed but unpublished translation of Part I (with Prologue at the Theatre and the Intermezzo omitted) and the Death of Faust from Part II by Professor Harry Wolcott Robbins of the English Department of Bucknell University. It will be remembered that Professor John F. L. Raschen has translated also considerable portions of Part II.

themselves are of unequal merit. Aside from the individual differences in linguistic preparation, there are two factors which have influenced the nature of the translations. The first of these was prejudice against certain parts of the drama. Lord Francis Leveson-Gower, John Stuart Blackie, and John Hills have omitted either parts or the whole of the Prologue in Heaven and other portions of the drama because they seemed to them impious and obscene. Carlyle Ferren MacIntyre desired to adapt his version for stage presentation, and he has, therefore, relegated the Dedication, the Prologue at the Theater, and the Walpurgis Night's Dream to the Appendix to the translation.

In the second place, some of the translators either had no definite theory of translation or followed a mistaken one. Some versions are, therefore, too literal, others too free; a few are in blank verse and a few in prose; while others, again, are defective on account of their stilted and unnatural language. Hence, only the best, like those of Anna Swanwick, Bayard Taylor, John Todhunter, William Page Andrews, Alice Raphael, and John F. L. Raschen, reproduce the form and spirit of the original in a highly pleasing if not entirely adequate manner.

Great progress toward a reasonably acceptable translation, however, has been made during the course of time. It is interesting to note that the versions of Part II have been uniformly better than those of Part I. The inspired First Part seems to have balked the endeavors of the most gifted translators, while the "dichterische Kunst" of Part II apparently lends itself better to the change from one language to another. A comparison of Martin's two parts brings this difference to the surface with great emphasis. It can be asserted also that the American versions, taken as a whole, are superior to the English, but one must bear in mind that the American translators have profited materially from the successes and failures of their English predecessors. To stress one further point, the translations by Anna Swanwick and Alice Raphael stand well to the fore and are to be preferred to most of those made by their masculine competitors.

Various fortunes have attended these translations during the course of years. Some, like those of Gower, Warburton Davies, Arthur Taylor, Syme, Birch, Hills, Colquhoun, Galvan, and Buchanan, have not yet gone beyond a first or second edition and in a few cases have become outstanding bibliographical rarities. Others, because of their intrinsic merit, or because they were accepted into some popular series, or because of the prominence of the translator in public life, have appeared in many editions. Outstanding among these are the translations by Abraham Hayward, Lewis Filmore, John Anster, Anna Swanwick, Sir Theodore Martin, and Bayard Taylor.

Notes

CHAPTER I

1. Goethe, *Faust* (trans. Bayard Taylor, Boston, 1871), Part II, Act IV, lines 10274-10284.
1a. In a letter from Ulrike von Pogwisch, Weimar, July 22, 1826, in *Goethes Werke* (Weimar edition, Weimar: Hermann Böhlau, 1890), Vol. XLI, Part IV, p. 97. (All later references to *Goethes Werke* will be to the Weimar edition.)
2. John Evans, *Lancashire Authors and Orators* (London: Houlston and Stoneman, 1850), p. 86.
3. *Dictionary of National Biography*, XVII, 153. (Cited hereafter as D. N. B.)
4. *London Times*, Thursday, February 19, 1857, p. 9.
5. Goethe, *Faust* (trans. into English Prose by A. Hayward, Esq., 2nd ed., London, 1834), p. xxx.
6. *Diary, Reminiscences, and Correspondence of Henry Crabb Robinson* (ed. Thomas Sadler, London: Macmillan, 1869), II, 432.
7. Quoted in Marshall Montgomery, "The First English Versions of Faust," *Publications of the English Goethe Society*, new series, III, 91.
8. *The Monthly Review*, LXII (1810), 491-95.
9. *The Complete Poetical Works of P. B. Shelley* (ed. William M. Rossetti, London, 1878), III, 320-36.
10. *The Liberal*, I (1822), 121-37.
11. *Goethes Werke*, Vol. X, Part III, p. 54.
12. *Ibid.*, Vol. XXXIX, Part IV, p. 210.
13. *Goethes Gespräche* (ed. F. W. von Biedermann, Leipzig, 1909-11), III, 485.
14. *Ibid.*, VII (1890), 154.
15. *Ibid.*, VII (1890), 155.
16. *Correspondence between Goethe and Carlyle* (ed. Charles Eliot Norton, London: Macmillan, 1887), p. 254.
17. *Annual Register*, LXII (1924), new series, p. 151.
18. *Who Was Who*, 1916-1928 (London: A. and C. Black, 1929), p. 143.
19. *Der Grosse Brockhaus* (Leipzig: F. A. Brockhaus, 1929), III, 441.
20. *Athenaeum*, LXXXI (1908), p. 302.
21. Goethe, *Faust*, Part I (trans. Sir George Buchanan, London, 1908).
22. *Athenaeum*, LXXXI (1908), p. 302.

CHAPTER II

1. Goethe, *Faust* (trans. Alice Raphael), from the revised but as yet unpublished edition, Part I, Study II, lines 1970-1979.
1a. *Edinburgh Review*, January, 1863, p. 42.
2. *The Hayward Letters* (ed. Henry E. Carlyle, London: John Murray, 1886), I, 7.

3. *D. N. B.*, IX, 308.
4. *Faust* (Hayward, 1834), p. xxix.
5. Erich Schmidt, "Ein verschollener Aufsatz Schlegels über Goethes Triumph der Empfindsamkeit," *Festschrift zur Begrüssung des Fünften Allgemeinen Deutschen Neuphilologentages* (Berlin, 1892), pp. 78-95.
6. *Ibid.*
7. *Goethes Werke*, Vol. XXVIII, Part I, p. 73. (Hayward's translation of Goethe's words.)
8. *The Hayward Letters*, I, 19.
9. *Ibid.*
9a. *Ibid.*
10. Hermann Kindt, "Goethe's Faust in England," *Die Gegenwart*, June 13, 1874, p. 376.
11. *Westminster Review*, XXV (1836), 384.
12. *D. N. B.*, II, 38.
13. [————], *Men of the Time* (London: David Bogue, 1856), p. 25.
14. *D. N. B.*, II, 38.
15. *Letters, Conversations, and Recollections of Samuel Taylor Coleridge* (ed. Thomas Allsop, London: Groombridge and Sons, 1858), p. 216.
16. *Men of the Time, loc. cit.*, p. 25.
17. *Biographia Epistolaris* (ed. A. Turnbull, London: G. Bell and Sons, 1911), II, 244 ff.
18. *Ibid.*
19. *Ibid.*
20. L. E. Watson, *Coleridge at Highgate* (New York: Longmans, Green and Co., 1925), pp. 99 ff.
21. Coventry Patmore, *The Table Talk and Omniana of Samuel Taylor Coleridge* (London: Oxford University Press, 1917), p. 207.
22. *Imperial Dictionary of Universal Biography* (ed. J. F. Waller, London: W. Mackenzie, 1865), I, 171.
23. Goethe, *Faustus* (trans. John Anster LL.D., London: Longman, Rees, Orme, Brown, Green, and Longman, 1835), p. viii.
24. Advertisement to *Faust* (Hayward, 1834).
25. *Edinburgh Review*, October, 1835, p. 37.
26. Goethe, *Faust*, Part I (trans. Honourable Robert Talbot, 2nd ed., London, 1839), p. xviii.
27. Westminster Review, XXV (1836), 284.
28. *Faustus* (Anster, 1835), p. xix.
29. *Gentleman's Magazine*, August, 1867, p. 250.
30. *Athenaeum*, VIII (1835), p. 614.
31. *A Genealogical and Heraldic History of Peerage and Baronetage* (ed. Sir Bernard Burke, London: Burke's Peerage, Ltd., 1928), p. 2234.
32. *Gentleman's Magazine*, May, 1835, p. 512.
33. *Faust* (Talbot, 1839), p. xvii.
34. *Ibid.* (1835), p. v.
35. *Ibid.*, Postscript, facing p. xiv.
36. *Ibid.*, p. iv.
37. *Ibid.*, p. x.
38. *Gentleman's Magazine*, May, 1835, p. 512.
39. *Archiv für das Studium der neueren Sprachen und Literaturen* (Begründet von Ludwig Herrig, herausgegeben von Alois Brandl und Adolf Tobler, Braunschweig: Georg Westermann, 1900), Vol. CVI (1901), pp. 355 f.
40. *Faust* (Talbot, 1839), pp. xvi ff.

41. *Ibid.*, pp. xxiii f.
42. *Enciclopedia universal ilustrada* (Barcelona: Espasa, 1907 (?) — 1930), XXX, 496.
43. *D. N. B.*, Supplement II, Vol. II, p. 578.
44. *Annual Register*, XLVII (1909), 130.
45. *Blackwood's Magazine*, September, 1909, pp. 453 ff.
46. *Ibid.*, p. 460.
47. *Ibid.*, pp. 453 ff.
48. Theodore Martin, *Essays on the Drama* (printed for private circulation, London, 1874), p. 126.
49. Goethe, *Faust*, Part II (trans. Theodore Martin, Edinburgh and London: William Blackwood and Sons, 1886), p. xiv.
50. *Ibid.*, p. viii.
51. *Atlantic Monthly*, LXVI (1890), pp. 733 ff.
52. *Annual Register*, XXV (1887), new series, p. 144.
53. *D. N. B.*, II, 117.
54. *Ibid.*
55. *Ibid.*
56. *Athenaeum*, LXXVI (1903), p. 685.
57. S. Austin Allibone, *Critical Dictionary of English Literature and British and American Authors* (Philadelphia: J. B. Lippincott and Co., 1870), III, 2621.
58. *Athenaeum*, LXXVI (1903), p. 685.
59. *Bibliotheca Cornubiensis* (ed. G. C. Boase and W. P. Courtney, London: Longmans, Green and Dyer, 1878), II, 859.
60. *Athenaeum*, LIV (1881), p. 393.
61. *Enciclopedia universal ilustrada* (Madrid: Espasa-Calpe, 1930), LXIX, 1704.
62. *Annual Register*, XLI (1903), new series, p. 164.
63. *Athenaeum*, LXXVI (1903), 685.
64. *Ibid.*
65. *Ibid.*
66. *Ibid.*
67. Goethe, *Faust* (trans. Thomas E. Webb, LL.D., London: Longmans, Green, and Co., 1880). See explanatory notes to Act I.
68. *Athenaeum*, LIV (1881), 393.

CHAPTER III

1. Goethe, *Faust* (trans. Alice Raphael), from the revised but as yet unpublished edition, Part I, Study, lines 1908-1922.
1a. Goethe, *Faust* (trans. John Stuart Blackie, 2nd ed., London: Macmillan and Co., 1880), Translator's Dedication.
2. *D. N. B.*, Supplement, I, 204.
3. *Blackwood's Magazine*, April, 1895, p. 662.
4. *Ibid.*, p. 664.
5. *The Letters of John Stuart Blackie to his wife* (ed. A. S. Walker, Edinburgh and London: William Blackwood and Sons, 1909), p. 29.
6. *Ibid.*
7. *Ibid.*, p. 37.
8. *Ibid.*, p. 38.
9. John Stuart Blackie, *Notes of a Life* (ed. A. S. Walker, Edinburgh and London: William Blackwood and Sons, 1910), p. 50.

10. *Ibid.*, p. 80.
11. *Ibid.*, pp. 80 f.
12. John Stuart Blackie, *The Wisdom of Goethe* (Edinburgh and London: W. Blackwood and Sons, 1883).
13. Goethe, *Faust* (trans. John S. Blackie, Edinburgh: William Blackwood; London: T. Cadell, 1834).
14. *Faust* (Blackie, 2nd ed., 1880), Translator's Dedication.
15. *Faust* (Blackie, 1834), p. vii.
16. *Faust*, Part I (Latham, 1902). These dedicatory lines, written by the translator's brother Harry Latham, A. G. L., appear on a fly-leaf at the beginning of Part I.
17. *Who's Who* (London: Macmillan, 1938), p. 1943.
17a. *Ibid.* (1942), p. 33.
18. This passage and those which follow, as well as much additional information about the translation, unless otherwise noted, are taken from the translator's letter to me dated January 20, 1931. This letter is now in the Speck Collection.
19. *Faust* (Latham, 1902), p. vii.
20. Latham's letter to me, January 20, 1931.
21. *Ibid.*
22. *Ibid.*
23. Goethe, *Faust* (trans. W. H. Van der Smissen, London and Toronto: J. M. Dent and Sons; New York: E. P. Dutton and Co., 1926), p. xviii.
24. *University of Toronto Monthly*, February, 1929, p. 192.
25. *Ibid.*
26. *Ibid.*
27. *Faust* (Van der Smissen). See Introduction by Robert A. Falconer.
28. *Ibid.*, Preface, p. xi.
29. *Ibid.*, p. xviii.
30. *Ibid.*
31. *Ibid.*, Prologue in Heaven, lines 33-35.
32. The facts concerning Professor Priest's life and literary activity were taken largely from *Who's Who in America*, 1936-1937 (ed. Albert Nelson Marquis, Chicago: A. N. Marquis Co., 1936), p. 1988.
32a. *The American German Review*, April, 1947, p. 35.
33. This information was obtained directly from Professor Priest.
34. *Faust*, Parts I and II (trans. George Madison Priest, New York: Covici-Friede, 1932), p. viii.
35. *Ibid.*
36. *Ibid.* (revised ed., New York, 1941), p. v.
37. The facts concerning Shawcross' life, as well as his comments on his efforts to translate *Faust*, are taken from letters to me dated June 25, 1935, and October 27, 1947. These letters are now in the Speck Collection.
38. Goethe, *Faust*, Part I (trans. John Shawcross, with a foreword by Dr. G. P. Gooch, London: Eric Partridge Ltd., 1934), p. v.
39. The facts concerning Professor Schmidt's life and his translation are taken from his letter to me dated April 22, 1935, and from *Who's Who in America*, 1940-1941. The letter is now in the Speck Collection.
40. Goethe's *Faust*, Part I (trans. Carlyle F. MacIntyre, Norfolk, Connecticut: New Directions [1941]). The last stanza of a poem, "Letter to a Young Poet," prefacing the translation.

41. Lawrence Clark Powell, "C. F. MacIntyre," *Wilson Bulletin for Librarians* (New York: H. W. Wilson Company, 1939), XIII, 462.
42. Letter from Professor MacIntyre to me dated March 30, 1942.
43. Powell, "C. F. MacIntyre," *loc. cit.*, p. 462.
44. *Ibid.*
45. *The Times Literary Supplement* (London: Times Publishing Co., February 27, 1937), p. 154.
46. *Twentieth Century Authors* (ed. Stanley J. Kunitz and Howard Haycroft, New York: H. W. Wilson Co., 1942), p. 877.
47. Letter from Professor MacIntyre to me, March 30, 1942.
48. *Ibid.*
49. *Ibid.*
50. *Ibid.*
51. *Faust,* Part I (trans. C. F. MacIntyre), p. 436. Translator's Note.
52. *Ibid.*
53. Letter from Professor MacIntyre to me, March 30, 1942.
54. *Who's Who in America,* 1948-1949 (Chicago: A. N. Marquis Co., 1948), XXV, 2026.
55. *Ibid.*
56. *Ibid.*
57. *Ibid.*
58. In a letter to me, dated January 10, 1949.
59. *Ibid.*

CHAPTER IV

1. Goethe, *Faust* (trans. Bayard Taylor), Part II, Act III, lines 9981 ff.
2. S. Austin Allibone, *Critical Dictionary of English Literature and British and American Authors* (Philadelphia: J. B. Lippincott and Co., 1880), II, 2322.
3. British Museum Catalogue, 1882.
4. Goethe, *Faust,* Part I (trans. Frank Claudy, Washington, D. C.: Wm. H. Morrison, 1886), p. iv.
5. British Museum Catalogue, 1895.
6. Goethe, *Faust,* Part I (trans. v. Beresford, Cassel and Göttingen: George H. Wigand, 1862).
7. Goethe, *Faust,* Part I (trans. John Wynniat Grant, London: Hamilton, Adams, and Co., 1867), "Address to the Muse" placed at the end of the translation.
7a. John Foster Kirk, *Supplement to Allibone's Critical Dictionary of English Literature and British and American Authors* (Philadelphia: J. B. Lippincott and Co., 1891), I, 702.
8. Goethe, *Faust,* Part I (trans. Charles Hartpole Bowen, London: Longmans, Green and Co., 1878).
9. Samuel Lewis, *Topographical Dictionary of Ireland* (2nd ed., London: [————], 1846), II, 435.
10. Goethe, *Faust,* Part I (trans. W. H. Colquhoun, London: Arthur H. Moxon, 1878).
11. Bayard Quincy Morgan, *Bibliography of German Literature in English Translation* (University of Wisconsin Studies in Languages and Literature, No. 16, Madison, 1922), p. 160.
12. Karl Goedeke, *Grundriss zur Geschichte der Deutschen Dichtung* (4 vols., 3rd ed., Dresden: L. Ehlermann, 1910-13), IV, 639.

13. *Faust* (Colquhoun), Preface.
14. Goedeke, *op. cit.*, p. 158.
15. In a letter to me from A. G. Berry, Foreign and English Book Seller, dated March 3, 1931.
16. Goethe, *Faust*, Part I (trans. Beta, London: David Nutt, 1895), p. iv.
17. Morgan, *op. cit.*, p. 158.
18. *Academy*, xxxi (1887), p. 79.
19. *Transactions of the Manchester Goethe Society* (Warrington: Mackie and Co., 1894), pp. 127 f.
20. *Faust* (McLintock, 1897), p. xxvii.
21. *Ibid.*, p. xxx.
22. *Ibid.*, p. viii.
23. *Ibid.*
24. *Academy*, XXXI (1897), p. 79.
25. Otto Heller, *Faust and Faustus: A Study of Goethe's Relation to Marlowe* (St. Louis: Washington University Press, 1931) p. 10.
26. *Transactions of the Manchester Goethe Society*, pp. 127 f.

CHAPTER V

1. Goethe, *Faust*, Part I (trans. Alice Raphael), from the revised but as yet unpublished edition, Before the Gate, lines 993-1006.
2. Goethe, *Faust* Parts I and II (trans. Anna Swanwick, London: George Bell and Sons, 1879), Prologue for the Theatre.
3. *D. N. B.*, XXXII, 398.
4. *Literary Gazette*, XXX (1846), 180.
5. *Ibid.*, p. 176.
6. Goethe, *Faust*, Part I (trans. Sir George Lefevre, M.D., 2nd ed., Frankfort: Charles Jugel, 1843).
7. *Ibid.*
8. *Ibid.*
9. British Museum Catalogue, 1897.
10. *Who Was Who*, 1916-1928, p. 1045.
11. Goethe, *Faust*, Part I (trans. John Todhunter, Oxford: Basil Blackwell, 1924), Acknowledgments.
12. *Ibid.*
13. *Ibid.*, p. xvi.
14. The facts concerning Dr. Coxwell's life, as well as quoted comments on his efforts to translate *Faust*, are taken from his letter to me dated May 6, 1936, and Mrs. Louise D. Coxwell's letter to me dated October 20, 1947.

CHAPTER VI

1. Goethe, *Faust*, Part I (trans. Alice Raphael), from the revised but as yet unpublished edition, Prologue in the Theatre, lines 148-157.
2. Goethe, *Faust*, Parts I and II ([trans. Arthur Taylor], London: Arthur Taylor, 1839).
3. British Museum Catalogue, 1888.
4. This information is taken from private correspondence with Professor William A. Rose, University of London.
5. Morgan, *Bibliography of German Literature in English Translation*, p. 162.
6. Samuel Halkett and Rev. John Laing, *Dictionary of Anonymous and*

Pseudonymus English Literature (Edinburgh: William Patterson, 1893), II, 905.
7. *D. N. B.*, XIII, 491.
8. *Gentleman's Magazine*, March, 1863, p. 390.
9. British Museum Catalogue, 1891.
10. Goethe, *Faust*, Part II, as completed in 1831 ([trans. William Bell Macdonald], Dumfries: D. Halliday, 1838).
11. *Ibid.* (2nd ed., London: William Pickering, 1842), Advertisement.
12. *Ibid.*
13. Ludwig Herrig, *Archiv für das Studium der Neueren Sprachen und Litteraturen* (hrsg. Alois Brandl und Adolf Tobler, Braunschweig: Georg Westermann, 1900), new series, V, 357.
14. *D. N. B.*, V, 65.
15. Goethe, *Faust*, Part I (trans. Jonathan Birch, Esq., London: Black and Armstrong, 1839), pp. ix f.
16. *Faust*, Part II (Birch, 1843), pp. vii f.
17. *Ibid.* (1839), p. x.
18. *Ibid.*, p. vi.
19. *D. N. B.*, V, 65.
20. *Faust*, Part I (Birch, 1839), p. x.
21. Herrig's *Archiv*, new series, V, 357.
22. *Faust*, Part II, [First five scenes of Act I] (Birch, London and Leipzig: [――――, 1840?]).
23. *Faust*, Part II (Birch, 1843), pp. vii f.
24. *Dublin Review*, IX (1840), 492.
25. Henry Crabb Robinson, *Blake, Coleridge, Wordsworth, Lamb* (ed. Edith J. Morley, Manchester: The University Press; London and New York: Longmans, Green and Co., 1922), p. 90.
26. Goethe, *Faust*, Part I (trans. John Hills, Esq., London: Whittaker and Co.; Berlin: Asher, 1840) p. iv.
27. *Ibid.*, p. 5.
28. *Ibid.*, pp. x f.
29. *Ibid.*, pp. xvi f.
30. *Illustrated London News*, June 7, 1890, p. 707.
31. *Modern English Biography* (ed. Frederic Boase, Truro: Netherton and Worth, 1892), V (Supplementary Vol. II), p. 293.
32. Goethe, *Faust*, Part I (trans. Lewis Filmore, London: William Smith, 1841), pp. iii ff.
33. Albert H. Smyth, *Bayard Taylor* (Boston and New York: Houghton, Mifflin and Co., 1896), p. 13.
34. In Bayard Taylor, *The Poet's Journal* (Boston: Ticknor and Fields, 1863), p. 182.
35. Smyth, *op. cit.*, p. 23.
36. Goethe, *Faust*, Part I (trans. Bayard Taylor, Boston: Fields, Osgood, and Co., [1870]), p. iii.
37. Smyth, *op. cit.*, p. 292.
38. *Faust* (Bayard Taylor, 1870), p. iii.
39. *Life and Letters of Bayard Taylor* (ed. Marie Hansen Taylor and Horace E. Scudder, Boston: Houghton, Mifflin and Co., 1884), II, 464.
40. *Ibid.*, II, 535.
41. Smyth, *op. cit.*, p. 193.
42. *Ibid.*, p. 121.
43. *Ibid.*, p. 113.

44. Quoted in *Life and Letters of Bayard Taylor*, I, 44.
45. *Ibid.*, II, 563.
46. *Ibid.*, II, 541.
47. *Ibid.*, II, 418.
48. Taylor, *The Poet's Journal*.
49. Smyth, *op. cit.*, p. 181.
50. *Life and Letters of Bayard Taylor*, II, 551.
51. *Ibid.*, II, 506.
52. *Faust* (Bayard Taylor, 1870), p. iii.
53. *Life and Letters of Bayard Taylor*, II, 510.
54. *Ibid.*, II, 506.
55. *Faust* (Bayard Taylor, 1870), p. xv.
56. *Ibid.*, p. xvi.
57. Juliana Haskell, *Bayard Taylor's Translation of Goethe's Faust* (New York: Columbia University Press, 1908), pp. 88 ff.
58. *Ibid.*, pp. 2 ff.
59. See Miss Haskell's chapter on "The Poetic Worth of Taylor's Translation," pp. 74 ff.
60. Introduction to Taylor's translation of *Faust* in the Modern Readers' Series (New York: Macmillan and Co., 1930), p. xxi. Another 1930 edition was published by the Modern Library, New York: Random House.
61. The information pertaining to the life of Frank Claudy was obtained by me from his son, Carl H. Claudy.
62. Frank Claudy, *Selections from the Translation of Goethe's Faust*, Washington, D. C., 1883.
63. Information from Carl H. Claudy.
64. *Ibid.*
65. *Menorah*, February, 1890, pp. 57 ff.
66. *New York Times*, July 12, 1886.
67. *Nation*, May 27, 1886, p. 451.
68. *Westminster Review*, January, 1887, p. 257.
69. *Menorah*, February, 1890, pp. 57 ff.
70. *Dictionary of Universal Biography* (ed. Albert M. Hyamson, London: George Routledge and Sons; New York: E. P. Dutton and Co., 1916), p. 320.
71. *D. N. B.*, Supplement II, Vol. II, 331.
72. *Dictionary of Universal Biography*, p. 320.
73. *D. N. B.*, Supplement II, Vol. II, 331.
74. *Ibid.*
75. I have obtained the facts concerning the life and works of William Page Andrews, unless otherwise noted, from a letter from his literary executor, Professor Karl E. Weston, of Williams College.
76. *Atlantic Monthly*, LXVI (1890), 733 ff.
77. William Page Andrews, "Goethe's Key to Faust: The Prologues"; "The Tragedy of the First Part"; "The Second Part of Faust,"*Atlantic Monthly*, LXVII (1891), 538 ff., 676 ff., 820 ff.
78. William Page Andrews, "Goethe's Key to Faust," *loc. cit.*, p. 676.
79. This letter is now in the Speck Collection.
80. *Atlantic Monthly*, LXVI (1890), 733 ff.
81. *Die Literatur*, February, 1931, p. 258.

CHAPTER VII

1. Goethe, *Faust*, Part I (trans. Alice Raphael), from the revised but as yet unpublished edition, Martha's Garden, lines 3431 ff.
2. *A Bibliographical List of the English Translations and Annotated Editions of Goethe's Faust* (comp. William Heinemann, London: Elliott Stock, 1882), p. 11.
3. Letter to Dr. Carl F. Schreiber from Professor R. Priebsch, London, August 7, 1931. This letter is in the files of the Speck Collection.
4. Sir Bernard Burke, *Genealogical and Heraldic History of the Landed Gentry* . . . (London: Burke's Peerage, Limited, 1939), p. 576.
5. Joseph Foster, *Alumni Oxoniensis* . . . *1715-1886* (Oxford, London, 1888), I, 35.
6. *Selections from the Letters and Correspondence of Sir James Bland Burges . . . Sometime Under-Secretary of State for Foreign Affairs* (ed. James Hutton, London: John Murray, 1885), p. 356.
7. Goethe, *Faust*, Part I (trans. Warburton Davies, London: Simpkin and Marshall, 1834), p. v.
8. *Ibid.*, p. vi.
9. *Ibid.*, pp. vi, vii.
10. *Ibid.*, p. vii.
11. *Ibid.*
12. *Enciclopedia universal ilustrada* (Barcelona, 1905), VIII, 358.
13. This letter is contained in Mr. William A. Speck's "Notes on the English Translation of the Second Part of *Faust* by Leopold J. Bernays" which are appended to *Offene Gegend*, a fragment of the Second Part of *Faust* in Goethe's hand (Rare item No. 5 in the Speck Collection).
14. *Ibid.*
15. Goethe, *Faust*, Part II (trans. Leopold J. Bernays, London: S. Lamb; Karlsruhe: A. Bielefeld, 1839), Dedication.
16. *Ibid.*, p. ix.
17. In Adolph Bernays' letter to Johann Peter Eckermann, dated November 28, 1839. (Cf. Note 13.)
18. *Faust*, Part II (Bernays, 1939), p. x.
19. *Literary Gazette*, XXIII (1839), p. 806.
20. *Foreign Quarterly Review*, XXV (1840), p. 103.
21. *D. N. B.*, XXIII, 354-55.
22. *London Times*, March 29, 1887, p. 8.
23. *Modern English Biography* (ed. Boase), I, 1260.
24. *Bibliotheca Cornubiensis* (ed. George Clement Boase and William Prideaux Courtney, London: Longmans, Green, Reeder, and Dyer, 1874-1882), III, 1210.
25. *English Review*, X (1848), 46-76.
26. Goethe, *Faust*, Part II (trans. Archer Gurney, London: Senior, Heathcote and Senior, 1842), pp. vii f.
27. *Ibid.*, p. 336.
28. Charles T. Brooks, *Poems, Original and Translated*, with a Memoir by Charles W. Wendte (ed. W. P. Andrews, Boston: Robert Brothers, 1885), p. 114.
29. *Ibid.*, p. 10.
30. *Ibid.*, p. 40.
31. *Ibid.*, p. 41.
32. *Ibid.*, p. 55.

33. Goethe, *Faust*, Part I (trans. Charles T. Brooks, Boston: Ticknor and Fields, 1856), p. 5.
34. *Life and Letters of Bayard Taylor*, II, 554, 555.
35. Brooks, *Poems, Original and Translated*, p. 14.
36. *Ibid.*, pp. 55, 56.
37. Brooks, *Poems, Original and Translated*, p. 88.
38. *D. N. B.*, Supplement II, Vol. II, 80.
39. *Athenaeum*, LXXV (1902), p. 129.
40. *Ibid.*, p. 129.
41. *Annual Register*, XL (1902), new series, p. 133.
42. Goethe, *Faust*, Part I (trans. Charles Kegan Paul, London: Simpkin and Marshall), Preface.
43. Walter G. Hart, *The Old School Lists of Tonbridge School* (London, [1933]), pp. 136, 137.
44. Joseph Foster, *Alumni Oxoniensis . . . 1715-1886* (Oxford, London, 1888), IV, 1263.
45. *The Register of Tonbridge* [Tunbridge] *School* (ed. W. O. Hughes-Hughes, London, 1893), p. 39. The information on the life of William Dalton Scoones taken from the sources listed above was made available to me by Professor Carl F. Schreiber.

CHAPTER VIII

1. Goethe, *Faust* (trans. Alice Raphael), from the revised but as yet unpublished edition, Part I, Before the Gate, lines 884-902.
2. *Publications of the English Goethe Society*, V, 191.
3. Goethe, *Faust*, Part I (trans. Captain C. H. Knox, London: John Ollivier, 1847), p. iv.
4. *Goethes Werke* (Tagebücher), Vol. II, Part III, pp. 20, 198.
5. *Modern English Biography* (ed. Boase), V, 835.
6. *Faust* (Knox, 1847), p. iii.
7. *Ibid.*, p. iv.
8. The information regarding Cookson's life and his translation was gathered from a letter addressed to Professor Carl F. Schreiber and from two letters to me, dated March 26, 1931, and October 17, 1947, respectively.

CHAPTER IX

1. Goethe, *Faust* (trans. Alice Raphael), from the revised but as yet unpublished edition, Part I, Night, lines 664-675.
2. *Alumni Dublinensis . . . New Edition* (Dublin, 1935), p. 315.
3. Goethe, *Faust*, Part I (trans. John Galvan, Dublin: William Robertson, 1860), title-page and p. ix.
4. D. J. O'Donoghue, *The Poets of Ireland* (Dublin, 1912), p. 158.
5. *Faust* (Galvan), p. vii.
6. *Ibid.*, p. ix.
7. *Ibid.*, p. viii.
8. Goethe, *Faust*, Parts I and II (trans. William Barnard Clarke, Freiburg im Breisgau: Schmidt; London: Bedford Row, 1865).
9. Morgan, *Bibliography of German Literature in English Translation*, p. 160.
10. Algernon Graves, *The Royal Academy of Arts* (London, 1905), II, 74.
11. British Museum Catalogue, 1881.

12. *Faust* (Clarke), Preface, p. xiii.
13. *Ibid.*
14. *Ibid.*
15. *Illustrated London News*, February 9, 1895, p. 184.
16. *Quarterly Journal of the Geological Society of London*, LI (1895), 64.
17. *Modern English Biography* (ed. Boase), IV (Supplementary Vol. I), 406.
18. Goethe, *Faust*, Part I (trans. James Adey Birds, London: Longman's, Green and Co., 1880), p. v.
19. *Ibid.*, p. vii.
20. *Ibid.*
21. *Faust II* (Birds, 1889), p. 3.

CHAPTER X

1. Goethe, *Faust* (trans. Bayard Taylor), Part II, Act III, lines 9365-9374.
2. *D. N. B.*, Supplement, III, 374.
3. *Annual Register*, XXVII (1889), new series, p. 174.
4. Mary L. Bruce, *Anna Swanwick, a Memoir* (London: T. Fisher Unwin, 1903), p. 25.
5. *Ibid.*
6. *Ibid.*, pp. 28, 34.
7. *Ibid.*, p. 25.
8. *Ibid.*, p. 39.
9. *Dramatic Works of Goethe* (trans. Anna Swanwick, London: Henry G. Bohn, 1850), p. vii.
10. Bruce, *op. cit.*, p. 40.
11. *Ibid.*, p. 98.
12. *Faust* (Swanwick, 1879), p. v.
13. William F. Hauhart, *The Reception of Goethe's Faust in the First Half of the Nineteenth Century* (New York: Columbia University Press, 1909), p. 132.
14. *Literary Gazette*, XXXV (1851), 141.
15. Bruce, *op. cit.*, p. 115.
16. *Ibid.*
17. All information and quoted material concerning the life and work of Alice Raphael, unless otherwise noted, has been taken from an autobiographical sketch prepared for me by the translator and her daughter Alice, and from subsequent letters to me from the translator.
18. From a letter written to Professor Carl F. Schreiber, January 4, 1931.
19. Goethe, *Faust* (trans. Alice Raphael, New York: Jonathan Cape and Harrison Smith, 1930), p. xviii.
20. Professor Carl F. Schreiber, *A Note on Faust Translations* (New York: Jonathan Cape and Harrison Smith, 1930), on a loose leaf accompanying the pamphlet.

BIBLIOGRAPHY

Bibliography

WILLIAM PAGE ANDREWS
Translation Limited to a Single Edition

1. *Goethe's *Faust*/ Part I/ Translated by William Page Andrews/ Edited and Revised by George M. Priest, Ph.D., Princeton University, and Karl E. Weston, M.A., Williams College/ Princeton University Press/ Princeton New Jersey/ 1929

Partial Edition

1. Numerous short passages appeared in the *Atlantic Monthly* for 1890, 1891.

JOHN ANSTER
Editions and Reprints

1. **Faustus*/ A Dramatic Mystery; The Bride of Corinth; The First Walpurgis Night*/ Translated from the German of Goethe and Illustrated with Notes/ By John Anster, LL.D., Barrister at Law/ Longman, Rees, Orme, Brown, Green, and Longman/ London/ 1835. 491 p. 8 vo.
2. **Faust*. Part I. Jügel's Pocket Novelists No. 19. Frankfurt A. Main. 1841. XLVI, 283 p. 8 vo.
3. **Faust*. Part I. New Edition. London. 1864. 8 vo.
4. **Faust*/ The Second Part/ From the German of Goethe/ By John Anster, L.L.S., M.R.I.A./ Regius Professor of Civil Law in the University of Dublin/ Longman, Green, Longman Roberts and Green/ London/ 1864. LXXXII, 485 p. 8 vo.
5. **Faust*/ Part I/ From the German/ By John Anster/ Bernhard Tauchnitz/ Leipzig and London/ 1867. XXIV, 295 p. 8 vo. In Collection of German Authors/ Vol. V.

* All items marked by an asterisk in this Bibliography are to be found in the William A. Speck Collection of Goetheana, Sterling Memorial Library, Yale University.

6. *Faust. Part I. G. Routledge and Sons. London and New York. 1885.
7. *Marlowe's *Faustus* and Goethe's *Faust*/ From the German/ By J. Anster/ With an Introduction/ By Henry Morley/ London/ 1883. 315 p. 8 vo. Also in Morley's Universal Library/ Vol. III/ London/ 1887
8. *Faust. Part I. With an Introduction/ By the Rev. Hugh Reginald Haweis. London and New York. 1886. 160 p. 12 mo. In Routledge's World Library.
9. Faust. Parts I and II. 8 vo. Routledge. London. 1886.
10. *Faust. Part I. With Marlowe's *Faustus*. Routledge. London. 1887. 8 vo.
11. *Faust. Part I. With an Introduction by Henry Morley. Illustrations by J. P. Lawrens. Routledge. London and New York. 1887.
12. *Faust. Parts I and II. Harper. New York. 1888. 2 vol.
13. Faust. Part I. With Introductory matter by Henry Morley and the Rev. Hugh R. Haweis. New York. 1888. V, 290 p. 8 vo. In Harper's Handy Series.
14. *Faust. Part I. Introduction by Burdett Mason and Illustrations by Frank M. Gregory. White and Allen. New York and London. [1888].
15. Faust. Part I. New York. 1888. III, 329 p. 8 vo. In Munro's Seaside Library No. 1043.
16. *Faust. Part I. Edition de grand luxe. Illustrations with ten aquarelles and many monochromes by Frank M. Gregory. J. C. Yorston and Co. London and New York. [1888?].
17. Faust. Part I. With Schiller's *Poems and Ballads*. Introduction by H. Morley. Routledge. London. 1889. 8 vo.
18. Faust. Part I. Illustrated by F. J. Boston. Vignette edition. New York. 1890; London. 1890? IV, 360 p. 8 vo. Also London. 1895. 240 p. 8 vo.
19. *Faust. Part I. Illustrated by F. J. Boston. Stokes. New York. [1890].
20. *Faust. Part I. Introduction by Henry Morley. G. Routledge and Sons. London and New York. 1891.
21. Faust. Parts I and II. Introduction by H. Morley. Routledge. London. 1893. VIII, 287 p. 8 vo. In Lubbock's One Hundred Books. 12th Edition. 1894.

Bibliography

22. *Faust. Part I. Introduction by Burdett Mason. Truslove and Hanson. London. 1894. 250 p. 8 vo.
23. *Faust. Part I. Introduction by Burdett Mason and Illustrations by Frank M. Gregory. Dodd, Mead and Co. New York. 1894.
24. Faust. Part I and Marlowe's Faustus. Introduction by H. Morley. London. 1897. 604 p. 8 vo.
25. Faust. Part I. In the Universal Library. London. 1902. 254 p. 12 mo.
26. Faust. Part I. In Caxton Series of Pocket Classics. London. New York. 1903. 250 p. 8 vo.
27. Faust. Part I. Newnes. London. 1903. 254 p. 12 mo.
28. Faust. Part I. In Hutchinson's Popular Classics. London. 1907.
29. Marlowe's Tragical History of Doctor Faustus and Goethe's Faust, Part I. Introduction by A. W. Ward. Frowde. London. 1908. XXX, 235 p. 8 vo. Appeared also in World's Classics. Oxford University Press. 1909. 16 mo.
30. Faust. Part I. People's Edition. London, New York, Toronto, Melbourne. 1909. 419 p. 8 vo.
31. *Faust. Part I. Illustrations by Harry Clarke. Dingwall-Rock Limited. New York. [1925].
32. *Marlowe's Tragical History of Dr. Faustus and Goethe's Faust Part I/ With an Introduction by Sir Adolphus William Ward, Litt. D., Master of Peterhouse, Cambridge/ Humphrey Milford/ Oxford University Press/ 1925/ London/ Edinburgh/ Glasgow/ Copenhagen/ New York/ Toronto/ Melbourne/ Cape Town/Bombay/ Calcutta/ Madras/ Shanghai.

Partial Edition

1. *Translation of extracts from Faust: Parts of Dedication; Prelude at the Theatre; Night (I); Parts of Witches' Kitchen; Gretchen's Song at the Spinning Wheel; and almost the entire Prison scene in Blackwood's Magazine, 1880, pp. 235-258.

THOMAS JAMES ARNOLD
Translation Limited to a Single Edition

1. *Faust/ A Tragedy/ By Johann Wolfgang von Goethe/ The First Part Translated in the Original Metres/ By Thomas James Arnold Esq./ F.S.A. (Metropolitan Police Magistrate,

England)/ With 50 illustrations after original designs by Alexander Liezen Mayer (Honorary member of the Royal Academy, Munich), and with vignettes, ornamental borderings etc. by Rudolf Seitz/ Published by Theo. Stroefer/ Munich;/ George Kirchner and Co./ New York/ 1877. 157 p.

LEOPOLD J. BERNAYS
Editions
1. *Goethe's *Faust*/ Part II/ With Other Poems, Original and Translated/ By Leopold J. Bernays/ S. Lamb/ London; A. Bielefeld/ Carlsruhe/ 1839. XX, 268 p. 8 vo.
2. *Ibid.* London and Carlsruhe. 1840.

Partial Edition
1. The larger part of the translation appeared in the *Monthly Magazine*, 1839, previous to the publication of the entire version in the same year.

BETA
Translation Limited to a Single Edition
1. *Goethe's *Faust*/ The First Part/ With a literal Translation and Notes for Students/ By Beta/ London/ David Nutt/ 1895. 384 p.

JONATHAN BIRCH
Editions and Reprints
1. **Faust*/ A Tragedy/ By J. Wolfgang von Goethe/ Translated into English Verse by J. Birch, Esq./ Author of "Fifty-One Original Fables and Morals," "Divine Emblems," etc./ Black and Armstrong/ London;/ F. A. Brockhaus/ Leipzig/ 1839/ With Engravings after Retzsch. XVII, 276 p. 8 vo.
2. *Ibid.* Same as above except for title-page, where "engravings after Retzsch" are not mentioned and advertisements left out.
3. **Faust*/ A Tragedy in Two Parts/ By J. Wolfgang von Goethe/ The Second Part/ Translated into English Verse/ By Jonathan Birch, Esq. Honorary Member of the Society for Home and Foreign Polite Literature in Berlin/ Embellished with Eleven Engravings on Steel/ By John Brain, after Moritz Retzsch/ Chapman and Hall/ London;/ F. A. Brockhaus/ Leipzig/ 1843. XXXIV, 342 p.

4. *Faust.* Part II. Rendered into English Verse, accompanied by a Dramatis Personae Raisonné and very copious Notes and Remarks. Embellished with Engravings after M. Retzsch by J. Brain. Black and Armstrong. London. [1863].
5. **Faust.* Part I. Published by Thomas Beecham. St. Helen's Lancashire. [1886]. Each page has at the bottom the words "Beecham's Pills."

Partial Edition

1. **The Prospectus and Temporary Title-page* has the following announcements: *Faust*/ The Second Part/ By von Goethe/ Rendered into English Verse, accompanied by a Dramatis Personae Raisonné, and Very Copious Notes and Remarks by J. Birch, Esq./ Embellished with Engravings after Moritz Retzsch, by J. Brain/ In Parts/ Part I/ Black and Armstrong/ London;/ F. A. Brockhaus/ Leipzig. No date. 80 p. Text, Notes, and Remarks, XVI p. 24½cm. Very probably the same as the edition listed by B. Q. Morgan and by Goedeke's *Grundriss* for 1840. Contains first five scenes of Part II.

JAMES ADEY BIRDS
Editions and Reprints

1. **Faust*/ A Tragedy/ By Goethe/ Translated chiefly in Blank Verse with Introduction and Notes by James Adey Birds, B.A., F.G.S./ Longmans, Green and Co./ London/ 1880. VIII, 460 p. 8 vo.
2. **Faust*/ A Tragedy/ By Goethe/ The Second Part Translated in verse with Introduction and Notes by James Adey Birds, B.A., F.G.S. Vol. II/ Longmans, Green and Co./ London;/ New York, 15 East 16th Street/ 1889. 450 p. 8 vo.
3. *Ibid.* Parts I and II. In 2 volumes. New York. 1889. 460 and 450 p. 8 vo.

Partial Edition

1. An analysis and observation on Part II accompanied with specimens of the translation in *Westminster Review* for April, 1886.

JOHN S. BLACKIE
Editions

1. *Faust/ A Tragedy/ By J. W. Goethe/ Translated into English Verse/ By John S. Blackie/ William Blackwood/ Edinburgh;/ T. Cadell/ London/ 1834. 288 p. 8 vo.
2. *Faust/A Tragedy/ By Goethe/ Translated into English Verse/ With Notes and Preliminary Remarks/ By John Stuart Blackie/ Second Edition/ Carefully Revised and Largely Rewritten/ Macmillan and Co./ London/ 1880. 296 p. 8 vo.

CHARLES HARTPOLE BOWEN
Translation Limited to a Single Edition

1. *Faust/ A Tragedy/ By T. W. [sic] von Goethe/ Translated into English Verse/ By Charles Hartpole Bowen/ Longmans, Green and Co./ London/ 1878. 247 p. 8 vo.

CHARLES TIMOTHY BROOKS
Editions and Reprints

1. *Faust/ A Tragedy/ Translated from the German of Goethe/ With Notes/ By Charles T. Brooks/ Ticknor and Fields/ Boston/ 1856. 234 p. 16 mo.
2. *Faust/ A Tragedy/ Translated from the German of Goethe/ With Notes/ By Charles T. Brooks/ Second Edition/ Boston/ Ticknor and Fields/ MDCCC LVII
3. Ibid. 1858.
4. Ibid. 1859.
5. *Faust/ A Tragedy/ Translated from the German of Goethe/ With Notes/ By Charles T. Brooks/ Third Edition/ Boston/ Ticknor and Fields/ MDCC LX
6. *Ibid. 1862. Fourth Edition.
7. *Ibid. 1864. Fifth Edition.
8. Ibid. 1865.
9. *Ibid. 1866. Sixth Edition.
10. Ibid. 1868.
11. Faust/ A Tragedy/ Translated from the German of Goethe/ With Notes/ By Charles T. Brooks/ Fields, Osgood and Company/ Boston/ 1869
12. *Ibid. 1871.

13. *Faust/ A Tragedy/ Translated from the German of Goethe/ With Notes/ By Charles T. Brooks/ James R. Osgood and Company/ Boston/ 1871/ Ninth Edition
14. *Ibid. 1873. Tenth Edition.
15. Ibid. 1874.
16. Ibid. 1875.
17. Faust/ A Tragedy/ Translated from the German of Goethe/ With Notes/ By Charles T. Brooks/ Houghton, Osgood and Company/ Boston/ 1878
18. Ibid. 1880.
19. Faust/ A Tragedy/ Translated from the German of Goethe/ With Notes/ By Charles T. Brooks/ Houghton, Mifflin and Company/ Boston/ 1882

Partial Edition

1. Goethe/ *The Song of the Angels*/ Translated by C. T. B.[rooks]. In *Literary World*. (New York, 1849). Vol. V., p. 349.
See Bibliographical Note p. 304 on Brooks.

SIR GEORGE BUCHANAN
Translation Limited to a Single Edition

1. *Faust/ By Goethe/ The First Part/ Translated into English Verse/ By Sir George Buchanan/ Alston Rivers/ London/ 1908. 200 p. 12 mo.

WILLIAM BARNARD CLARKE
Translation Limited to a Single Edition

1. *Translation of Goethe's *Faust*/ 1st and 2nd Part/ By William Barnard Clarke/ Schmidt/ Freiburg im Breisgau/ And Bedford Row/ London/ 1865. 460 p. 8 vo.

FRANK CLAUDY
Editions

1. *Faust/ A Tragedy/ By Johann Wolfgang von Goethe/ The First Part/ Translated in the Original Metres/ By Frank Claudy/ Wm. H. Morrison/ Washington, D. C./ 1886. 182 p.
2. *Ibid. Second Edition. 1899. 182 p.

Partial Editions

1. *Selections from the Translation of Goethe's Faust/ By Frank Claudy/ Washington, D. C./ 1883. 8 p.
2. *Ibid. Second Edition. 1884.

W. H. COLQUHOUN
Translation Limited to a Single Edition

1. *The Faust of Goethe/ Part I/ In English Verse/ By W. H. Colquhoun/ Arthur H. Moxon/ London/ 1878. 216 p.

GEOFFREY M. COOKSON
Translation Limited to a Single Edition

1. *Goethe's Faust/ Part I/ Translated by Geoffrey M. Cookson/ With an Introduction by J. G. Robertson/ George Routledge and Sons/ London;/ E. P. Dutton and Co./ New York/ (Broadway Translation). Date of publication not given in the translation, but Cookson writes that it was first published in 1925.

C. FILLINGHAM COXWELL
Translation Limited to a Single Edition

1. *Goethe's Tragedy of Faust/ Translated with Notes and a Life of Goethe/ By C. Fillingham Coxwell/ Author of Siberian and Other Folk Tales/ Translator of Russian Poems/ The C. W. Daniel Company/ London/ Forty-six Bernard Street, W. C. 1./ 1932. Life of Goethe pp. 9-122. Faust pp. 123-326. Notes pp. 327-344.

WARBURTON DAVIES
Translation Limited to a Single Edition

1. *Faustus/ A Tragedy/ Translated from the German [By Warburton Davies]/ Published by Simpkin and Marshall/ Stationers' Hall Court/ London/ 1834. VIII, 231 p. 12 mo.

LEWIS FILMORE
Editions and Reprints

1. *Faust/ A Tragedy/ By Goethe. Translated Expressly for this Series/ By Lewis Filmore/ William Smith/ London/ 1841. In Smith's Standard Library. VI, p. 64, 8 vo.

2. *Faust.* Part I. Reprint of 1841 Edition without Notes.
3. *Faust/ A Tragedy/ by Goethe/ Translated by Lewis Filmore London/ William Smith, Fleet Street/ George Routledge and Co., Soho Square. (No date but with Introduction and Notes).
4. *Faust.* Part I. London. 1843. XIX, 64 p. 12 mo.
5. *Faust.* Part I. New Edition. London. 1847. 12 mo.
6. *Faust.* Part I. New Edition. Ingram, Cooke and Co. London. 1853. With Translations of *Wallenstein* in the Universal Library of Poetry. Vol. I.
7. *Faust.* Part I. New Edition. London. 1861. 8 mo.
8. *Faust.* Part I. New Edition. With Notes and Appendix. London. Griffin. 1866. 64 p. 8 mo.
9. *Faust.* Part I. In Masterpieces of Foreign Literature. Griffin. London. 1866. 8 mo.

JOHN GALVAN
Editions

1. *Faust/ A Tragedy/ Part the Second/ Rendered from the German of Goethe/ By John Galvan/ William Robertson/ Dublin/ 1860;/ Simpkin, Marshall and Co./ London/ 1860. 252 p. 16 cm.
2. *Ibid.* John M. O'Toole and Son. Dublin. 1862.

JOHN WYNNIAT GRANT
Translation Limited to a Single Edition

1. *Faust/ A Dramatic Poem/ By Goethe/ Translated by John Wynniat Grant/ Hamilton, Adams, and Co./ London/ 1867. 162 p. 8 vo.

ARCHER GURNEY
Translation Limited to a Single Edition

1. *Faust/ A Tragedy/ Part the Second/ Rendered from the German of Goethe/ By Archer Gurney/ Senior Heathcote and Senior/ Foreign Booksellers [London]/ 49 Pall Mall/ 1842. 8 vo.

ABRAHAM HAYWARD
Editions and Reprints

1. *Faust* [Part I]/ A dramatic poem/ By Goethe/ Translated

into English prose, with remarks on former translations, and notes, by the translator of Savigny's *Of the Vocation of Our Age for Legislation and Jurisprudence*/ Edward Moxon/ London/ 1833. LXXXVII, 291 p. 8 vo.

2. **Faust*/ A Dramatic Poem/ By Goethe/ Translated into English Prose/ By A. Hayward, Esq./ Second Edition/ Edward Moxon/ London/ 1834. 350 p. 8 vo.
3. *Faust.* Part I. Third Edition. Edward Moxon. London and New York. 1838. 8 vo.
4. **Faust.* Part I. D. Appleton and Company, New York. 1840.
5. **Faust.* Part I. Reprinted from the third English edition, corrected and revised. Printed for Ludwig Hillsenberg. Erfurt and Leipzig. 1842. IV, 172 p. 12 mo.
6. *Faust/ A Dramatic Poem/ By Goethe/ Translated into English Prose, with Notes, etc./ By A. Hayward, Esq./ Second American from the third London edition/ Lowell Bixby and Whiting/ 1845
7. **Faust.* Part I. Fourth Edition. Edward Moxon. London. 1847. 8 vo.
8. *Faust.* Part I. Fifth Edition. Edward Moxon. London. 1851. 12 mo.
9. *Faust.* Part I. Boston. 1854. 16 mo.
10. **Faust.* Part I. Sixth Edition. Edward Moxon. 1855. XXXVI, 245 p. 8 vo.
11. **Faust.* Part I. Ticknor and Fields. Boston. 1859.
12. *Faust.* Part I. Seventh Edition. London. 1860. 8 vo.
13. *Faust.* Part I. Eighth Edition. London. 1864. XXXVI, 245 p. 8 vo.
14. *Faust.* Part I. Ninth Edition. With increased notes, etc. London. 1874. 12 vo.
15. *Faust.* Part I. Tenth Edition. London. 1880.
16. **Faust*/ A Dramatic Poem/ By Goethe/ Translated into English Prose, with Notes, etc./ By A. Hayward/ A New Edition/ Boston/ James R. Osgood and Company/ 1882
17. **Faust.* Part I. Together with Anna Swanwick's translation in the five-volume edition of Goethe's Works. Noa and Hedge. Boston. 1882.
18. *Faust.* Part I. Eleventh Edition. London. 1890. 282 p.
19. **Faust*/ Part I [German Text]/ together with the prose translation, notes and appendices of the late Abraham Hayward,

Bibliography

Q. C./ Carefully revised, with introduction by C. A. Buchheim/ G. Bell and Sons/ London and New York/ 1892. XXVI, 497 p. 8 vo. Also a large paper edition with same imprint.

20. *Faust.* Part I. With [30] illustrations by Mr. Willy Pogany. Hutchinson and Co. London. 1908. 230 p. 8 vo.
21. **Faust*/ By Goethe/ Translated by Abraham Hayward/ With Illustrations by Willy Pogany/ New York/ George H. Doran Company. (No date).
22. **Faust.* Part I. D. Estes and Company. Boston. [1911].

Partial Editions

1. "Inhaltsangabe" of Second Part of Faust with the translation of numerous passages from Part II by A. Hayward: *Foreign Quarterly Review.* (1833). No. 23, pp. 81-109.
2. Hayward's translation of Gretchen's Dungeon Song: in *Psyche aus Franz Horns Nachlass.* Ausgewählt von Gustav Schwab und Friedrich Förster. Leipzig. 1841. Cf. Vol. 3, p. 229 ff. A version of Gretchen's Song at the Spinning Wheel reprinted from the Addenda to Hayward's 1834 edition is here erroneously attributed to Hayward. Hayward himself (p. 301) says he has received it from someone else.

JOHN HILLS
Editions

1. *Faust/* Part I/ A Drama/ Translated into English Prose/ By John Hills/ Whittaker/ London/ 1839. 8 vo. The existence of this edition is exceedingly doubtful.
2. **Faust*/ A Tragedy/ By Goethe/ Translated into English Verse/ By John Hills, Esq./ Whittaker and Co./ London;/ Asher/ Berlin/ 1840. 369 p. 16 mo.

ALFRED HENRY HUTH
Editions

1. **The Tragedy of Faustus*/ By Johann Wolfgang von Goethe/ The First Part/ Translated in the original Rhyme and Metre/ By Alfred Henry Huth/ Sampson Low, Marston, Searle and Rivington/ London/ 1889. 373 p.
2. Second edition. Sampson Low, Marston, Searle and Rivington. London. 1911.

CAPTAIN CHARLES HENRY KNOX
Editions

1. *Faust/ A Tragedy/ By J. W. von Goethe/ Translated By Captain Knox/ John Ollivier/ London/ 1847. 338 p. 8 vo.
2. *Faust/ A Tragedy/ By J. W. von Goethe/ Translated by Colonel C. H. Knox/ New Edition/ Harrison/ London. (no date). 338 p. 8 vo. See Bibliographical Note, pp. 302-3.

ALBERT G. LATHAM
Editions and Reprints

1. *Goethe's Faust/ Part I/ Translated by Albert G. Latham/ J. M. Dent/ Temple Classics/ London and New York/ 1902. 282 p. 8 vo.
2. *Faust/ Part II/ Translated and edited by Albert G. Latham/ With frontispiece/ J. M. Dent/ Temple Classics/ London/ 1905. X, 411 p. 16 mo.
3. *Faust/ Parts I and II/ Translated by Albert G. Latham/ Dutton/ Everyman's Library/ New York/ 1908. 468 p. 16 mo.
4. *Ibid. Dent. Everyman's Library. London. 1909. 468 p.
5. Ibid. 1910.
6. Ibid. 1912.
7. Ibid. 1914.
8. Ibid. 1919.
9. Ibid. 1925.

SIR GEORGE LEFEVRE
Editions

1. *Goethe's Faust/ Translated into English Verse/ By Sir George Lefevre, M.D./ Nutt/ London/ 1841. 202 p. 12 mo.
2. *Goethe's Faust/ Translated into English Verse/ By Sir George Lefevre, M.D./ Second Edition/ Printed by Charles Jugel/ Frankfort O. M./ 1843. 207 p.

LORD FRANCIS LEVESON-GOWER
Editions

1. *Faust/ A Drama in verse/ By Goethe/ And Schiller's *Song of the Bell*/ Translated by Lord Francis Leveson-Gower/ J. Murray/ London/ 1823. 304 p. 8 vo.

Bibliography

2. *Faust/ A Drama by Goethe/ With translations from the German/ By Lord Francis Leveson-Gower/ Second edition/ John Murray/ London/ 1825. 201, 205, p. 2 volumes.

Partial Editions

1. *John Galt, The Bachelor's Wife, a Selection of curious and interesting extracts with cursory observations. Edinburgh. 1824. Pp. 255-285: German Genius. Several longer extracts from Gower's translation.
2. *Horae Germanicae, on Goethe's Faust. Prefaced by three quotations in the original from Goethe. Extracts from Gower's translation. Knickerbocker. New York. 1833.

WILLIAM BELL MACDONALD
Editions

1. *Faust/ A Tragedy/ By J. W. Goethe/ Part II as completed in 1831/ Translated into English Verse [by William Bell Macdonald]/ D. Halliday/ Dumfries, [Scotland] 1838. 84 p. Paper cover. 25 cm.
2. *Faust/ A Tragedy/ By J. W. Goethe/ Part II as completed in 1831/ Translated into English Verse [by William Bell Macdonald]/ Second Edition/ William Pickering/ London/ 1842. 351 p. 18 cm.

CARLYLE F. MACINTYRE
Translation Limited to a Single Edition

1. *Goethe's Faust/ A New American Translation/ By Carlyle F. MacIntyre/ With Illustrations by Rockwell Kent/ Together with the German Text/ New Directions/ Norfolk, Connecticut. [1941]. 436 p. 26 cm.

THEODORE MARTIN
Editions and Reprints

1. *Faust/ Part I/ A Dramatic Poem by Goethe/ Translated into English verse/ By Theodore Martin/ William Blackwood and Sons/ Edinburgh and London/ 1865. 239 p. 8 vo.
2. *Faust. Part I. Second edition. William Blackwood and Sons. London. 1866.

3. *Faust. Part I. Third edition. William Blackwood and Sons. London. 1870. 227 p. 8 vo.
4. Goethe's *Faust*/ Part II/ Translated by Theodore Martin [Edinburgh and London/ William Blackwood and Sons/ 1886]
5. *Goethe's *Faust*. Part I and II. In the Weimar Edition. 1908.

R. McLINTOCK
Translation Limited to a Single Edition

1. *Goethe's *Faust*/ (The so-called First Part, 1770-1808)/ Together with the scene "Two Imps and Amor," the Variants of the Göchhausen Transcript, and the complete *Paralipomena* of the Weimar Edition of 1887/ In English, with Introduction and Notes/ By R. McLintock/ D. Nutt/ London/ 1897. XXXVII, 375 p.

CHARLES KEGAN PAUL
Translation Limited to a Single Edition

1. *Faust/ A Tragedy by Goethe/ Translated in Rime/ By C. Kegan Paul/ Henry S. King and Co./ London/ 1873. 229 p. 19 cm.

GEORGE MADISON PRIEST
Editions and Reprints

1. *J. Wolfgang von Goethe/ *Faust*/ Parts I and II/ Translated from the German/ By George Madison Priest, Professor of German Literature, Princeton University/ Covici-Friede/ New York [1932]. IX, 420 p. 24 cm. Edition Limited to 500 copies. The translation follows the text of the Standard Edition of Goethe's Works, the "Jubiläumsausgabe" or "Jubilee Edition."
2. *Ibid. Reprint of First Edition. Covici-Friede. New York. [1932]. 420 p. 24 cm. In half leather binding. Limited Edition.
3. *Revised Edition. Alfred A. Knopf. New York. 1941. 425 p. 24 cm.

ALICE RAPHAEL
Editions and Reprints

1. *Faust/ A Tragedy/ By Johann Wolfgang von Goethe/ Trans-

lated by Alice Raphael/ With an Introduction for the Modern Reader by Mark Van Doren and Woodcuts by Lynd Ward/ Jonathan Cape and Harrison Smith/ New York [November, 1930]. 262 p. 22½ cm.

2. *Ibid.* Second Edition November, 1930. Limited Edition. In half linen binding with blue and gold modernistic design. Only 501 copies printed (490 for sale). Copy in the William A. Speck Collection contains inscription by the translator in her own hand. 262 p. 24½ cm.

3. *Faust/ A Tragedy/ The First Part/ By Johann Wolfgang von Goethe/ In a Modern Translation by Alice Raphael/ With an Introduction by Carl F. Schreiber and a Note by Mark Van Doren/ With ten full page multicolored designs by René Clarke/ This Edition consists of fifteen hundred copies for the Members of the Limited Editions Club/ By the Bartlett Aldus Press of New York/ Issued March 22, 1932, to mark the Centenary of the Author's Death/ Copy number 35 in the Speck Collection signed by René Clarke. 112 p. 31 cm.

4. *Faust/ By Johann Wolfgang von Goethe/ A Tragedy in a modern translation/ By Alice Raphael/ Illustrated with eighteen lithographs by Eugene Delacroix/ With an introduction by Carl F. Schreiber, the Translator's Foreword and a Note by Mark Van Doren/ New York/ The Heritage Club [1939]

JOHN FREDERICK LOUIS RASCHEN
Translation Limited to a Single Edition

1. Goethe/ *Faust,* Part I and Selected Sections of Part II in the German Original/ With an English Translation/ by J. F. L. Raschen/ The Thrift Press/ Ithaca, New York. 360 p.

F. G. G. SCHMIDT
Translation Limited to a Single Edition

1. *Faust/ Translated into English Prose/ With Introduction and Notes/ By F. G. G. Schmidt, Ph.D./ Professor of Germanic Languages and Literature, University of Oregon, Eugene/ Emil Rehmkopf/ Leipzig/ 1935

WILLIAM DALTON SCOONES
Translation Limited to a Single Edition

1. *Faust/ A Tragedy by Goethe/ Translated into English Verse

By William Dalton Scoones, B.A./ Trübner and Co./ London/ 1879. 230 p. 17 cm.

JOHN SHAWCROSS
Translation Limited to a Single Edition
1. *The First Part of Goethe's *Faust*/ Translated from the German/ By John Shawcross, M.A./ With a Foreword/ By Dr. G. P. Gooch, President of the English Goethe Society/ Eric Partridge Limited/ London/ At the Scholartis Press,/ 30 Museum Street/ 1934. 189 p. The firm which published this translation went into liquidation before the publication was complete, so that only a few copies reached the public.

ANNA SWANWICK
Editions and Reprints
1. *Dramatic Works of Goethe/ Comprising *Faust, Iphigenia in Tauris, Torquato Tasso, Egmont*/ Translated by Anna Swanwick/ And *Goetz von Berlichingen*/ Translated by Sir Walter Scott/ Carefully Revised/ London/ Henry G. Bohn/ York Street, Covent Garden/ 1850. XVI. 504 p. *Faust* 154 p. 8 vo. In Bohn's Standard Library.
2. *Ibid. Neue Titelauflage. 1851.
3. *Faust. Part I. H. G. Bohn and J. Mitchell. London. [1852].
4. *Dramatic Works of Goethe/ Comprising *Faust, Iphigenia in Tauris, Torquato Tasso, Egmont*/ Translated by Anna Swanwick/ And *Goetz von Berlichingen*/ Translated by Sir Walter Scott/ And carefully revised by Henry G. Bohn/ London/ Bell and Daldy/ York Street/ Covent Garden/ 1867
5. *Ibid. 1871.
6. *Faust. Part I*, and selected Portions of *Part II*. Illustrations after Retzsch. Bell. London. 1878. Two Parts. XVI, 350 p. 8 vo. Also London, 1879. 366 p.
7. *Goethe's *Faust* in Two Parts/ Translated by Ann Swanwick/ The first part revised, and the second newly translated/ George Bell and Sons/ London/ 1879. XLIII, 437 p. 8 vo. In Bohn's Library.
8. *Faust/ Part II/ Together with *Clavigo* and *Egmont*/ Tr. by Miss Swanwick, and *Wayward Lover* Tr. by E. A. Bowring/

Bibliography

T. Y. Crowell Co. New York. [1882]. 455 p. 8 vo. In Crowell's Red-Line Edition of Poets. Illustrations by A. von Kreling.

9. *Faust/ Parts I and II/ In Goethe's Works/ People's Edition/ Volume I/ Edited and revised by F. H. Hedge and L. Noa/ Boston. 1882. Volume I also contains Hayward's prose version of *Part I*.
10. *Faust/ Parts I and II/ Together with *Clavigo* and *Egmont*/ Tr. by Miss Swanwick, and *Wayward Lover* Tr. by E. A. Bowring/ S. E. Casino/ Boston. 1882.
11. *Faust. Parts I and II. J. B. Lippincott and Co. Philadelphia. 1883.
12. *Faust. Part II. T. Y. Crowell and Co. New York. [1883?]. 16 mo. In White, Stokes, and Allen's Poets. Vol. 6.
13. *Goethe's *Faust*/ Translated by Anna Swanwick/ Translator of *Aeschylus*, etc./ New York/ White, Stokes, and Allen/ 1884
14. *Faust. Parts I and II. J. W. Lovell Company. New York. [1884]. 405 p. 16 mo.
15. *The Works of Goethe/ With Biographical Introduction/ By Hjalmar H. Boyesen, Ph.D./ Copyright George Barrie/ Phila., New York, and Boston/ 1885. *Faust* is contained in Volume II of this series. Cf. Bibliographical Note p. 305.
16. *Faust. Part I. White, Stokes, and Allen. New York. 1886. Also with Heine's *Book of Songs*.
17. Faust. Parts I and II. Bell. London. 1886. 437 p. 18 cm.
18. *Faust. Part I. In Bohn's Shilling Library. G. Bell and Sons. London. 1888. 167 p. 8 vo.
19. *Faust. Parts I and II. Hurst and Co. New York. [1888?].
20. *Goethe's *Faust*/ Translated by Anna Swanwick/ Translator of *Aeschylus*, etc./ New York/ Wm. L. Allison/ Nos. 93 Chambers & 75 Reade Sts.
21. *Faust. Part I. W. L. Allison Co. New York. [1890?].
22. Faust. Part I. New illustrated edition. Stokes. New York. 1893.
23. *Faust. Part I. G. Bell and Sons. London and New York. 1893.
24. Faust. Part I. Revised Edition with Retzsch's Illustrations. Bell. London. 1895. 167 p. 8 vo.

25. *Faust. Part I.* With an Introduction by E. Brooks, Jr. McKay. Philadelphia. 1898. 213 p. 16 cm.
26. *Goethe's *Faust*/ In Two Parts/ Translated by Anna Swanwick, LL.D./ Translator of *Aeschylus*, etc./ London/ George Bell and Sons/ 1900
27. **Faust. Part I.* Chatterton-Peck Co. New York. [19-?].
28. *Faust. Part I.* Revised edition. With an Introduction and Bibliography by Karl Breul. Macmillan. London. 1905. LXX. 437 p. 8 vo.
29. **Faust. Parts I and II.* A. L. Burt Company. [New York]. [19-?].
30. *Faust* [Part I]/ A Dramatic Poem by Johann Wolfgang von Goethe/ Translated by Anna Swanwick/ With Biographical Sketch and Explanatory Introduction/ With Sixteen Full Page Half Tone Illustrations/ A. L. Burt Company/ Publishers/ New York
31. *Faust. Parts I and II.* Bell. London. 1905. 508 p. 12 mo.
32. **Faust. Part I.* E. P. Dutton and Co. New York. 1906.
33. *Faust. Parts I and II.* Bell. London. 1909. 437 p. 18 cm.
34. *Faust. Part I.* Collier. New York. 1909. 431 p. 22 cm. In Harvard Classics.
35. **Faust. Parts I and II.* Edited by Karl Breul. Macmillan Company. London and New York. 1914. 437 p. In Bohn's Popular Library Series.
36. **Faust. Parts I and II.* G. Bell. London. 1914. 400 p. 12 mo.
37. **Faust. Parts I and II.* Haldeman-Julius. Girard, Kansas. [1925].
38. *Goethe's *Faust*/ In Two Parts/ Translated by Anna Swanwick, Translator of *Aeschylus*, etc./ Chicago and New York/ Belford, Clarke and Company, Publishers. [No date].
39. **Faust*/ In Two Parts/ By J. W. Von Goethe/ Translated by Miss Anna Swanwick/ In two volumes/ Volume I/ Library Edition/ New York/ The Publishers Plate Renting Co. [No date].
40. *Goethe's *Faust* [Part I]/ Translated by Anna Swanwick, LL.D./ Edited, with Introduction and Bibliography, By Karl Breul, (Hon.) M.A., Litt.D., Ph.D./ Fellow of King's College, Cambridge/ Schröder Professor of German in the Uni-

versity of Cambridge/ Vice-President of the English Goethe Society London/ G. Bell and Sons, Ltd./ 1928.

DAVID SYME
Translation Limited to a Single Edition
1. *Faust/ A Tragedy. Translated from the German of Goethe/ By David Syme/ Adam and Charles Black/ Edinburgh;/ Fleischer/ Leipzig/ 1834. 241 p. 20 cm.

THE HONORABLE ROBERT TALBOT
Editions
1. *The Faust of Goethe/ Attempted in English Rhyme/ By The Honorable Robert Talbot/ Smith, Elder and Co./ London/ 1835. 263 p. 8 vo.
2. *The Faust of Goethe/ Part the First/ Translated into English Rhyme/ By the Honorable Robert Talbot/ Second Edition/ Revised and much Corrected/ With the German Text on Alternate Pages, and Additional Notes/ J. Wacey/ London/ 1839. 569 p. 8 vo.

ARTHUR TAYLOR
Translation Limited to a Single Edition of Fifty Copies
1. *Faust/ A Tragedy/ In Two Parts/ By Göthe. Rendered into English Verse [By Arthur Taylor]/ Vol. I [and II]/ Printed by Arthur Taylor/ London/ 1838

BAYARD TAYLOR
Editions and Reprints
1a. *Faust/ A Tragedy/ By Johann Wolfgang von Goethe/ The First Part/ Translated in the Original Metres/ By Bayard Taylor/ [four lines of verse by Goethe]/ Boston. Fields Osgood and Co. 1871. 405 p. 8 vo. [But note on verso of title-page of Vol. I reads: "Entered according to act of Congress, in the year 1870, by Bayard Taylor, in the office of the Librarian of Congress, at Washington." G. H. Baker and Co., Cat. 70, 1937, lists copy of Vol. I with inscription by the translator: "Richard Henry Stoddard, with the love of Bayard Taylor, Dec. 14, 1870." Part I of first edition was, therefore, printed and ready for distribution December, 1870.]

b. *Faust/ A Tragedy/ By Johann Wolfgang von Goethe/ The Second Part/ Translated, in the Original Metres/ By Bayard Taylor/ [Five lines of verse from Goethe's *Tasso*]/ Boston. James R. Osgood and Company/ (Late Ticknor and Fields, and Fields, Osgood, and Co.)/ 1871. [First edition of Part II. 8 vo.]

2a. *Faust.* Part I. Title-page same as for 1a., but publisher's name reads: "Boston. James R. Osgood and Co." (Late Ticknor and Fields, and Fields, Osgood, and Co. 1871.)

b. *Faust.* Part II. Title-page same as 1b., except date is here given as 1872.

3. *Faust.* Parts I and II. Strahan and Co. London. 1871. XXIV, 386 and XX, 507 p. 8 vo.

4. *Faust/ A Tragedy/ By John Wolfgang von Goethe/ Translated in the original metres/ By Bayard Taylor/ The First Part/ Strahan and Co., Publishers/ 56, Ludgate Hill, London/ 1871. (Vol. II contains The Second Part.)

5. *Faust.* Parts I and II. Authorised edition. Brockhaus. Leipzig. 1872. XXIV, 308 p.

6. *Faust.* Parts I and II. J. R. Osgood and Co. Boston. 1873. XVI, 536 p. 8 vo.

7. *Faust.* Part I. Stroefer and Kirchner. New York. [1874].

8. *Faust.* Parts I and II. J. R. Osgood and Co. Boston. 1875. 378 and 478 p.

9. *Faust.* Part II. Authorised edition. Brockhaus. Leipzig. 1876. XX, 404 p. 8 vo.

10. *Faust.* Part I by Goethe. Translated by B. Taylor. Illustrated by E. Seibertz, A. Liezen-Mayer, and L. Hofmann. New York. 1876. Fol.

11. *Faust.* Parts I and II. J. R. Osgood and Co. Boston. 1876.

12. *Faust.* Parts I and II. Authorized edition. Ward, Lock, and Co. London. 1877. XX, 636 p. 8 vo.

13. *Faust/ A Tragedy/ By Johann Wolfgang von Goethe/ The First Part/ Translated, in the original metres/ By Bayard Taylor

Wer die Dichtkunst ———
——— in Dichters Lande gehen.
Goethe

Boston/ Houghton, Osgood and Company/ The Riverside Press/ Cambridge/ 1879

Bibliography

14. *Faust*. Parts I and II. Houghton, Osgood and Co. Boston. 1879.
15. *Faust*. Parts I and II. (Kennet edition). Houghton, Osgood and Co. Boston. 1879. 2 vols. in 1.
16. Faust. Part I. Second edition. Brockhaus. Leipzig. 1881. 308 p. 8 vo.
17. *Faust*. Parts I and II. Houghton, Mifflin. New York. 1882.
18. Faust. Parts I and II. With Konewka's illustrations. Roberts. Boston. 1883.
19. *Faust*/ A Tragedy/ By Johann Wolfgang von Goethe/ Translated, in the Original Metres/ By Bayard Taylor/ Two Volumes in one/
    Wer die Dichtkunst ———
    ——— in Dichters Lande gehen.
                                    Goethe
Seventh Edition/ Boston/ Houghton, Mifflin and Company/ The Riverside Press/ Cambridge/ 1884.
20. *Faust*. Parts I and II. J. Stark. London. 1884. Eighth edition. 2 vols. 8 vo.
21. Faust. Parts I and II. Strahan and Co. London. 1884. Eighth edition.
22. Faust. Part I. Ward, Lock and Co. London. 1886. 152 p. 8 vo.
23. *Faust*. Parts I and II. F. Warne and Co. London and New York. [1886]. In two editions: Chandos Classics; Londsdowne Poets.
24. Faust. Parts I and II. With biographical Introduction and Illustrations after Retzsch. Reduced format. London. 1886.
25. *Faust*/ A Tragedy By Johann Wolfgang von Goethe/ The First Part/ Translated, in the Original Metres/ By Bayard Taylor/
    Wer die Dichtkunst will verstehen,
    Muss in Land der Dichtung gehen:
    Wer den Dichter will verstehen,
    Muss in Dichters Lande gehen.
                                    Goethe
Ninth edition/ Boston/ Houghton, Mifflin and Company/ New York: 11 East Seventeenth Street/ The Riverside Press/ Cambridge. (no date).

26. *Faust.* Parts I and II. Strahan and Co. London. 1886. Ninth edition.
27. *Faust.* Parts I and II, and Part I alone. Since 1886 several illustrated editions in various series with Introduction by G. T. Bettany. Minerva Library, Popular Library of Literary Treasures, Moxon's Popular Poets, etc. Ward, Lock and Co.
28. *Faust.* Parts I and II/ A Tragedy of J. W. von Goethe/ Translated in the original metres with copious notes/ By B. Taylor/ Published by special arrangement with Mrs. Bayard Taylor/ With a biographical introduction, and Retzsch's plates, in reduced format/ London/ 1886
29. **Faust.* Parts I and II. Authorised edition. Ward, Lock and Co. London. [1887]. 636 p. 8 vo.
30. *Faust.* Part I. Boston. 1887. 16 mo.
31. *Faust.* Parts I and II. Ward, Lock and Co. London. 1889. New edition 8 vo.
32. *Goethe's *Faust.* With some of the minor Poems. Edited by Elizabeth Craigmyle, author of "Poems and Translations," etc. The Walter Scott Publishing Co., Ltd. London and Newcastle-on-Tyne. (no date).
33. *Faust.* Part I. With some of the minor poems, edited by Elizabeth Craigmyle. Scott. London and New York. 1889. 278 p. 14 cm. (Canterbury poets).
34. *Faust.* Parts I and II. Second edition. Ward, Lock and Co. London. 1889?
35. *Faust.* Parts I and II. Third edition. Ward, Lock and Co. London. 1890. 636 p. 8 vo.
36. **Faust.* Parts I and II. Houghton, Mifflin and Co. Boston and New York. [1890?]. 2 vols.
37. **Faust.* Parts I and II. Houghton, Mifflin and Co. Boston and New York. 1891. 2 vols in 1.
38. **Faust.* Parts I and II. Houghton, Mifflin and Co. London and New York. [1898]. In two editions. Two volumes and two volumes in one respectively.
39. **Faust.* Parts I and II. Large Paper edition with illustrations from A. Liezen-Mayer and M. Retzsch. Houghton, Mifflin and Co. Boston and New York. 1906. 4 vols. 28 cm.
40. *Faust.* Parts I and II. Ward, Lock and Co. London. 1911. 664 p.

Bibliography

41. *Faust*. Part I. Houghton, Mifflin and Co. Boston and New York. [1911]. 368 p. 18 cm.
42. *Faust*. Parts I and II. Introduction by Robert H. Fife. The Macmillan Co. New York. 1930. (The Modern Readers Series). XXIV, 562 p. 18½ cm.
43. *Faust*. Parts I and II. Bennett A. Cerf: Donald S. Klopfer. New York. [1930]. (The Modern Library Publishers). XX, 258 p. 17 cm.
44. *Faust*. Parts I and II. Introduction by Marshall Montgomery and Notes by Douglas Yates. Oxford University Press. London. [1932].
45. *Faust*/ By Johann Wolfgang von Goethe/ With Illustrations/ By Harry Clarke/ Translated into English, in the Original Metres, by Bayard Taylor/ New York/ Illustrated Editions Company/ 100 Fifth Avenue. [1932].
46. *Faust*/ Part I/ Translated in the original metres/ By Bayard Taylor/ Illustrated by Harry Clarke/ (Cameo Classics)/ Grosset/ New York. 1936. 251 p.
47. *Faust*/ By Johann Wolfgang von Goethe/ With Illustrations By Harry Clarke/ Translated into English, in the Original Meters/ By Bayard Taylor/ Grosset & Dunlap/ New York/ Cameo Classics/ (no date)
48. *Faust*. Johann Wolfgang von Goethe/ With Illustrations/ By Harry Clarke/ Translated into English, in the original Metres,/ By Bayard Taylor/ De Luxe editions/ (no date)
49. *Faust*/ Part I/ By Johann Wolfgang von Goethe/ Translated in the original meters/ By Bayard Taylor/ New York/ F. S. Crofts & Co./ MCMXLVI/ Crofts Classics/ Edited by B. Q. Morgan

Partial Editions

1. "Prelude to the Second Part of Faust," *Atlantic Monthly*, 1871, XXVII, 349.
2. *Selections from the Translation of* Bayard Taylor. With 26 steel plates by M. Retzsch. Estes and Lauriat. Boston. 1874.
3. *Songs and Scenes from Faust*. Translated by Bayard Taylor. (Paragon Series No. 17). Illustrated from designs by A. Liezen-Mayer and A. Lalauze. Estes and Lauriat. 1884 and 1901. 48 p.

4. *Der König von Thule* in Adolf Jensen, Song Album. Vol. 4. New York. G. Schirmer. [1884].
5. Many short passages in recent literary magazines.

JOHN TODHUNTER
Translation Limited to a Single Edition

1. *Goethe's *Faust*/ First Part/ Translated by John Todhunter/ With an Introduction/ By J. G. Robertson/ Basil Blackwell/ Oxford/ 1924. XIV, 188 p. 12 cm.

W. H. VAN DER SMISSEN
Translation Limited to a Single Edition

1. *Goethe's *Faust*/ Done in English Verse in the Original Metres/ With Commentary and Notes/ By W. H. Van der Smissen, M.A., Ph.D., Emeritus Professor of German Language and Literature in University College, Toronto/ Editor of Shorter Poems of Goethe and Schiller, etc./ With an Introduction/ By Sir Robert Falconer, K.C.M.G., LL.D., D.Litt., etc./ London and Toronto/ J. M. Dent and Sons Ltd.;/ New York/ E. P. Dutton and Co./ 1926. XXIV, Text 435 p. Commentary 58 p.

v. BERESFORD
Translation Limited to a Single Edition

1. **Faust*/ Translated from the German/ By v. Beresford/ George H. Wigand/ Cassel and Göttingen/ 1862. 226 p. 8 vo.

THOMAS E. WEBB
Editions

1. **Faust*/ From the German of Goethe/ By Thomas E. Webb, LL.D., one of her Majesty's Counsel; sometime Fellow of Trinity College; now Regius Professor of Laws and Public Orator in the University of Dublin/ Hodges, Figgis, and Co., Dublin, Grafton Street;/ Longmans, Green and Co., London, Paternoster Row 1880. Dublin University Series.
2. Second Edition. Longmans, Green and Co. London. 1881.
3. *Second Revised Edition with the *Death of Faust* from the Second Part. Longmans, Green and Co. London and New York. 1898.

BIBLIOGRAPHICAL NOTES

Bibliographical Notes

ON THE SUPPOSED TRANSLATION OF PART I BY LEOPOLD J. BERNAYS

The question whether Bernays translated both parts of *Faust* or only Part II was discussed in 1926 by Mr. William A. Speck in an article entitled: *Notes on the English Translation of the Second Part of Faust by Leopold J. Bernays.*

Mr. Speck calls attention to the circumstance that practically all the bibliographers of the *Faust*, including Heinemann and Engel, down to Oswald, have with slight variation erroneously followed Franz Peter's entry: "*Faust*, Part I, Part II, with other poems original and translated by Leopold J. Bernays. Carlsruhe. 1840." (Franz Peter, *Die Literatur der Faustsage bis Ende des Jahres 1850.* Friedrich Voigt, Leipzig, 1851, p. 30.) Mr. Speck finds also that although Oswald mentions only a translation of *Faust*, Part II, by Bernays, it is Lina Baumann in her book *Die Englischen Übersetzungen von Goethes Faust* (1907), who first questions the existence of Part I by Bernays, and that although the 1912 edition of Goedeke's *Grundriss* (IV, Part III, p. 633) calls attention to Lina Baumann's caution, it still lists both parts by Bernays.

Then citing Adolph Bernays' letter to Eckermann, Mr. Speck concludes from the whole tone of the correspondence, and the lack of any reference to Part I as translated by his son, that Leopold Bernays never translated Part I. The important passage in the letter in question reads: "Übrigens ist seine übersetzung, obgleich wir deren 8 oder 9 vom ersten Theile haben, die erste vom Zweiten, welche je in der englischen Sprache erschienen ist."

To what has been said above, may be added that the British Museum Catalogue of 1885, although it lists ten titles of books by Bernays, mentions only "*Faust*, Part II . . . with other poems original and translated. 1839." Also Hermann Kindt, in an extensive article called "Goethe's Faust in England" (*Die Gegenwart*, No. 25, June 20, 1874, p. 394), refers only to Part II by Bernays.

It seems natural to believe that if Bernays had planned to translate both parts, he would have started with Part I, but there is no indication in the letter that he had this in mind. On the contrary, it is quite evident from Adolph Bernays' statement and from the words of J. A. Heraud (referred to in the section on Bernays in this book) that the younger Bernays wished to supply what he considered to be already long in demand—a translation of *Faust*, Part II. He was aware of the fact that a number of translations of Part I existed, but not that there were any of Part II. Therefore, upon the strength of Bernays' letter to Eckermann, the British Museum Catalogue, Hermann Kindt's article, and, finally, because no first part by Bernays is known to exist anywhere, the present writer agrees with Mr. Speck that Leopold J. Bernays translated only *Faust*, Part II.

On the So-called English Translation of Goethe's *Faust* by L. E. Peithmann

The so-called "Analytical Translation" of Part I by L. E. Peithmann, which appeared in 1840, has been listed in bibliographical works for many years under the English versions of *Faust*. However, since the volume is only a reprint of the German text with copious grammatical notes and vocabularies, it is not considered in this book. In reality Peithmann is only editor and not translator. A second edition of this work appeared in 1856.

On the Editions of the Translation of Goethe's *Faust* by Captain Charles Henry Knox

William Heinemann in his work *A Bibliographical List of English Translations and Annotated Editions of Goethe's Faust* (Elliot Stock, London, 1882) comments, page eleven, on the first edition of Knox's translation of *Faust*, supposedly published in 1834: "This edition is only mentioned in a Bibliography of some English translations of Goethe's *Faust*, which appeared in the Literary World, Boston, 13th of August, 1881 [*sic*]. I have never seen a copy, nor is there notice of it in the edition of Knox's translation published in 1847."

Unfortunately, even now, more than half a century later, no additional information concerning the 1834 edition of *Faust* by Knox has come to light. However, since the publication of Heinemann's *List of English Translations*, at least two copies of a *Titelauflage* of the 1847 edition have become available in America. Some years ago I was fortunate enough to acquire one of these for my private

Bibliographical Notes 303

library, and the Speck Collection possesses another copy. In this edition the title-page *in toto* reads as follows: "Faust, A Tragedy, By J. W. von Goethe. Translated by Colonel C. H. Knox, Author of 'Rittmeister's Budget,' 'Harry Mowbray,' 'Day Dreams,' &c. New Edition. London: Harrison, 59, Pall Mall." The date of publication is not given, but since the translator was advanced from "Captain of 94 foot" to the rank of "lieut. Col. Royal Glamorgan militia" in 1853, this *Titelauflage,* in spite of the fact that the date of the Preface is 1846, cannot have been published before 1853.

On the Supposed 1849 Edition of Anna Swanwick's Translation of *Faust*

There is considerable confusion in regard to the date of the first publication of Miss Swanwick's translation of *Faust,* Part I. The British Museum Catalogue certainly is mistaken when it cites both parts by Miss Swanwick as published in 1846. Beginning with *The English Catalogue* of 1864, all strictly bibliographical works mentioning *Faust* refer to an 1849 edition under some such title as the following: "Faust and Schiller. Selections from. Translated by Swanwick. 8vo. Manwaring, 1849."

However, *The English Publishers' Circular* for 1849, a volume purporting to list all works published in Great Britain for that year, does not mention an 1849 edition. The circular for 1850 carried the notice of the 1850 edition in Bohn's Standard Library. The failure to mention any 1849 edition of *Faust* is significant and already makes its existence doubtful. Furthermore, Franz Peter in his *Literatur der Faustsage* (1850), although he mentions the 1850 edition, says nothing about an 1849 edition. Most significant of all are Miss Swanwick's own words in the Translator's Preface to the Bohn edition of 1850: "My translation of *Iphigenia* and the first act of *Tasso* have already appeared in a volume entitled *Selections from the Dramas of Goethe and Schiller*. The remainder of the *Tasso,* together with my versions of *Faust* and *Egmont,* are published now for the first time." This Preface is dated "London, November, 1850." We are compelled to accept the author's own statement: "My versions of *Faust* and *Egmont,* are now published for the first time." It is possible that Manwaring may have first acquired the right to Miss Swanwick's translation, and actually announced its forthcoming publication, but that H. G. Bohn bought these rights from him before Manwaring could carry out his plans.

To me, therefore, there seems sufficient ground to assume that Anna Swanwick's version of *Faust* first appeared in 1850.

ON THE EDITIONS OF THE TRANSLATION OF GOETHE'S *Faust* BY CHARLES TIMOTHY BROOKS

The Houghton Mifflin Company, the present successors to Ticknor and Fields, have kindly supplied me with some of the facts relative to the publication of Brooks's translation. Their letter dated February 7, 1938, states: "Printings up to and including 1868 were made by Ticknor and Fields, that in 1869 by Fields, Osgood and Company, the next four by James R. Osgood and Company, the two in 1878 and 1880 by Houghton Osgood and Company, and the sixteenth and last by Houghton, Mifflin and Company. There is no indication on our cards of any changes in the plates from time to time and there is but one copyright claim that we know of, that in 1856. The work is described as being 16 mo., containing 234 pages, and the price always seems to have been one dollar."

The above statement, however, does not account for all the editions and reprints of the translation by Brooks. See items 2, 5, and 12 under Editions and Reprints.

ON THE SO-CALLED TRANSLATION OF GOETHE'S *Faust* BY G. G. ZERFFI

Like L. E. Peithmann in 1840, G. G. Zerffi was the author of what might be called a school edition of the German text of Goethe's *Faust*, supplied with critical and explanatory notes. In no sense can Zerffi be called a translator. This volume was first published by Simpkin Marshall & Company, London, 1859. Several later editions of this work are listed in the British Museum Catalogue (XXI, 170).

ON THE REPORTED ENGLISH TRANSLATION OF GOETHE'S *Faust* BY J. CARTWRIGHT

Nothing definite is known about J. Cartwright or the translation of *Faust* attributed to him. The *English Publisher's Circular* for 1862, which contains a list of all the new books printed during the year, does not mention this volume, nor does any collection of Goetheana contain it. Mr. William A. Speck and Mr. Frank Claudy, diligent American collectors of Goetheana, after half a century of fruitless search for this version in both Europe and

America, came to the conclusion that such a translation never existed. Professor Carl F. Schreiber, the present curator of the William A. Speck Collection of Goetheana, Yale University, has ventured the opinion that the translation may have been made and its forthcoming publication announced, but that for some reason it was never actually published.

Allibone's *Dictionary of Authors* (John Foster Kirk, *Supplement to Allibone's Critical Dictionary of English Literature and British and American Authors*, Philadelphia: J. B. Lippincott and Co., 1891, I, 298) lists a J. A. M. Cartwright as the translator of three works from the German: "Goethe's *Torquato Tasso:* translated into English verse by C., London, 1861; *Translations from Euripides*, Lond. 1866; and Schiller's *William Tell*, London, 1869." Goedeke's *Grundriss* (Karl Goedeke, *Grundriss zur Geschichte der Deutschen Dichtung*, 3rd ed., Dresden: L. Ehlermann, 1910-13, IV, 293, 341, 636) confirms the translation of *Tasso* by "J. Cartwright, London, 1861," and furnishes the additional information that *Hermann and Dorothea* was translated into "English verse by John Cartwright, London, 1862" and "*Faust* . . . by J. Cartwright, London, 1862." It is possible that J. A. M. Cartwright, John Cartwright, and J. Cartwright are one and the same individual, but until more convincing circumstantial evidence is available, or at least a single copy of a translation of Goethe's *Faust* by J. Cartwright is discovered somewhere, it will probably be prudent to assume the non-existence of such a translation.

ON THE SO-CALLED TRANSLATION OF GOETHE'S *Faust*
BY H. BOYESEN, 1885

Attention must be called here to the *Faust* translation loosely and erroneously attributed to Hjalmar H. Boyesen. Goedeke's *Grundriss*, 1912, under the *English Translations*, has the following item: "H. Boyesen (beide Teile): Goethe's Works illustr. by the best German artists. Philadelphia. 1885." From a comparison of this edition with Miss Swanwick's translation, it appears that the text of Boyesen's Part I is nearly always the same as Miss Swanwick's revised version of 1879 and the text of Boyesen's Part II is identical in all respects with Miss Swanwick's Part II published in 1879. In the future Miss Swanwick should be credited with this edition and Professor Boyesen mentioned solely as editor.

A CHRONOLOGICAL ARRANGEMENT OF THE TRANSLATORS ACCORDING TO NATIONALITY

The British Translators of Goethe's *Faust*
Lord Leveson-Gower, Part I, 1823
Abraham Hayward, Part I, 1833
John Stuart Blackie, Part I, 1834
David Syme, Part I, 1834
Warburton Davies, Part I, 1834
John Anster, Part I, 1835; Part II, 1864
The Honorable Robert Talbot, Part I, 1835
William Bell Macdonald, Part II, 1838
Arthur Taylor, Parts I and II, 1838
Jonathan Birch, Part I, 1839; Part II, 1843
Leopold J. Bernays, Part II, 1839
John Hills, Part I, 1840
Sir George William Lefevre, Part I, 1841
Lewis Filmore, Part I, 1841
Archer Thompson Gurney, Part II, 1842
Captain Charles Henry Knox, Part I, 1847
Anna Swanwick, Part I, 1850; Part II, 1879
John Galvan, Part I, 1860
v. Beresford, Part I, 1862
William Barnard Clarke, Parts I and II, 1865
Sir Theodore Martin, Part I, 1865; Part II, 1886
John Wynniat Grant, Part I, 1867
Charles Kegan Paul, Part I, 1873
Thomas J. Arnold, Part I, 1877
Charles Hartpole Bowen, Part I, 1878
William H. Colquhoun, Part I, 1878
William Dalton Scoones, Part I, 1879
Thomas E. Webb, Part I, 1880
James Adey Birds, Part I, 1880; Part II, 1889
Alfred Henry Huth, Part I, 1889
Beta, Part I, 1895

List of Translators

R. McLintock, Part I, 1897
Albert G. Latham, Part I, 1902; Part II, 1905
Sir George Buchanan, Part I, 1908
John Todhunter, Part I, 1924
Geoffrey Montagu Cookson, Part I, 1925
C. Fillingham Coxwell, Part I, 1932
John Shawcross, Part I, 1934

THE AMERICAN TRANSLATORS OF GOETHE'S *Faust*

Charles Timothy Brooks, Part I, 1856
Bayard Taylor, Part I, 1870; Part II, 1871
Frank Claudy, Part I, 1886
William H. Van der Smissen, Parts I and II, 1927 (Canadian)
William Page Andrews, Part I, 1929
Alice Raphael, Part I, 1930
George Madison Priest, Parts I and II, 1932, 1941
F. G. G. Schmidt, Part I, 1935
Carlyle F. MacIntyre, Part I, 1941
John Frederick Louis Raschen, Part I, 1949

A NUMERICAL TABLE OF THE EDITIONS AND REPRINTS OF EACH TRANSLATION

Andrews	1	Latham	9
Anster	32	Lefevre	2
Arnold	1	Leveson-Gower	2
Bernays	2	Macdonald	2
Beta	1	MacIntyre	1
Birch	5	Martin	5
Birds	3	McLintock	1
Blackie	2	Paul	1
Bowen	1	Priest	3
Brooks	19	Raphael	4
Buchanan	1	Raschen	1
Clarke	1	Schmidt	1
Claudy	2	Scoones	1
Colquhoun	1	Shawcross	1
Cookson	1	Swanwick	40
Coxwell	1	Syme	1
Davies	1	Talbot	2
Filmore	9	Taylor, Arthur	1
Galvan	2	Taylor, Bayard	49
Grant	1	Todhunter	1
Gurney	1	Van der Smissen	1
Hayward	22	v. Beresford	1
Hills	2	Webb	3
Huth	2		
Knox	2		249

INDEX

Index

Aberdeen, Lord George Gordon, 18
Adams, Professor John Couch, 238
Alford, R. G., 218, 219
Aldrich, Thomas B., 159
Alger, Rev. William R., 205
Allsop, Thomas, 25
Anderson, Mary, 171
Andree, Dr. Karl, 156
Andrews, Rebecca Scudder, 180
Andrews, Samuel, 180
Andrews, William Page, xx, 22, 77, 78, 116, 117, 126, 131, 169, 180-87, 200, 204, 221, 222, 252, 253, 257, 259, 275, 307, 308; works of, 181
Anster, John, xix, 16, 24-30, 50, 108, 112, 113, 123, 162, 200, 243, 260, 275, 276, 277; works of, 26
Argelander, John, 140
Arnold, Thomas J., xix, 16, 45-49, 50, 256, 277, 306, 308; works of, 46
Auerbach, Berthold, 156

Bancroft, George, 205
Bankel, J., 47
Barry, William F., 167
Baumann, Lina, 301
Beck, Professor Charles, 205
Bellamy, Rev. J. W., 197
Bernays, Dr. Adolph R., 195, 197, 200, 301, 302
Bernays, Leopold J., xx, 24, 139, 162, 189, 195-200, 204, 243, 278, 301, 302, 306, 308; works of, 200
Berry, A. G., xviii, III
Beta, ix, xxi, 50, 84, 100, 111-13, 112, 278, 306, 308.
Beutler, Hans, 90
Birch, Jonathan, xx, 131, 140-47, 196, 199, 200, 243, 256, 257, 260, 278, 306, 308; works of, 140
Birds, James Adey, xx, 112, 216, 226, 233-35, 235, 256, 279, 306, 308

Birds, William Taylor, 233
Blackie, John Stuart, xix, 29, 31, 50, 55-61, 101, 106, 113, 221, 222, 256, 257, 259, 280, 306, 308; works of, 56, 59
Bloch, Richard, 248
Bloede, Mrs. Marie, 162
Böckh, Professor August, 57
Bohn, Henry G., 239, 303
Bonaparte, Napoleon, 3
Boozey and Sons, xvi
Borrow, George, x, xvi
Botta, Anne Charlotte Lynch, 164
Bowen, Charles Hartpole, xix, 100, 108-10, 123, 306, 308
Boyesen, Professor Hjalmar, xvi, 305
Brooks, Rev. Charles Timothy, xx, 158, 161, 172, 189, 204-10, 256, 257, 280, 304, 307, 308; works of, 206, 207
Bruce, Mary L., 237
Buchanan, Sir George, xix, 3, 11-15, 256, 257, 260, 281, 307, 308
Buckle, Henry Thomas, 176
Bufleb, August, 157
Bufleb, Mrs. August, 157
Byron, George Gordon, 58, 257

Cameron, Professor Charles A., 227
Carl August, Duke, 156
Carlyle, Dr. John, 5
Carlyle, Thomas, 5, 11, 20, 22, 34, 63, 89, 142, 257
Carr, Samuel, 4
Cartwright, J., xvi, 304, 305
Catlin, Caroline, 171, 175
Catlin, Mary Josephine Dillon, 167
Chamisso, Adelbert von, 20
Clarke, Frederick, 230
Clarke, William Barnard, xx, 40, 41, 226, 230-32, 256, 281, 307, 308; works of, 230
Claudy, Carl Harry, 167, 171

Claudy, Frank, xx, 29, 64, 83, 131, 166-76, 182, 189, 256, 257, 281, 304, 306, 308
Claudy, Mrs. Frank, 170
Closs, A., 190
Coleridge, Samuel Taylor, 22, 25, 81, 149, 257
Colquhoun, W. H., xix, 100, 110-11, 180, 228, 260, 282, 306, 308
Cookson, Geoffry Montagu, xvii, xx, 72, 73, 93, 222-25, 256, 257, 282, 307, 308; works of, 223
Cornwall, Barry, 5
Corvinius, Jacob, 210
Coxwell, C. Fillingham, xvii, xix, 119, 126-30, 256, 282, 307, 308; works of, 127
Czernin, Countess Otto, 13

Davies, Anna Baillie, 191, 192
Davies, Thomas Henry, 191, 192
Davies, Warburton, xvi, xx, 101, 189-95, 260, 282, 306, 308
Deininger, J. F., 47
Derby, Lord Edward Geoffry Smith, 18
Deutschbein, Professor Max, 88, 90
Devonshire, Duke of, 4
Dingwall, E. J., xviii
Disraeli, Benjamin, 18
Dowden, Professor Edward, 40, 124, 125, 244
Downes, T. W., 189
Dryden, John, 90

Eckermann, Johann Peter, 20, 90, 195, 196, 301
Eckstein, Henry J., 246
Elster, Professor Ernst E., 88, 90
Engel, Carl Dietrich, 301
Ense, Varnhagen von, 20
Everett, Alexander H., xvi

Falconer, Robert A., 69
Fields, James T., 159, 162, 205
Fife, Professor Robert H., 166
Filmore, Captain Abraham, 151
Filmore, Lewis, xx, 63, 131, 151-55, 256, 260, 282, 283, 306, 308; works of, 152
Förster, Friedrich, 8, 9
Follen, Dr. Karl, 205
Forberg, E., 47

Fouqué, Baron de la Motte, 20
Frantz, Adolf I., ix, x, xi, xiii
Fraser, W., 5
Frederick William III, 140
Frederick William IV, 140
Freiligrath, Ferdinand, 157, 205, 207
Froude, J. A., 18, 36
Furness, Dr. William H., 162

Galvan, Bartholomew, 227
Galvan, John, xi, xx, 108, 123, 180, 226, 227-30, 256, 257, 260, 283, 306, 308; works of, 227
Gerok, Dr. Karl, 210
Gerstäcker, Friedrich, 158
Gladstone, William, 18, 238
Gleichen-Russworm, Baron von, 156
Goethe, Johann Wolfgang von, 4, 6, 7, 8, 9, 36, 46, 58, 207, 219
Goethe, Ottilie von, 18, 20, 219
Goethe, Wolfgang von, 156
Goff, William, 218
Golberg, G., 47
Gooch, Professor G. P., 81
Goodfield, Rev. Charles Old, 212
Gräf, Hans Gerhard, viii
Grant, John Wynniat, xix, 100, 105-7, 283, 306, 308; works of, 106
Granville, A. B., 7
Grimm, Herman, viii
Grimm, Jacob, 20
Grimm Brothers, 18, 142
Grün, Anastasius, 205
Gurney, Archer Thompson, xx, 139, 189, 199, 200-4, 256, 283, 306, 308; works of, 201
Gutzkow, Karl, 156, 243

Hallam, Henry, 22, 200
Hamann, Professor Richard, 88
Hammer, Julius, 156
Hanau, Prince Maurice of, 104
Hansen, Marie, 156
Hansen, Peter Andreas, 157
Haskell, Juliana, 163, 164
Haslewood, Joseph, 133
Hauhart, William F., 241
Hebbel, Christian Friedrich, 160
Heeren, Professor Arnold H., 57
Heine, Heinrich, 88
Heinemann, William, 189, 301, 302
Heller, Otto, 115
Henel, Heinrich, xii

Herder, Johann Gottfried, 156
Hewett, Professor Waterman Thomas, 158
Hills, John, xx, 131, 147-50, 257, 259, 260, 285, 306, 308
Hitzig, Dr. Julius Edward (?), 20
Hinkle, Dr. Beatrice M., 246, 247
Hoefer, Dr. Edward, 210
Hoffmannsthal, Hugo von, vii
Hogg, Thomas Jefferson, 46
Holtzendorf, Madame von, 160
Hook, Theodore, 4
Horn, Franz, 20
Howells, William D., 159
Howley, William, 4
Hughes, Thomas, 211
Huth, Alfred Henry, xx, 131, 176-80, 256, 285, 306, 308; works of, 177
Huth, Henry, 176
Huxley, Aldous, 89

Irving, Henry, 63

James, William, 247
Jean Paul. *See* Richter, J. P. F.
Jerdan, Churchill, 5
Jevons, Dr. F. B., 65
Johnson, Rev. James, 189, 192
Jung, Dr. Carl G., 246, 247

Kelvin, Lord William Thomson, x
Kent, Rockwell, 89, 93
Kindt, Hermann, 22, 38, 39, 301, 302
Kingsley, Charles, 210
Kippenberg, Anton, 90, 132
Kitchin, Very Rev. George William, 65
Klein, Dr. Edward E., 127
Knox, Captain Charles Henry, xx, 218-22, 256, 286, 302, 306, 308; works of, 220
Krumpelmann, Professor John T., xviii

Lachmann, Karl, 142
Lamb, Charles, 20
Lang, Professor A. E., xviii
Latham, Professor Albert G., xvii, xix, 55, 61-68, 77, 79, 93, 256, 286, 307, 308; works of, 62
Lefevre, Sir George William, xix, 119-23, 222, 256, 257, 259, 286, 306, 308; works of, 120
Leveson-Gower, Lord Francis, xi, xv, xix, 3, 4-11, 27, 32, 59, 60, 83, 121, 147, 149, 193, 210, 218, 256, 257, 260, 286, 287, 306, 308
Lewes, George Henry, 5
Loewe, J., 124
Longfellow, Henry Wadsworth, 158, 159, 208
Lowell, James Russell, 159, 238

Macaulay, Thomas Babington, 18
MacCormac, Sir William, 127
Macdonald, William Bell, xx, 131, 135-39, 162, 196, 198, 256, 287, 306, 308; works of, 137
MacIntyre, Carlyle Ferren, xvii, xix, 55, 86-93, 256, 257, 259, 307, 308; works of, 88
Maginn, Dr. William, 4, 5
Marlowe, Julia, 171
Marschal, Count, 219
Marschal, Mrs., 219
Martin, Sir Theodore, x, xix, 16, 22, 36-45, 50, 113, 117, 180, 214, 244, 256, 260, 287, 306, 308; works of, 37, 38
Maurice, F. D., 211
Mayer, Liezen, 47
McLintock, R., xix, 100, 113-17, 288, 307, 308; works of, 113
Mendelssohn-Bartholdy, Jakob Ludwig, 58
Mérimée, Prosper (?), 18
Mierow, Herbert Edward, vii
Mignet, François Auguste, 18
Miller, Professor, University of Göttingen, 19
Moir, G., 5
Morgan, Professor Bayard Quincy, xviii, 112, 135, 230
Mueller, Max, 238
Mueller, Victoria E., xviii
Müller, Ottfried, 57
Musset, Alfred de, 12

Neander, Johann August Wilhelm, 57
Nebel, Dr. Heinrich, 70
Needler, Professor George H., 70

North, Christopher. *See* Wilson, Professor John
Norton, Charles Eliot, 205

Oppenheim, James, 247
Osgood, James R., 159
Oswald, E., 301

Palmer, Professor George Herbert, 182
Palmerston, Lord Henry John Temple, 18
Parker, Theodore, 206
Paul, Rev. Charles, 210
Paul, Rev. Charles Kegan, xx, 47, 48, 189, 210-14, 256, 288, 306, 308; works of, 212
Peacock, Thomas Love, 46
Peithmann, L. E., xvi, 302, 304
Peter, Franz, 301, 303
Petrarch, Francesco, 158
Petsch, Robert, 95
Phillips, J. B., 160, 161
Philpots, Henry, 4
Platinius, 210
Potocki, Count Augustus, 121
Powell, Lawrence Clarke, 87
Pradez, Georges, 112
Priebsch, R., xviii, 190
Priest, Professor George M., xvii, xix, 55, 76-80, 126, 130, 182, 253, 256, 288, 307, 308; works of, 77

Raphael, Alice, xvii, xx, 22, 116, 126, 237, 244-54, 256, 257, 258, 259, 288, 307, 308; works of, 246
Raphael, Gabriel Matthews, 245
Raphael, Mrs. Gabriel Matthews, 245
Raschen, Professor John F. L., xv, xvii, xix, 22, 55, 83, 94-99, 256, 258, 259, 289, 307, 308; works of, 95
Reed, Lillian Espy, 145
Reinhardt, Max, 251
Retzsch, Moritz, 20, 145
Richardson, G. F. (?), 219
Richter, J. P. F. (Jean Paul), 205, 207
Rilke, Rainer Maria, 89
Robbins, Professor Harry Wolcott, 258

Robertson, Professor John G., 124, 125, 223
Robinson, Henry Crabb, 6, 147, 148, 200, 218
Rogers, Samuel, 22
Rolleston, T. W., 124
Rose, Professor William, xviii
Rückert, Friedrich, 160, 207
Ruland, Dr. C., 218, 219

Saalfeld, Professor Frederick S., 57
Sabatier, François, 112
Sachs, Dr. Julius, 245
Savigny, Frederick Charles von, 18, 19
Schade, Miss Anita, 168, 171
Schiller, Friedrich, 46, 156, 207
Schlegel, August Wilhelm, 20, 21, 33, 144, 145, 149, 256
Schleiermacher, Friedrich Daniel, 57
Schmeller, Johann Joseph, 218
Schmidt, Erich, 113
Schmidt, Professor F. G. G., xvii, xix, 24, 58, 83-86, 256, 289, 307, 308; works of, 84
Schreiber, Professor Carl F., vii-xiii, xvii, 190, 191, 192, 254, 258, 305
Schwab, Gustav, 210
Scoones, William, 214
Scoones, William Dalton, xx, 189, 214-16, 257, 289, 306, 308; works of, 215
Scott, Sir Walter, xvi, 5, 200, 257
Scudder, Horace E., 180, 182
Seitz, Rudolf, 47
Shakespeare, William, 20, 51
Shawcross, John, xix, 55, 80-83, 256, 258, 290, 307, 308; works of, 81
Shelley, Percy Bysshe, x, xvi, 46, 81, 166, 257
Shelley, Mrs. (Mary Wollostonecraft Godwin ?), 18
Simison, Barbara, 191
Southey, Robert, 5, 22, 200
Speck, William A., xvi, 5, 132, 166, 171, 175, 248, 250, 301, 302, 304
Speck Collection of Goetheana, xvi, xvii, 33, 58, 132, 138, 146, 159, 166, 169, 189, 251, 320
Stedman, Edmund Clarence, 162
Stein, Baron von, 156
Stein, Frau von, 156
Stoddard, Richard Henry, 164

Index

Swanwick, Anna, x, xii, xv, xvi, xx, 22, 41, 43, 44, 77, 79, 93, 112, 113, 180, 236, 237-44, 256, 259, 260, 290, 291, 292, 293, 303, 304, 305, 306, 308; works of, 239, 240
Swanwick, Mary, 237
Syme, David, xix, 31, 50, 100, 101-3, 260, 293, 306, 308; works of, 101

Talbot, The Honorable Robert, xix, 16, 27, 30-36, 144, 222, 256, 293, 306, 308
Taylor, Arthur, xvi, xix, 131-35, 137, 146, 196, 199, 243, 260, 293, 306, 308; works of, 132, 133
Taylor, Bayard, x, xii, xv, xx, 22, 29, 41, 43, 44, 45, 47, 48, 55, 64, 65, 70, 75, 76, 77, 79, 93, 112, 113, 117, 126, 131, 151, 155-66, 167, 169, 176, 180, 184, 185, 186, 207, 208, 209, 210, 234, 243, 244, 251, 252, 253, 256, 259, 260, 293, 294, 298, 307, 308; works of, 157, 158, 159, 160
Taylor, Mrs. Marie Hansen, 169
Taylor, William, 7, 255
Tennyson, Alfred, 37
Terry, Ellen, 63
Thackeray, William Makepeace, 18
Thomas, Professor Calvin, 95
Tieck, Ludwig, 18, 20
Todhunter, John, xix, 108, 119, 123-26, 256, 259, 298, 307, 308; works of, 123, 124
Translation, theories of, xi, xii, 21, 22, 32, 40, 51, 65, 66, 71, 74, 77, 81, 82, 90, 91, 92, 101, 124 149, 181, 183, 194, 202, 206, 207, 212, 213, 231, 233, 234, 240, 241
Translators, prejudice of against *Faust*, 8, 9, 26, 40, 52, 53, 59, 71, 93, 101, 114, 149, 193
Trippel, Alexander, 159
Tuson, George, 17

Ude, Louis Eustache, 5
Uhland, Johann Ludwig, 207

Van der Smissen, Professor William H., xix, 55, 69-76, 76, 128, 298, 307, 308; works of, 70
Van Doren, Mark, 254
Vandreuil, Count, 218
v. Beresford, xix, 100, 103-5, 170, 257, 306, 308; works of, 103
Victoria, Queen, 36, 37

Webb, Thomas E., xix, 16, 50-53, 108, 123, 256, 298, 306, 308; works of, 50-51
Wendte, Charles W., 206
Weston, Professor Karl E., xviii, 181, 182, 183, 184
Wieland, Christoph Martin, 157
Wilson, Professor John (Christopher North), 4, 5
Wittels, Dr. Fritz, 246
Wordsworth, John, 147
Wordsworth, William, 5, 22, 147, 200

Zerffi, G. G., xvi, 304
Zumpt, Professor at Kriegsschule, Berlin, 237, 238

www.ingramcontent.com/pod-product-compliance
Lightning Source LLC
Chambersburg PA
CBHW021353290426
44108CB00010B/223